T0305310

Post Keynesian Economics

KEY DEBATES AND CONTENDING PERSPECTIVES SERIES

Academic debate is an essential component in the development of understanding and knowledge-creation within and across disciplines. Advancing, challenging and deliberating different points of view can promote problem solving, stimulate innovative thinking and build links between ideas.

By engaging with diverse international perspectives and inspiring intellectual exchanges, each book in this series presents an up-to-date, critical appraisal of the most important debates shaping the field and provides a rich resource to enable a deeper understanding of the topic in question.

For a full list of Edward Elgar published titles, including the titles in this series, visit our website at www.e-elgar.com.

Post Keynesian Economics

Key Debates and Contending Perspectives

Edited by

Therese Jefferson

John Curtin Distinguished Professor Emeritus, School of Accounting, Economics and Finance, Curtin University, Australia

John E. King

Emeritus Professor of Economics, La Trobe University, Australia

KEY DEBATES AND CONTENDING PERSPECTIVES SERIES

Cheltenham, UK • Northampton, MA, USA

Published by
Edward Elgar Publishing Limited
The Lypiatts
15 Lansdown Road
Cheltenham
Glos GL50 2JA
UK

Edward Elgar Publishing, Inc.
William Pratt House
9 Dewey Court
Northampton
Massachusetts 01060
USA

A catalogue record for this book
is available from the British Library

Library of Congress Control Number: 2023951202

This book is available electronically in the **Elgar**online
Economics subject collection
http://dx.doi.org/10.4337/9781803922232

ISBN 978 1 80392 222 5 (cased)
ISBN 978 1 80392 223 2 (eBook)

Printed and bound by CPI Group (UK) Ltd, Croydon, CR0 4YY

Contents

Contributors

Philip Armstrong – The Gower Initiative for Modern Money Studies, United Kingdom

Riccardo Bellofiore – University of Bergamo and University of Modena and Reggio Emilia, Italy

Jonathan M. Harris – Tufts University and Boston University, United States of America

Neil Hart – University of New South Wales, Australia and University of Economics Ho Chi Minh City, Vietnam

Therese Jefferson – Curtin University, Australia

John E. King – La Trobe University, Australia

Peter Kriesler – University of New South Wales, Australia

Marc Lavoie – University of Ottawa, Canada and University of Sorbonne Paris Nord, France

Melanie G. Long – The College of Wooster, United States of America

Neil Perry – Western Sydney University, Australia

Steven Pressman – New School for Social Research and Monmouth University, United States of America

Louis-Philippe Rochon – Laurentian University, Canada

Malcolm Sawyer – University of Leeds, United Kingdom

Giovanna Vertova – University of Bergamo, Italy

1. Introduction to *Post Keynesian Economics*

Therese Jefferson and John E. King

This book aims to provide readers with up-to-date, critical appraisals of the most important debates shaping the field of Post Keynesian economics and provide a rich resource to enable a deeper understanding of each topic in question. It forms part of a series aiming to produce such appraisals from different disciplines. The book's format as an edited collection is intended to accommodate a diversity of views on each topic, so that key debates and challenges are represented.

The selection of topics was, initially, a decision made by the editors, motivated by a wish to cover contemporary developments where Post Keynesian insights seem to be particularly relevant and productive. While our original hope was to source significantly differing perspectives the outcome, in some cases, is a matter of complementarity between authors. This is discussed in more detail below but at a general level suggests that while Post Keynesian theoreticians and fellow travellers may disagree on theory, the translation of theory to policy can have very similar outcomes, albeit ones that differ significantly from the mainstream or received 'wisdom'. The contributions also demonstrate links between the somewhat arbitrary dividing lines drawn between different chapters or topics. Again, these are discussed further below.

The first broad topic to be discussed is the relationship between Post Keynesian economics and other heterodox schools of thought. Neil Hart and Peter Kriesler open the book with a discussion of the connections between the Post Keynesians and two other heterodox strands. Sraffian economics, they argue, is fundamentally inconsistent with the underlying principles of Post Keynesian economics, while institutional economics and Post Keynesianism, while different in some important respects, are essentially compatible. They begin by setting out the five main features of the Post Keynesian school. The first is a denial of the usefulness of general theory. Second is the treatment of the capitalist economy as a historical process in which uncertainty is fundamental. Third, and closely related to this, is an underlying concern with historical rather than logical time. Fourth is the belief that institutional and sociopolitical forces are critically important in shaping economic events. Fifth, and finally, the roles of effective demand and money are critical in determining levels of employment and output.

Hart and Kriesler devote the first substantial section of their contribution to a consideration of the methodological foundations of Post Keynesian economics, which they identify as a denial of any universally applicable general theory (somewhat ironically, in view of the title of Keynes's great book!), and an underlying emphasis on the role of effective demand, in particular the significance of investment expenditure by oligopolistic enterprises that have the power to influence governments and institutions. Again, this involves a strong emphasis on the role of money and finance.

In section two they play close attention to the contrasting methodologies of Post Keynesian and Sraffian economics, noting that the Sraffians make a great deal of the existence of long-run centres of gravity and thus, in effect, to equilibrium outcomes. The critical element here is the Sraffian insistence on a tendency towards a single equilibrium rate of profit throughout the economy. This is enough, Hart and Kriesler maintain, to render Sraffian economics incompatible with Post Keynesianism, where both methodological presumptions and empirical evidence regarding the weakness of competitive forces in 21st-century capitalism render equilibrium analysis unacceptable. Post Keynesians thus deny the applicability to modern capitalist economies of the Sraffian emphasis on long-period positions, which is impossible to reconcile with the evolutionary and cumulative nature of capitalist macro-dynamics. Hart and Kriesler conclude in this section that these methodological differences are so great that they do indeed render the Sraffian and Post Keynesian theoretical frameworks incompatible.

Institutional economics, on the other hand, has a great deal in common with Post Keynesian economics, as Hart and Kriesler argue in section three. The business environment that is portrayed by the institutionalists is very similar to the Post Keynesian representation of firms and the industries in which they operate, which are overwhelmingly oligopolistic. The two schools also agree on the prevalence of mark-up pricing and the role of excess capacity, and regard the capitalist economic system as embedded within evolutionary processes. Hart and Kriesler do note, however, that the institutionalists and the Post Keynesians do have some important differences, most notably with respect to the role and limitations of formal modelling. Nonetheless, they conclude that while the Sraffians and the Post Keynesians are indeed incompatible bedfellows, there are strong synergies between institutionalism and Post Keynesianism.

In his contribution, Louis-Philippe Rochon compares Post Keynesian economics with the theory of the monetary circuit, a well-established approach to the analysis of endogenous money that originated in France and Italy but has also proved influential in the English-speaking world. Both are rooted in the work of Keynes, or at least in their respective interpretations of the *General Theory*, and thus share intellectual roots, As Rochon observes, one of the contributors to the present volume, his own former teacher Marc Lavoie, is a leading authority in both schools.

In the first section of his contribution, Rochon outlines the early institutional links between Post Keynesian economics and circuit theory, stressing the friendship between Lavoie, Alain Parguez and Mario Seccareccia. As he notes, the history of the theory of the monetary circuit has not been well documented, at least in the English-language literature, so that it represents an important missing piece in the history of Post Keynesianism. Rochon sets this right with an extended account of the early history of the circuit approach in France and Italy (where the principal theorist was Augusto Graziani). As he shows, the most important ideas soon spread to Canada, where Parguez was a frequent visitor and established a close friendship with Lavoie and Seccareccia, the former undertaking postgraduate studies in Paris where he deepened his understanding of circuit theory. Rochon explains how academic conferences brought the Post Keynesians and the circuit theorists together in the 1980s and provides a detailed survey of the relevant publications at this time.

Next Rochon discusses the institutional links between the Post Keynesians and the circuit authors, under five headings: the nature of the economic system, endogenous money, social classes and income distribution, effective demand and uncertainty. On the first question, and in opposition to neoclassical theory, both the Post Keynesians and the circuit theorists resist the use of equilibrium analysis, regarding capitalist economy as fragile and unstable and stressing the role of effective demand in the determination of output and employment. As regards the second issue, there is again broad agreement on the importance of the endogeneity of money, which had already featured in the work of early Post Keynesians like Joan Robinson and Nicholas Kaldor. He notes the existence of further important similarities between the two heterodox schools, which both reject methodological individualism and insist on the importance of the class-based nature of the capitalist system. This, Rochon suggests, places the distribution of income and wealth at the core of their analysis, highlighting the importance of power asymmetries and emphasising the role of class conflict over the distribution of income, which both schools regard as the fundamental cause of inflation.

Fourth, Rochon maintains, the circuit theorists and the Post Keynesians broadly agree in identifying effective demand as the driving force of capitalist economic activity, rejecting Say's Law and insisting on the need for a monetary theory of output and employment. Finally, there are also clear similarities (but also some significant differences) in their understanding of the role that must be played by uncertainty in determining macroeconomic outcomes. Given the shared intellectual roots of these two heterodox schools, Rochon concludes, it is unsurprising that the relationship between them has grown closer in recent decades.

The second topic is Modern Monetary Theory. The first perspective, provided by Philip Armstrong, examines the case for considering Modern Monetary Theory as a contribution to and part of broadly defined, heterodox communities in economics (though his discussion of 'splitters' and 'lumpers' also has much in common with the chapter by Hart and Kriesler). Armstrong identifies history, time (or sequence) and an understanding of contemporary mechanisms and structures as key elements of Post Keynesians and others in the heterodox community. This is particularly relevant to understandings of the invention (or origins) of money and development of its role in the economy. Armstrong argues that this is an important attribute of Modern Monetary Theory, one of the distinguishing features of which, compared with main-stream approaches to monetary economics, is its explicit grounding in specific historic and institutional contexts.

The commonalities between Post Keynesian economics and Modern Monetary Theory do not, however, imply complete agreement between contributors to discussions and debate. Armstrong presents an argument, closely based on Mosler's work, that Modern Monetary Theory goes beyond Post Keynesian economics in its explanation of inflation and, from there, the development of policy implications. The differences identified between Modern Monetary Theory and Post Keynesian contributors may be minor in comparison to their disagreements with orthodox approaches but, as Lavoie later discusses, have had particular importance within the two communities. Ultimately, Armstrong contends that the 'taxes drive money' approach that underlies Modern Monetary Theory distinguishes it from other heterodox schools, including Post Keynesianism, and constitutes a legitimate school within the heterodox community. This is one difference between his analysis and that of Marc Lavoie's contrasting contribution, that Modern Monetary Theory is 'part of the Institutionalist branch of post-Keynesian economics'.

Further, while Armstrong emphasises complementarities between Post Keynesians and the Modern Monetary Theory section of the heterodox community, Lavoie summarises the complexity and confusion evident in debates about Modern Monetary Theory. Some contributions to debate, from both the Post Keynesian and mainstream communities, are described as 'ugly', perhaps for their complexity but also, it seems, for the avoidance or obscuring of key issues. Lavoie argues that some of this can be attributed to two significant categories of Modern Monetary Theory debate and discussion. One, described as 'specific' or 'academic' gives priority to particular, existing institutional arrangements and processes. The second, variously labelled 'popular', 'vulgar', or 'general' simplifies explanations of Modern Monetary Theory by, for example, consolidating the roles of the government and central bank. Ironically, this simplification detracts from fully understanding institutional arrangements and processes, a key distinguishing element of Modern Monetary Theory's development. In doing so, arguments may be simplified but become open to significant criticism. Ultimately discussions arise that can be at cross-purposes. In addition, however, Lavoie identifies unedifying claims about who deserves recognition for producing Modern Monetary Theory and its key insights as a second key element of the 'ugly'.

Regardless of whether Modern Monetary Theory is identified as inside or separate from Post Keynesianism, Armstrong's and Lavoie's insights have strong areas of alignment. Each identifies the importance of rejecting a conjectural theory of the origin of money and the importance of existing institutional arrangements for understanding the role of money/credit in the operation of specific economies. Lavoie extends this argument by providing examples of specific arrangements in the United States, Canada, the eurozone and Chile to illustrate the relevance of Modern Monetary Theory in each context. Similarly, there is large agreement on policy implications, including the need for a Job Guarantee, that also feature in both chapters. Together, the two chapters provide a range of insights into both Modern Monetary Theory and the state of debate in some other sections of the heterodox community.

Sadly, unforeseen circumstances mean that we have only one chapter on issues of race and gender. Fortunately, Chapter 6 by Melanie G. Long provides a thorough, comprehensive and enlightening discussion of these important questions. She begins by noting how the COVID pandemic had reconfirmed the extent of racial and gender disparities in Americans' exposure to risk, which a purely class-based approach would miss. Post Keynesian economics, she argues, offers unique analytical tools for studying attitudes towards risk, the role of financial markets and the associated macroeconomic implications. But it would benefit from paying closer attention to the contributions of feminist and stratification economics.

Long outlines the fundamental characteristics of these two modes of thought, according to which agents are socially embedded in specific cultural, temporal and economic contexts and, in their treatment of discrimination, emphasise power as an important source of group disparities. She notes that Post Keynesians also focus on power relations, linking themselves to the feminist structuralist macroeconomics that is derived from Kalecki but adds to it an analysis of women's unpaid caregiving activities. Closer attention to nonmarket processes, Long maintains, would deepen the explanatory power of Post Keynesian growth and distribution models.

She finds further analogies in the treatment of financial exclusion and the very uneven operation of credit markets. Post Keynesians, Long suggests, would have done well to pay more attention to the role of gender and ethnicity in their analysis of the 2008 Global Financial Crisis, extending the valuable

Minskyan model from firms to households. The so-called 'Minsky moment' involved more than social class relations. Financial instability was magnified by racial inequalities, which resulted in black borrowers being exploited due to their vulnerability. This, Long argues, helps to explain why the financial bubble became as large as it did before it finally burst. Similar observations apply to single households headed by women.

Related issues arise in the recently increased Post Keynesian focus on the distribution of wealth, where race and gender are again crucial determinants. Post Keynesians have suggested that the level of household assets affects the level of household consumption and should thus be included as a variable in the macroeconomic consumption function. This is important in the present context, since the distribution of wealth by race and gender is even more unequal than by socio-economic status.

Long next discusses the implications of all this for macroeconomic policy, with both monetary and fiscal policy having serious racial and gender biases which are insufficiently recognised by Post Keynesians. Additional research is needed on these questions, she maintains, to establish the size of their impact on policy outcomes and to indicate the potentially substantial scope for policy improvement. She concludes by providing a comprehensive set of references to the relevant academic literature on all these important questions.

In his contribution to the section of the book devoted to the Green New Deal, Jonathan M. Harris begins by setting out the underlying goals of such proposals, which involve a transition to a low-carbon economy based on renewable energy and improved energy efficiency, the protection of forests and wetlands, more sustainable farming and increased employment in green dimensions that will include renewable energy, ecological efficiency, infrastructure investment and ecological resilience. He concentrates on what he terms the 'green Keynesian' approach, which is intended to delink traditional carbon-intensive economic growth from employment creation and increased well-being. This is in part a technological issue, he concedes, but it will also require a shift in consumption patterns from energy-intensive to energy-conserving and service-oriented forms of consumption. As Harris notes, these ideas have proved to be politically quite influential, especially in the United States, where resolutions in support of them have often been debated in Congress.

He next sets out the principal features of Keynesian economics, which fell out of favour with many economists and politicians during the period of 'great moderation' from 1980 to 2007 but has revived since the fiscal crisis of 2007–08. Like the Great Depression of the early 1930s, which led to the introduction of the Roosevelt administration's original New Deal, the 'Great Recession' of the post-2007 period has had profound theoretical consequences, bringing Keynesian (especially Post Keynesian) ideas to the fore and reawakening interest in both class inequalities (as stressed by Kalecki) and financial instability.

Harris proceeds to discuss the relationship between ecological economics and the Green New Deal and the debates with advocates of de-growth, and the associated literature on 'absolute' versus 'relative decoupling', before returning to a consideration of the fundamental goals of a Green New Deal. To achieve these goals, he maintains, three major policy changes are required. First, existing private economic activity has to be redirected in a green direction via carbon taxes, elimination of perverse carbon-promoting subsidies and the introduction of sensible subsidies for genuinely green investment projects. Second, huge public investment is required in such projects. Finally, large-scale employment creation programmes are needed in areas like health, education and community services.

The fiscal implications of these proposals are set out at some length. Budget deficits should be incurred only if they are necessary to maintain full employment; otherwise, corporate and high-income individual taxes will have to be increased. Harris notes the regressive nature of carbon taxation, which will need to be offset by flat-rate individual tax rebates or social investment that benefits low-income citizens. He then cites work from the University of Massachusetts/Amherst demonstrating that the job creation effects of green investment may be very considerable and criticising the relevant US legislation for not going nearly far enough. Harris concludes by agreeing with Keynes that the faults of the capitalist economy can only be put right by significant and sustained government intervention, which will promote prosperity and increased employment in addition to stabilising both the economic and the ecological systems.

Neil Perry is in broad agreement with Jonathan M. Harris on almost all these questions, and indeed he begins with a brief discussion of absolute and relative decoupling, but his approach is very different. His is by far the most technically sophisticated of all the contributions to this volume, with no less than 21 equations and three elaborate diagrams. Perry uses a model of growth and distribution derived from Michał Kalecki to set out his understanding of the Green New Deal. As he notes at the outset, its proponents in the United States, most notably Bernie Sanders, have a strong resonance with Post Keynesian economics. For Perry the critical issues linking ecological economics to the Green New Deal can best be understood via the IPAT equation, an identity where total environment impact (I) equals the population (P) multiplied by consumption per capita, or affluence (A), multiplied by the inverse of environmental efficiency, that is, the environmental impact per unit of consumption (T). Environmental efficiency is the target for advocates of the Green New Deal, and there is continuing debate over the need for green growth or de-growth. It all depends on whether technological improvements will be sufficient to allow P and A to continue to increase.

Perry then introduces environmental efficiency into the underlying macroeconomic model, which is a long-run version of Kalecki's own short-run model of the economy. The crucial elements in this model are the demand regime, the productivity regime and the class distribution of income. Perry focuses on the probable impact of the Green New Deal on green productivity and technical change, the mark-up, depreciation and the budget deficit, which are all affected by the demand and productivity regimes. These impacts are modelled in the first 12 of Perry's equations and his three diagrams, which illustrate the impact of a Green New Deal on environmental efficiency and hence on environmental sustainability via its effect on the demand regime (the DR line) and the productivity regime (the PR line). He concludes that the degree of sustainability will depend on the size of the shifts that can be achieved in these two critical variables and several parameters which are related to the green productivity equation, the rising propensity to save, the profit share and the parameters of the investment function.

Perry next turns to the prospects for achieving net zero carbon emissions and the potential contribution of a Green New Deal. Again, the distinction between relative and absolute decoupling is an essential part of the analysis, and he suggests that there may well be a strong case for advocating de-growth, depending of course on the values of the parameters. He also models the role of carbon offsets, using Post Keynesian tax incidence theory and invoking the Keynesian principle of increasing risk. He concludes by noting again that green productivity improvements and government spending on renewable energy are double-edged, reducing carbon emissions per unit of output but also increasing the rate of growth of output. Nothing is simple in environmental macroeconomics.

As the title of their chapter indicates, the contribution by Riccardo Bellofiore and Giovanna Vertova is easily the most far-ranging and ambitious in the book. Their account of macroeconomic theory and policy in what they describe as 'the capitalism of permanent catastrophe' deals with some profoundly important issues in the political economy of the 21st century, drawing on the work of radical and Marxist scholars (in particular Michał Kalecki). They begin by noting how Keynes himself had regarded World War I and its aftermath as a major watershed in the history of global capitalism, more important than the Great Depression or World War II. In a similar vein, Bellofiore and Vertova argue that our present-day reality puts into question many economic and social features that had previously been taken for granted. This 'polycrisis' offers a huge challenge, since fundamental change is urgent but its character, and its attainability, poses some very large questions.

Bellofiore and Vertova identify four major shocks: the Global Financial Crisis of 2007–08, the COVID pandemic, the climate crisis and the Ukraine war. Together they raise fundamental macroeconomic issues, not merely relating to the level of employment but also to what employment is for: 'how', 'what', 'how much' and 'for whom' to produce. Using the Keynesian (and, more radically, the Marxian) notion of the 'socialisation of employment', they draw on the recent work of Mario Draghi, Adam Tooze and Jan Kregel, summarising their related but rather different interpretations of the COVID crisis and placing special emphasis on Kregel's interpretation of the pandemic as a clear example of true Keynesian uncertainty and his associated critique of the policy responses of the major national governments.

Bellofiore and Vertova endorse Kregel's insistence on the need for a return of the state to exercise much greater influence that it had done in the era of neo-liberal capitalism. This, they maintain, has profound implications for the operation of monetary and fiscal policy, since there is now a clear need for an alternative to the 'privatised capitalism' that has relied entirely on budget deficits and cheap money. Capitalist logic, they argue, is instead becoming even more ferocious, giving priority to the private sector while maintaining austerity for the working and middle classes. Returning to the COVID crisis, Bellofiore and Vertova see it as a crisis of the capitalist social form of production and consumption. It should be seen not as a 'shock' but rather as 'a catastrophic event bringing to light the pathological content behind the supposed normality of our everyday life', thereby revealing the pathological nature of the existing capitalist system. It should certainly not be seen as nothing more than a shocking surprise.

There are big implications for macroeconomics, similar in magnitude and extent to those that led Keynes to develop the monetary theory of production. Bellofiore and Vertova favour the interpretation of Keynes set out by Hyman Minsky in the 1975 book in which he stressed the contradiction between the production of authentically social use-values and production for profit. For Minsky, as arguably also for Keynes, one phase of capitalism was dying, and the characteristics of the next stage remained highly uncertain. Bellofiore and Vertova also cite the contemporaneous writings of Joan Robinson on 'the second crisis of economic theory' that had been initiated by the fierce class warfare of the 1960s and early 1970s in many parts of Europe. Similar concerns had been raised by Kalecki, but in his celebrated 1943 article on the political aspects of full employment, not in his later work with Tadeusz Kowalik on the apparently successful subsequent reform of capitalism. They conclude by reaffirming the need to create a very different and very much better society, warning against the danger of reformist illusions and asserting the need for a genuinely socialist future.

Malcolm Sawyer's contribution has a much narrower focus, dealing exclusively with COVID, but some of the many criticisms that he makes of British government reactions to the pandemic are entirely consistent with the more general arguments of Bellofiore and Vertova. Sawyer notes the very significant macroeconomic effects of the pandemic, with a sharp fall in GDP in 2020 that was soon very largely (but not entirely) reversed, and a decline in employment, but very little impact on unemployment. He then turns to the policy responses of the British government, which involved significant fiscal loosening, with the old rules for budget deficits and debt levels being quickly abandoned to allow for income and employment support measures, along with loans and grants to firms. Monetary policy was also loosened, with the Bank of England reducing the bank rate from 0.75 per cent to 0.1 per cent and engaging in Quantitative Easing. The ratio of government spending to GDP rose from 39.1 per cent in 2019–20 to a peak of 51.6 per cent in 2020–21 before falling back to 44.5 per cent in 2021–22, while government debt rose from 82.8 per cent of GDP in 2020 to 95.5 per cent in 2022.

Sawyer next discusses the three crucial interfaces between the public and private sectors: 'test and trace' activities, the acquisition of Personal Protective Equipment (PPE) and the development and roll-out of effective vaccines. He is highly critical of government policy in the first two areas, noting evidence of poor performance by the private companies contracted to test and trace for COVID and the excessive profits that they made. The companies relied on to produce PPE did not always meet quality standards, leading to accusations of cronyism in the awarding of contracts, and they were able to charge much higher prices than normal. By contrast, the vaccine roll-out was quite successful. On the implementation and effectiveness of the government's policies, Sawyer finds evidence of similar abuses to those encountered in the test and trace and PPE programmes. However, the COVID Job Retention Scheme (CJRS), or 'furlough', was effectively administered and at its peak was supporting no fewer than 8.9 million jobs, or a quarter of the entire workforce. Significantly, it had challenged the traditional crisis response by the British state of non-intervention in the labour market.

Sawyer stresses the unequal impacts of both the COVID pandemic itself and the policy responses to it. The shutdown of schools, he convincingly argues, and the use of online and home learning, increased the socio-economic divide in educational attainment, with pupils from better-off homes faring much better in their learning than their poorer counterparts. Similarly for adults, whose loss of employment and earnings was greater among the lower paid than the more highly paid, and significantly greater for workers from ethnic minorities. There were also significant disparities in illness and death rates by age, region and ethnicity. He concludes that the strong package of financial measures did reduce the effect of the lockdown on employment, but the lack of preparedness led to the rushed implementation of poorly designed programmes and other policy failures. As we noted earlier, these criticisms of neo-liberal capitalism and its continued subordination to a rapacious form of capitalism seem to be in essence quite consistent with the broader case made by Bellofiore and Vertova. The success of the furlough programme, in particular, suggests that a significant increase in government intervention can indeed greatly improve macroeconomic outcomes.

The two final contributions deal with economic inequality, with particular reference to the work of Thomas Piketty on this important question. John E. King begins by noting three reasons why Post Keynesians are concerned with inequality. First, a change in the degree of inequality will have serious effects on the level of aggregate demand, since poor people save a much smaller proportion of their incomes than the wealthy. Second, there are huge ethical questions involved in the assessment of inequality. Third, Post Keynesians have been alarmed at the sharp rise in inequality since the 1970s, some seeing it as evidence of a new and unpleasant stage in the history of capitalism. In the second part of his contribution King surveys the Post Keynesian literature on wage-led growth, focusing on Michał Kalecki's work on this question. Kalecki argued that while wage reductions would benefit the individual capitalist, they would probably damage the interests of the capitalist class as a whole, as they would reduce effective demand and so damage aggregate profitability. In his celebrated 1970 discussion of the 'crucial reform' of the system after 1939, which had first reduced inequality and then ensured that real wages rose at least as fast as productivity, he argued that a large majority of capitalists had come to recognise the benefits that they, too, gained from these political changes. Ironically, they were on the cusp of a dramatic reversal in the neo-liberal era.

King identifies three lessons from all this. First, the economy is profoundly affected by political changes. Second, the mainstream faith in micro-reduction is completely wrong, as revealed by the evident fallacy of composition identified by Kalecki on the effects of wage cuts. Third, there is a huge policy question: can capitalism be reformed, quickly and decisively, to greatly reduce inequality, or do we need to establish a new, basically noncapitalist, mode of production?

In the next two sections King discusses Piketty's two great books, *Capital in the Twenty-First Century* and *Capital and Ideology*. He notes that these are very different works, the first setting out what Piketty originally regarded as the two fundamental laws of capitalism, which connect the profit share first to the capital–output ratio and the rate of profit, and then to the rate of economic growth and the savings ratio. He argued that the relationship between the profit rate and the rate of growth was critical to the tendency for the distribution of wealth to become first less unequal (between 1914 and 1970) and then more unequal (after 1970). King summarises the critical literature on *Capital in the*

Twenty-First Century and Piketty's reaction to it. By the time *Capital and Ideology* was published, Piketty had lost confidence in the two fundamental laws and the policy proposals that seemed to flow from them, and instead stressed the essential role of political and, especially, ideological change, and the need for economics to draw on the other social sciences to explain major changes in the degree of inequality. He now laid out a set of principles for a new participatory socialism that went far beyond anything that he had earlier being willing to accept. As King notes in his conclusion, Piketty was now deeply interested in the ethics of distribution.

Steven Pressman takes a very different approach to Piketty's work on inequality, though in the final analysis his conclusions are not greatly different from those of John E. King. He begins with the very substantial similarities between Piketty's ideas and those of the Post Keynesians, including an emphasis on real historical time, on the nonoptimality of unregulated market outcomes and on the need for government intervention (and especially progressive taxation policy) to overcome these defects. Pressman continues with an exposition of Piketty's ideas on the causes of inequality, as set out in *Capital in the Twenty-First Century*, stressing the relationship between the rate of profit and the rate of growth and providing some time-series evidence. He proceeds by explaining the treatment of the relationship between *r* and *g* in Post Keynesian theory, using some simple algebra to demonstrate the importance of the capitalists' savings ratio in determining this relationship and hence also the upward or downward trend in wealth inequality.

In section four Pressman outlines the rather different views of Piketty and the Post Keynesians on the consequences of excessive inequality, which include such microeconomic problems as increased crime and deteriorating health and especially the adverse macroeconomic consequences, such as reduced effective demand and the resulting higher unemployment and slower productivity growth. He then turns, in section five, to their rather different views on public debt. Pressman begins by contrasting the ideas of Modern Monetary Theory and of John Maynard Keynes on this vital question, before introducing the balanced budget multiplier as a concept that might help to reconcile the apparently opposing opinions of Piketty and Keynes on questions of fiscal policy. As Paul Samuelson had maintained in the 1940s, taxing the rich, who had a much higher propensity to save, and then spending the tax revenues, would promote consumer spending and increase economic growth without the need for greatly increased public debt. In section six Pressman notes that, for all their differences, Piketty and the Post Keynesians had got a lot right in their analysis of inequality, but also quite a lot wrong. Returning to the theme with which he began, Pressman concludes that they do have a great deal in common, being politically left of centre, deeply concerned about inequality and confident that a more egalitarian fiscal policy will generate higher employment and faster rates of growth.

We hope to have shown in this book that Post Keynesians have contributed to some of the most interesting and important theoretical and policy questions of the present day, agreeing on many points but disagreeing on others, usually, if not always, in a friendly and courteous manner. The five broad issues that our authors were asked to address were not, of course, the only topics that Post Keynesians are debating in 2023. We considered soliciting contributions on issues of economic methodology, including the thorny chestnut of providing micro-foundations for macroeconomics; on the political implications of Post Keynesianism, which might be seen as 'liberal socialist', social democratic or basically conservative. Perhaps a second volume, edited by younger colleagues in 2033, will cover some of these fascinating controversies.

2. On the compatibility of post-Keynesian, Sraffian and evolutionary economics

Neil Hart and Peter Kriesler

INTRODUCTION

In attempting to understand the economy, different traditions within political economy emphasise different fundamentals and have quite contrasting visions. One important question is the extent to which these differing traditions may be compatible and may complement each other. According to John E. King, 'post-Keynesian economics emerged as a distinct school of thought, in the 1960s, as a reaction against … perversions of Keynes's original vision' (King, 2003, xiv). Its origins lie in a rejection of the core methodological foundations of mainstream economics particularly with the use of comparative static equilibrium method.

Post-Keynesian is a portmanteau term covering a number of different strands of thought. Originally, the main uniting theme was a reaction against the mainstream, and a critique associated with the Cambridge capital controversies. From this has arisen a number of alternative theoretical structures, with differing methodological foundations. There has been some debate amongst these economists as to the compatibility of these new approaches and as to whether they can all be considered as post-Keynesian.

What the approaches share is that they are inspired by the contributions of Keynes, particularly *The General Theory of Employment, Interest and Money* (1936). However, in addition, they all incorporate elements of classical, Marxian and institutional economic thought and have been influenced by the work of Kalecki, who developed a theory of effective demand reaching similar conclusions to Keynes, but embodied in a broader framework of economics, incorporating Marx's schemas of reproduction, imperfectly competitive market structures, income distribution and the dynamics associated with cycles and growth.

Subsequently, there have been a number of surveys and attempts to clarify exactly what is meant by the designation 'post-Keynesian economics', with some disagreement as to the exact nature of the enterprise. The next section contains a brief overview of what we see as the main methodological features of post-Keynesian economics.

In a Festschrift for John E. King, we considered the question of the coherence of post-Keynesian and Sraffian economics and concluded that 'Serious and irreconcilable methodological differences exist between Sraffians and post-Keynesians about the validity of comparisons of long-run equilibrium positions, the role of historical versus logical time, the significance of imperfect competition and of uncertainty and of the consequences of money' (Hart and Kriesler, 2016). These issues are revisited in the next section. Some of the parallels between post-Keynesian and evolutionary economics are considered in the subsequent section.

WHAT IS THIS THING CALLED POST-KEYNESIAN ECONOMICS?

The vision of capitalist economies which underlies post-Keynesians' view of the economy is as part of a historical process, with the unchangeable past influencing the present, and with inherent uncertainty about the future. Within this, class divisions dominate – with unequal access to power, wealth and income. As a result, the emphasis of their analysis is on historical time, with expectations having significant and unavoidable impacts on economic events. Given that most important economic decisions are made within an environment of fundamental uncertainty, conventions, rules of thumb and satisficing behaviour arise as a method of dealing with this, with institutions also taking on a paramount role (Kriesler, 1999; Halevi, Hart and Kriesler, 2013).

In a previous attempt to consider its coherence, we outlined five main features which characterised post-Keynesian economics:

1. The denial of the validity or the usefulness of a general theory;
2. The view of the economy as being a historical process, with the unchangeable past influencing the present, hence the key role of uncertainty;
3. Concern with historical time, the future is uncertain and expectations have a significant and unavoidable impact on economic events;
4. The importance of institutions, social and political forces in shaping economic events;
5. The central role of effective demand and of money/finance in determining the levels of employment and output. (Hart and Kriesler, 2016, 190)

As a result of these considerations, economic action is seen to occur in the short run in response to the impacts of both short-period and long-period factors on decision-making. This approach overcomes the disconnect between the short period and the long period, which is most apparent in the incoherence of the medium period/run in mainstream analysis (Solow, 2000; Kriesler, Nevile and Harcourt, 2014). In terms of growth, all the economic growth rates identified by Harrod – the actual rate of growth, the expected rate of growth, the natural rate of growth (given by the growth rate of the workforce and of their productivity) and the warranted growth rate (the growth rate which fulfils the plans of decision-makers) – are interdependent and influence each other, giving rise to the cyclical growth models associated especially with Goodwin (1967) and Kalecki (1968).

Cumulative causation processes identified by Adam Smith and developed during the last century by Veblen, Myrdal, Allyn Young and Kaldor play important roles in post-Keynesian analysis. These processes characterise important markets – such as the stock exchange, foreign exchange markets, housing markets – and even whole economic systems. In these markets stocks dominate flows, and expectations and speculation dominate traditional economic fundamentals in the determination of prices and quantities (Kaldor, 1939). As a result, cumulative causation dominates any equilibrating tendencies.

Associated with this is the rejection of the validity of static comparative equilibrium analysis based on logical time which plays a particularly important role in mainstream economics. Joan Robinson has been particularly critical of the reliance on logical time, arguing that economics should be based on historical time which is continuous and irreversible (Robinson, 1974). This means that what happens today is vitally dependent on the history of the economy. The size and composition of the capital stock – human and physical – as well as the economic, political and social institutions are all the legacies of irreversible decisions made in the past on the basis of imperfect information in an environment of uncertainty. Over time all of these will change as a result of decisions being continuously made and revised. This means that change is cumulative, resulting from decisions made in the past. As a result, 'long-run' positions can't exist independently from 'short-run' adjustments – and so are determined by the path the economy has taken. Importantly, the past is irreversible – we can't undo the consequences of past decisions – while the future is unknowable. Path determinacy implicit with historical time is central to post-Keynesian analysis, so, to explain the current position of the economy, or to make predictions about the future, it is vital to know how the economy came to be there – its history.

As stated by Joan Robinson, the post-Keynesian objections to equilibrium-based theory (similar to those expressed by evolutionary economists): 'The point is that the very process of moving has an effect upon the destination of the movement, so that there is no such thing as a position of long-run equilibrium which exists independently of the course which the economy is following at a particular date' (Robinson, 1953a, 177).[1]

In this environment, the consequence of uncertainty on all aspects of economic behaviour is fundamental. To deal with this, historically and conventionally determined behaviour alongside the evolution of institutions become the norm for determining outcomes. This means that, from a post-Keynesian perspective, the stylised facts of capitalism and of the specific economy being observed become the starting point of the analysis, rather than abstract theorems based on behaviour postulates that don't relate to the specifics.

Conventions and institutions, such as rules of thumb and satisficing behaviour, have evolved as ways of dealing with uncertainty. As these conventions and behaviours evolve differently, they will vary between economies and over times, which explains why most post-Keynesian economists deny the usefulness of general theories to explain all economic activity. Rather, they argue that analysis needs to start from the institutional basis of the economy, stressing the importance of institutions' economic and political forces in shaping economic events. According to Kalecki 'the institutional framework of a social system is a basic element of its economic dynamics' (Kalecki, 1970, 311). Of course, all of these evolve with the economy, with important feedbacks between all the components. Consequently, they take a 'horses for courses' approach, in which development of key institutions, both social and economic, will influence the underlying dynamics of the economy, so that the choice of most appropriate analysis vitally depends on the nature of the economy being considered.

Overall, post-Keynesians have an ambiguous response to the use of equilibrium theory. Many post-Keynesians reject it out of hand. This is because in an economy in historical time with fundamental uncertainty it is unclear if the process of getting into equilibrium can actually be modelled. Elsewhere, we have identified a number of views as to the usefulness of equilibrium analysis and argued that, according to post-Keynesian economists, 'Equilibrium is not a useful concept, as the economy is always on a dynamic path that does not tend toward any equilibrium' (Halevi et al., 2013, 176). For example, Setterfield (1997b), although favouring path determinacy over equilibrium nevertheless sees some purpose in using it as a reference point, while Chick (2023) takes a nuanced view not totally rejecting equilibrium analysis. Nevertheless, both authors favour more path-determined analysis with a slight concession to the possible usefulness of equilibrium as a reference point.

Post-Keynesian economists argue that capitalism has evolved beyond its initial 'competitive' stage and is imperfectly competitive, characterised by oligopolistic market structures – increasingly multinational corporations. Firms within these structures have significant market power, which enables them to dominate domestic markets and influence both governments and institutions. This can be compared to the analysis of classical economists, there competition was associated with the free movement of capital in response to profit rate differentials, leading to a strong tendency towards a uniform rate of profits. Rather, barriers to entry inhibit the free mobility of capital and play important roles in allowing significant profit rate differentials between firms and industries. The industrial barriers are reinforced by the financial sector where the ability and terms of borrowing by firms for accumulation are determined, to a large extent, by the size of the firm – reinforcing existing market power (Kalecki, 1937).

Within this methodological framework, the emphasis is on effective demand as the main factor determining the level of employment and output, as well as being a causal factor of economic growth. Although domestic consumption is the major component of demand, the analysis of investment is seen as crucial due to its volatility. It is in the explanation of investment that money and finance play key roles, resulting in their non-neutrality. For post-Keynesian economists, monetary factors influence and are influenced by real factors in both the short and the long period (Harcourt, 2012; Kriesler, 1997).

POST-KEYNESIAN AND SRAFFIAN ECONOMICS, CONTRASTING METHODOLOGIES[2]

Due to the influence of Sraffa on post-Keynesian economists, in particular the fundamental contribution to the critique of mainstream economic theory, the Sraffian school was initially considered as part of that tradition. However, as the main characteristics of post-Keynesianism began to be articulated, many of its proponents started doubting the compatibility of the Sraffa school with key elements outlined in the previous section. Sraffians' objects of analysis are the long-run centres of gravity which serve as the equivalent of equilibrium positions to which the economy tends. The problem for post-Keynesians is not so much analysis of these positions, as their independence of the path taken to get there.

Sraffian economics focuses on the production process and the relationships between different sectors of the economy and emphasises the role of technical conditions and institutional arrangements in shaping economic outcomes. At the heart of Sraffian economics is the concept of a 'circular production system', which refers to an economy in which the outputs of one industry are used as inputs in other industries, and vice versa. According to Sraffians, prices of goods and services are determined by the technical conditions of production and the institutional arrangements that govern the distribution of income. In a circular production system, the prices of goods and services cannot be determined by supply and demand in individual markets, as assumed by neoclassical theory. Instead, prices are determined by the interdependent relationships between different sectors of the economy.

Sraffian economics offers a critique of neoclassical economics and emphasises the importance of understanding the technical conditions of production while providing a theoretical framework for analysing the interdependent relationships between different sectors of the economy. It does so by considering long-run positions of the economy, which it considers to be centres of gravitation, focusing on the microeconomic level.

The Sraffa equations, derived from the technical input–output equations for all sectors of the economy, show the long-run positions of prices around which market prices are assumed to oscillate with output given. The central problem for the analysis is to show the determination of long-period prices, so price theory forms the core of the analysis and is important for its own sake. Within the analysis, competitive processes push the economy to the long-run position. In particular, a strong tendency towards a uniform rate of profits across the economy is both the driving force towards equilibrium and part of the definition of long-run positions. The tendency to a uniform profit rate plays a fundamental role in Sraffian theory as the main force driving market prices to their long-period positions. This is the view that dominated classical economics, where this tendency was synonymous with the role of competition. It also played a key role in the analysis of Marx. However, Marx also thought that, with the development of capitalism, this form of competition would be eroded by firms exerting political and economic power. For post-Keynesians, competition works in very different ways, with any tendency towards uniform profit rates being overwhelmed by other forces – particularly those associated with increased concentration and the rise of powerful oligopolies (Halevi and Kriesler, 1991).

The adjustment process for Sraffians occurred as competitive processes were assumed to lead to increased investment in areas making above the normal rate of profits, while investment would fall (even to negative net levels) in those sectors making below normal profits. The resulting increase (decrease) in capital would increase (decrease) supply, pushing prices down until normal profits are established. However, investment associated with this process is likely to advantage profitable firms in a cumulative way, strengthening their competitive edge and overwhelming any tendency to uniform profit rates. In addition, such processes are associated with technical progress and structural changes which will cause new production processes and new products to emerge in a process of cumulative causation (Young, 1928; Myrdal, 1957). This reinforces the argument that path dependency rather than long-period equilibrium positions is the best way to understand competitive processes.

As a result, profit differentials may grow due to the increased investment in the sector. Even if there were long-period positions to which the economy gravitated, as we have argued in the previous section, these would be path determined and could not be analysed independent of the path the economy takes to achieve them. However, the evolutionary and cumulative nature of growth and dynamics makes most post-Keynesian economists doubt the validity of any long-period position, particularly if, as with the Sraffians, they are independent of the movements of the economy when not in those long-run positions, i.e. when path determinacy is ignored.

Most post-Keynesians would argue that modern capitalist economies have evolved in such a way that the competitive process will no longer provide forces which push economies to long-period positions, if they ever did. This critique of the Sraffian analysis is reinforced by the methodological critique of comparative static analysis discussed above. As a result, we would argue that the methodological differences between Sraffians and post-Keynesian economists are so fundamental as to render their analytical frameworks incompatible.

POST-KEYNESIAN AND EVOLUTIONARY ECONOMICS: COMPATIBLE BEDFELLOWS[3]

In 2011, the Veblen–Commons Award from the Association for Evolutionary Economics in recognition of significant contributions to evolutionary and institutional economics was awarded jointly to Geoff Harcourt and Jan Kregel, two preeminent developers of what has come to constitute post-Keynesian economics (Prasch, 2011). In this section some key aspects of evolutionary economics of interest to post-Keynesian economists will be noted. These connections are often recognisable implicitly in the work of the two schools of thought, together with the many common objections they have to what they perceive to be representative of mainstream economics. Indeed, it is somewhat surprising that a greater cross-fertilisation of ideas between the two approaches has not been developed further.

Evolutionary economics draws on principles from evolutionary biology, complex systems theory and institutional economics to explain economic phenomena. At its core, it posits that economic systems are dynamic, adaptive and self-organising, and that they evolve over time through a process of variation, selection and replication. It sees economic systems as akin to living organisms that adapt and change in response to environmental pressures, such as technological change, market conditions, international influences or regulatory interventions. It recognises that economic agents, such as firms, consumers and institutions, have limited information, bounded rationality and diverse preferences, and that they interact with each other in complex and often unpredictable ways. As a result, like post-Keynesian economics, it also emphasises the role of institutions, both formal and informal, in shaping economic behaviour and outcomes, with institutions providing the rules, norms and routines that guide economic activities and coordinate social interactions. They can also create path dependencies, whereby past decisions and events influence future choices and outcomes. Evolutionary economics focuses on the microeconomic level and emphasises the role of innovation, learning and adaptation in driving economic change and growth.

Evolutionary/institutional economics has had a long and interesting history, including the well-known contributions of the likes of Thorstein Veblen and Joseph Schumpeter, with the emergence of modern evolutionary economics most often associated with Nelson and Winter's (1982) substantive volume. Nelson and Winter's positive contribution had emerged from a dissatisfaction with the treatment of firm behaviour and long-run economic development processes within mainstream economics (Nelson and Winter, 1974). These criticisms parallel in many respects those found in the post-Keynesian literature. Nelson (1973, 1980, 1981) was particularly critical of the orthodox 'neoclassical' equilibrium-based treatment of growth and technical progress, instead emphasising the implications arising from the uncertain and disorderly nature of such processes. Winter's (1964, 1971) concerns were related directly to the simplistic behavioural assumptions that formed the basis of the maximisation conditions describing the decision-making behaviour of firms within the mainstream equilibrium-based models. It was from this critical perspective that Winter developed the idea that the behaviour of business organisations could be more effectively explained in terms of general habits and strategic orientations emanating from the firm's past.

The literature that followed Nelson and Winter has been constructed from a variety of ontological, methodological and theoretical foundations. A working definition of what constitutes modern evolutionary economics is provided in the 2008 *New Palgrave Dictionary of Economics*:

> Evolutionary economics focuses on the processes that transform the economy from within and investigates their implications for firms and industries, production, trade, employment, and growth. These processes emerge from the activities of agents with bounded rationality who learn from their own experience and that of others and who are capable of innovating. The diversity of individual capabilities, learning efforts, and innovative activities results in growing, distributed knowledge in the economy that supports the variety of coexisting technologies, institutions, and commercial enterprises. The variety drives competition and facilitates the discovery of better ways of doing things. The question in evolutionary economics is therefore not how, under varying conditions, economic resources are optimally allocated in equilibrium given the state of individual preferences, technology and institutional conditions. The questions are instead why and how knowledge, preferences, technology, and institutions change in the historical process, and what impact these changes have on the state of the economy at any point in time. (Witt, 2008, 1873)[4]

The notion of evolutionary change indicates an ongoing process of transformation and growth which is both cumulative and irreversible in time. Central is the

accumulation, acquisition and application of new knowledge, which becomes
the basis of new routines that govern human and organisational behaviour,
and which define the state of technology at a point in time. Investment in
physical and human capital is central to both creativity and adaptation, which
is the source of adaptive economic change (Metcalfe, Foster and Ramlogan,
2006). Most importantly, investment enhances productive capabilities, both
for the aggregate economy and for individual firms. The growth in productive
capabilities is uneven amongst individual firms, consequently providing the
impetus for further investment opportunities.

By their nature, the outcomes of evolutionary processes are uncertain and
often unpredictable, and it is in this setting that economic questions are formulated and sought to be resolved. These processes are not reducible to mechani-
cal laws, and the outcomes observed at any point in time cannot be interpreted
as 'optimal' in the sense of being best fitted to current circumstances. However,
evolutionary change does not imply instability, as order can be established
through behavioural routines and forms of organisations and institutional
arrangements (including government policy) that have evolved through time.
Importantly, stability does not entail equilibrium, as systems in equilibrium do
not, and cannot, evolve. Therefore, notions such as 'long-period equilibrium',
and 'equilibrium growth path', defy logic. Similarly, prediction based on static
equilibrium analysis has no operational role to play within this framework,
given the cumulative and path-dependent nature of change. Formal modelling
does play an important role in evolutionary studies; however, this largely
takes the form of rather sophisticated simulation studies where alternative
scenarios can be considered and evaluated. This reinforces the view shared by
both post-Keynesian and evolutionary economists of the importance of path
determinacy and the limitations of equilibrium analysis.

In place of the traditional exogenous and endogenous equilibrium-based
approaches to growth theory, as discussed in the previous section, many
economists following Nicholas Kaldor, within the post-Keynesian approach,
have adopted notions of cumulative causation. Not surprisingly, this mode of
thinking was championed by the pioneering evolutionary economist, Veblen:

> And this last recourse has in our time been made available for the handling of
> schemes of development and theories of a comprehensive process by the notion
> of a cumulative causation. The great deserts of the evolutionist leaders – if they
> have great deserts as leaders – lie, on the one hand, in their refusal to go back to
> the colorless sequence of phenomena and seek higher ground for their ultimate syn-
> theses, and, on the other hand, in their having shown how this colorless impersonal
> sequence of cause and effect can be made use of for theory proper, by virtue of its
> cumulative character. (Veblen, 1898, 377)

The cumulative causation approach embraces a number of different specifications, however, its defining characteristics can be found in the common themes informing the work of Gunnar Myrdal and Kaldor (Kaldor, 1972, 1985), and earlier Allyn Young, and their followers. Cumulative causation is seen as an extended and open-ended sequence of causal linkages. First, there is the notion of 'circular causation' which emphasises the multicausal nature of the complex linkages between core variables. Similarly, 'cumulative causation' occurs as positive feedback processes magnify and multiply the impact of these interactions through time. Negative feedback effects may also move the system in opposite directions, with endogenous contradictions often embedded in the cumulative causation processes (Berger, 2008).

Although cumulative causation analysis does offer a very useful framework in which the implications of evolutionary change can be described, it does not provide a systematic portrayal or explanation of such processes. While there is a legitimate debate to be held over the virtues of analytical tractability and rigour, and empirical substance, evolutionary economics does provide the opportunity to incorporate a range of tools and techniques that can investigate these processes more formally.[5] More importantly, evolutionary economics can address what Geoffrey Hodgson (1989) argued was the lack of institutional foundations within the cumulative causation studies, which, therefore leads to a failure to adequately consider the inherited institutional structures and social practices that affect growth and development.[6]

While evolutionary economics offers a powerful vehicle through which the nature of qualitative economic change can be investigated, post-Keynesian theory sheds light on the determination of prices and economic aggregates that emerge from such processes, and which in turn place limits on the ability of economic systems to adapt to change and create new possibilities for change. These explanations escape the restrictions imposed by equilibrium-based theories which, as post-Keynesian economists have demonstrated, are divorced from the realities of economic systems evolving through historical time. Evolutionary economics also offers the opportunity to broaden the multidisciplinary dimension of economic analysis, as is illustrated, for example, in the emerging literature on evolutionary economic geography (Boschma, 2012; Kogler, 2016; Frenken, 2007).

The business environment portrayed within evolutionary economics is closely aligned with that of the post-Keynesian representation of firms and industry organisation. Following the approach advocated by Michał Kalecki and based on the empirical studies by Hall and Hitch (1939) and others, post-Keynesians observe that the majority of goods and services are produced in industries characterised by imperfect competition and oligopolistic markets. The assumption of myopic profit-maximising behaviour is replaced with a notion of mark-up pricing where prices are depicted as being a 'mark-up' on expected average costs of production. Excess capacity exists as a buffer against unanticipated changes in demand for the product. The mark-up itself is a function of several factors, including those relevant to financial and strategic considerations targeting survival and growth. In an evolutionary economics setting, the mark-up pricing principle can be seen as a 'rule of thumb' pricing routine adaptable to the variable and uncertain environment in which corporations seek to survive and grow.

When considering organisations, evolutionary economics highlights the effectiveness and changing nature of routines through time that guide their behaviour, leading to a representation of competition among firms where innovation, survival and growth are key outcomes. Schumpeterian notions of technological competition, invention and innovation as the dynamic of capitalist development are combined with the biological analogies associated with natural selection, together with behavioural theories of the firm, initially inspired by the work of Alchian (1950) and Simon (1959) in particular. These general themes signpost several different approaches, including, for example, the development of what has been termed the 'organisational capabilities' theories of the firm. These theories emphasise the significance of interfirm relationships and markets, along with implications arising from imperfections and asymmetries in knowledge about how to produce and coordinate activities (Langlois and Foss, 1999; Winter, 2003). The strategic efforts to build and improve the set of operative capabilities as reflected in its array of accumulated strategic routines are considered. Most importantly, an explicit role for the cognitive powers of human beings is found in these theories, in particular relating to how these powers help shape organisational forms in response to changes in the environment in which interactions occur (Loasby, 1999).

The discussion above indicates close parallels between post-Keynesian and evolutionary schools of thought, both in terms of what they reject and what they agree upon. Indeed, it may be useful to think of the post-Keynesian depiction of the operation of economic systems as being embedded within evolutionary processes. Certainly, some methodological differences and disputes may arise between the two schools of thought, particularly in relation to the role and limitations of formal modelling. However, to some extent, these differences also mirror debates within the respective approaches. Importantly, evolutionary economics provides an opportunity to delve more deeply into the behavioural observations that form the basis of post-Keynesian analysis. At the same time, the analytical tools developed by post-Keynesian economists add clarity to the consideration of policy issues that in turn have a major impact on the operation of the processes being described by evolutionary economists.

CONCLUSION

As Geoff Harcourt (2006, 2) observed, post-Keynesianism is an extremely broad church, with significant overlap with some other schools of thought that oppose aspects of mainstream theory and method. This chapter has investigated the extent to which the Sraffian framework and evolutionary economics may sit comfortably within this broad church. We have argued that, to a significant extent, Sraffians and post-Keynesians are incompatible bed-fellows, for reasons similar to those stated by the pioneering post-Keynesian Joan Robinson, namely due to deep methodological differences. Despite her profound regard for Sraffa's intellectual influences, and her complete endorsement of his critique of the marginalist theories, Robinson was unable to satisfactorily 'reconcile' Sraffa's perspective of the 'classical' tradition with her vision of the Keynesian tradition:

> Sraffa habitually uses the language of change but, properly speaking, there are no events in his world except for the cycle of self-reproduction and the flow of net output to wages and net profits … there is no movement from one position to another, merely a comparison of positions corresponding to different levels of the rate of profits. (Robinson, 1980a, 139)

> All of this is a purely logical structure – an elaborate thought experiment. There is no causation and no change. At each moment, in any one system, the stock of inputs required for its technology and its growth rate has already come into existence, which implies that in the past, when stocks were being replaced, there must have been correct foresight of what 'today' would be like, so that the profit-maximising variety of technology has been installed – in short the distinction between the future and the past, as viewed from 'today', has been abolished. (Robinson, 1980b, 132)

On the other hand, as discussed in the previous section, evolutionary economics is concerned with economic systems that are undergoing continuous change and transformation, and the behaviour of individuals, groups and institutions within these evolving systems. Recognition of the connections and synergies existing between the post-Keynesian approach and evolutionary economics adds considerably to the explanatory capabilities of both methods of analysis.

NOTES

1. See also Robinson (1953b).
2. This section develops analysis from Halevi and Kriesler (1991) and Hart and Kriesler (2016).
3. Discussion in this section incorporates material referred to in Hart (2013).
4. Recent accounts of the current themes in evolutionary economics include Nelson et al. (2018) and Hodgson (2019).

5.   See, for example, discussion in Fagerberg (2003) and Foster and Metcalfe
      (2004).
6.   On the other hand, Hodgson (1999, 174) defends the method of theorising in
      Nelson and Winter's work by arguing that it 'does not exhibit formalism for its
      own sake but is a genuine attempt to rebuild economics as an operational and
      empirically enriched science'. Setterfield (1997a) provided an early attempt to
      address these issues within the cumulative causation framework.

REFERENCES

Alchian, A. A. (1950). Uncertainty, Evolution, and Economic Theory. *Journal of
    Political Economy*, *58*(2), 211–21.
Berger, S. (2008). Circular Cumulative Causation à la Myrdal and Kapp – Political
    Institutionalism for Minimizing Social Costs. *Journal of Economic Issues*, *42*(2),
    357–66.
Boschma, R. A. (ed.) (2012). *The Handbook of Evolutionary Economic Geography*.
    Edward Elgar Publishing: Cheltenham, UK and Northampton, MA, USA.
Chick, V. (2023). Should equilibrium be abandoned by heterodox economists?, in
    Negru, I. and Hawkins, P. (eds) *Economic Methodology, History and Pluralism*
    (pp. 108–21) Routledge: London.
Fagerberg, J. (2003). Schumpeter and the Revival of Evolutionary Economics: An
    Appraisal of the Literature. *Journal of Evolutionary Economics*, *13*(2), 125–59.
Foster, J. and J. S. Metcalfe (eds) (2004). *Frontiers of Evolutionary Economics:
    Competition, Self-Organisation and Innovation Policy*. Edward Elgar Publishing:
    Cheltenham, UK and Northampton, MA, USA.
Frenken, K. (2007). *Applied Evolutionary Economics and Economic Geography*.
    Edward Elgar Publishing: Cheltenham, UK and Northampton, MA, USA.
Goodwin, R. M. (1967). A growth cycle, in Feinstein, C. H. (ed.) *Socialism, Capitalism
    and Economic Growth: Essays Presented to Maurice Dobb* (pp. 54–58) Cambridge
    University Press: Cambridge, reprinted in Goodwin, R. M. (1982). *Essays in
    Economic Dynamics* (pp. 165–70) Palgrave Macmillan: London.
Halevi, J., N. Hart and P. Kriesler (2013). The traverse, equilibrium analysis and
    post-Keynesian economics, in Harcourt, G. C. and Kriesler, P. (eds) *Oxford
    Handbook of Post-Keynesian Economics Volume 2: Critiques and Methodology*
    (pp. 175–97) Oxford University Press: New York.
Halevi, J. and P. Kriesler (1991). Kalecki, Classical Economics and the Surplus
    Approach. *Review of Political Economy*, *3*(1), 79–92.
Hall, R. L. and C. J. Hitch (1939). Price Theory and Business Behaviour. *Oxford
    Economic Papers*, *2*(1), 12–45.
Harcourt, G. C. (2006). *The Structure of Post-Keynesian Economics: The Core
    Contributions of the Pioneers*. Cambridge University Press: Cambridge.
Harcourt, G. C. (2012). On the concept of period and run in economic theory, in Gehrke,
    C., Salvadori, N., Steedman, I. and Sturn, R. (eds) *Classical Political Economy and
    Modern Theory: Essays in Honour of Heinz Kurz* (pp. 257–65) Routledge: London.
Hart, N. (2013). *Alfred Marshall and Modern Economics: Equilibrium Theory and
    Evolutionary Economics*. Palgrave Macmillan: Basingstoke, UK.
Hart, N. and P. Kriesler (2016). Keynes, Kalecki, Sraffa: coherence within pluralism?,
    in Courvisanos, J., Millmow, A. and Doughney, J. (eds) *Reclaiming Pluralism in*

Economics: Essays in Honour of John E. King (pp. 186–202) Routledge: London. SSRN: https://papers.ssrn.com/sol3/papers.cfm?abstract_id=2393724.

Hodgson, G. M. (1989). Institutional Rigidities and Economics Growth. *Cambridge Journal of Economics*, *13*(1), 79–101.

Hodgson, G. M. (1999). *Evolution and Institutions: On Evolutionary Economics and the Evolution of Economics*. Edward Elgar Publishing: Cheltenham, UK and Northampton, MA, USA.

Hodgson, G. M. (2019). *Evolutionary Economics: Its Nature and Future*. Cambridge University Press: Cambridge.

Kaldor, N. (1939). Speculation and Economic Activity. *Review of Economic Studies*, *7*(1), 1–2.

Kaldor, N. (1972). The Irrelevance of Equilibrium Economics. *Economic Journal*, *82*(328), 1237–55.

Kaldor, N. (1985). *Economics without Equilibrium*. University College of Cardiff Press: Cardiff, UK.

Kalecki, M. (1937). The Principle of Increasing Risk. *Economica: New Series*, *4*(16), 440–47.

Kalecki, M. (1968). Trend and Business Cycles Reconsidered. *Economic Journal*, *78*(310), 263–76, reprinted in Ositaynski, J. (ed.) (1991). *Collected Works Volume II: Capitalism: Economic Dynamics* (pp. 435–50) Oxford University Press: Oxford.

Kalecki, M. (1970). Theories of Growth in Different Social Systems. *Scientia*, *64*(5), 311–16.

Keynes, J. M. (1936). *The General Theory of Employment, Interest and Money*. Palgrave Macmillan: London.

King, J. E. (2003). *The Elgar Companion to Post-Keynesian Economics*. Edward Elgar Publishing: Cheltenham, UK and Northampton, MA, USA.

Kogler, D. (2016). *Evolutionary Economic Geography: Theoretical and Empirical Progress*. Routledge: Abingdon.

Kriesler, P. (1997). Keynes, Kalecki and the General Theory, in Harcourt, G. C. and Riach, P. (eds) *A 'Second Edition' of The General Theory* (pp. 300–22) Routledge: London.

Kriesler, P. (1999). Harcourt, Hicks and Lowe: incompatible bedfellows?, in Sardoni, C. and Kriesler, P. (eds) *Keynes, Post-Keynesianism and Political Economy: Essays in Honour of Geoff Harcourt Volume 3* (pp. 400–17) Routledge: London.

Kriesler, P., Nevile, J. and Harcourt, G. C. (2014). *Why myths in neoclassical economics threaten the world economy: A post-Keynesian manifesto*, UNSW Australian School of Business Research Paper No. 2013–36, http://papers.ssrn.com/sol3/papers.cfm?abstract_id=2374960.

Langlois, R. N. and N. J. Foss (1999). Capabilities and Governance: The Rebirth of Production in the Theory of Economic Organization. *Kyklos*, *52*(2), 201–18.

Loasby, B. J. (1999). *Knowledge, Institutions and Evolution in Economics*. Routledge: London.

Metcalfe, J. S., J. Foster and R. Ramlogan (2006). Adaptive Economic Growth. *Cambridge Journal of Economics*, *30*(1), 7–32.

Myrdal, G. (1957). *Economic Theory and Underdeveloped Regions*. Gerald Duckworth: London.

Nelson, R. A., G. Dosi, C. E. Helfat, A. Pyka, P. Saviotti, K. Lee, S. G. Winter, K. Dopfer and F. Malerba (2018). *Modern Evolutionary Economics: An Overview*. Cambridge University Press: Cambridge.

Nelson, R. R. (1973). Recent Exercises in Growth Accounting: New Understanding or Dead End? *American Economic Review*, *63*(3), 462–68.

Nelson, R. R. (1980). Production Sets, Technological Knowledge and R&D: Fragile and Overworked Constructs for Analysis of Productivity Growth? *American Economic Review*, *70*(2), 62–67.

Nelson, R. R. (1981). Research on Productivity Growth and Productivity Differences: Dead Ends and New Departures. *Journal of Economic Literature*, *29*(3), 1029–64.

Nelson, R. R. and S. G. Winter (1974). Neoclassical vs. Evolutionary Theories of Economic Growth: Critique and Prospectus. *Economic Journal*, *84*(4), 886–905.

Nelson, R. R. and S. G. Winter (1982). *An Evolutionary Theory of Economic Change.* Harvard University Press: Cambridge, MA, USA.

Prasch, R. E. (2011). The 2011 Veblen–Commons Award Recipients: Geoffrey Harcourt and Jan Kregel. *Journal of Economic Issues*, *45*(2), 257–60.

Robinson, J. (1953a). 'Imperfect Competition' Revisited. *Economic Journal*, *63*(251), 579–93, reprinted in Robinson, J. (1978). *Contributions to Modern Economics* (pp. 166–81) Basil Blackwell: Oxford.

Robinson, J. (1953b). A Lecture Delivered at Oxford by a Cambridge Economist, reprinted in Robinson, J. (1980). *Collected Economic Papers IV* (pp. 254–63) Basil Blackwell: Oxford.

Robinson, J. (1974) History versus Equilibrium. *Thames Papers in Political Economy*. Thames Polytechnic: London, reprinted in Robinson, J. (1980). *Collected Economic Papers V* (pp. 48–58) Basil Blackwell: Oxford.

Robinson, J. (1980a). Misunderstandings in the Theory of Production, in Robinson, J. (1980). *Further Contributions to Modern Economics* (pp. 135–40) Basil Blackwell: Oxford.

Robinson, J. (1980b). Retrospect: 1980, in Robinson, J. (1980). *Further Contributions to Modern Economics* (pp. 131–34) Basil Blackwell: Oxford.

Setterfield, M. (1997a). 'History versus Equilibrium' and the Theory of Economic Growth. *Cambridge Journal of Economics*, *21*(3), 365–78.

Setterfield, M. (1997b). Should Economists Dispense with the Notion of Equilibrium? *Journal of Post-Keynesian Economics*, *20*(1), 47–76.

Simon, H. A. (1959). Theories of Decision Making in Economics and Behavioral Science. *American Economic Review*, *49*(3), 253–83.

Solow, R. M. (2000). The Neoclassical Theory of Growth and Distribution. *Banca Nazionale del Lavoro Quarterly Review*, *53*(215), 349–81.

Veblen, T. B. (1898). Why Is Economics Not an Evolutionary Science? *Quarterly Journal of Economics*, *12*(3), 373–97.

Winter, S. G. (1964). Economic 'Natural Selection' and the Theory of the Firm. *Yale Economic Essays*, *4*(1), 225–72.

Winter, S. G. (1971). Satisficing, Selection and the Innovation Remnant. *Quarterly Journal of Economics*, *85*(2), 237–61.

Winter, S. G. (2003). Understanding Dynamic Capabilities. *Strategic Management Journal*, *24*(10), 991–95.

Witt, U. (2008). Evolutionary economics, in Durlauf, S. N. and Blume, E. (eds) *The New Palgrave Dictionary of Economics* (pp. 1873–79) Palgrave Macmillan: London.

Young, A. (1928). Increasing Returns and Economic Progress. *Economic Journal*, *38*(152), 527–42.

3. Credit, money, and production: post-Keynesian[1] economics and the circuit traditions[2]

Louis-Philippe Rochon

INTRODUCTION

As King (2013, p. 1) wrote a decade ago now, "The relations between Post Keynesians and other economists have never ceased to be of great interest." While this is undoubtedly true, at least in the eyes of this author as well, writing a chapter on the similarities between post-Keynesian economics and other approaches poses a number of interesting challenges, especially when comparing it to the theory of the monetary circuit.

Chief among these is how to define the circuit approach, let alone how we tackle the thorny issue of what is post-Keynesian economics. Indeed, within each tradition, there are considerable challenges in clearly defining their respective core characteristics. As Lavoie (2014, p. 38) writes, "All post-Keynesians were not created alike."

None of this of course comes as a surprise. In identifying who is a post-Keynesian, for instance, the views of, say, Paul Davidson are not the same as those of Marc Lavoie or John E. King. Is this a matter of substance or simply of emphasis?

At the heart of this interesting inquiry is who is a post-Keynesian economist? Do we adopt a big tent approach and include, say, Sraffians, Institutionalists, and Kaleckians and, if we do, should we even refer to ourselves as post-Keynesians? Perhaps we should use post-Kaleckians, heterodox, post-classical, or nonorthodox, among some of the many names that have been proposed? Post-autistic? My preference is for the use of 'post-Keynesian' for historical reasons, on the understanding that we must accept a bigger tent. This said, I also use the expression heterodox interchangeably.

The problem of identifying post-Keynesian economics – or what Davidson (2005, p. 393) calls "the boundary lines that encompass Post Keynesian economic" – was on full display in Davidson's book review of King's (2002)

A History of Post Keynesian Economics – to which both King and Lavoie in turn replied (see King, 2005; Lavoie, 2005; Davidson, 2003–04, 2005, among many other articles by various other authors).

The same problem applies to the circuit approach, where the views of Alain Parguez are at times different from those of Augusto Graziani. In turn, both of these approaches can at times be very different from the approach developed independently by Bernard Schmitt – or from quantum macroeconomics, as followers of this last group now call themselves. Indeed, as Deleplace and Nell (1996, p. 10) argue, "This diversity of sources explains why the circulation approach does not present a unified front, as an integrated school." As a result, as Lavoie (1987, p. 67) writes, "it is not easy to identify with certainty the fundamental ideas of circulationists", although he would later write that Parguez's views on the circuit "bore an extraordinary resemblance to that being promoted independently in Italy by Augusto Graziani" (Lavoie, 2003, p. 12) (see also Passarella, 2014).

Despite what is just written, identifying similarities between post-Keynesian economics and the theory of the monetary circuit should not be a complicated task as both approaches are "related" (Rousseas, 1996, p. 677). But to be successful, we must remain at the level of general statements and avoid getting too deep into details, otherwise we risk a complete unravelling. For instance, while both approaches certainly accept the notion of endogenous money (general statement), the precise details differ from one approach to the other. Circuit writers would argue that money was always endogenous because of its relationship to credit and debt (the *nature* of money), while some post-Keynesians would argue that money became endogenous through the creation or behaviour of central banks. This is what Rochon and Rossi (2013) have called the revolutionary and evolutionary theories of endogenous money, respectively. Lavoie (1996, p. 533) summarizes well the differences between the two approaches: "accommodation or the lack of it, liability management or the lack of it, and financial innovations or the lack of it are second-order phenomena compared to the crucial causal story that goes from debt creation to the supply of means of payment." Nevertheless, as stated above, as long as we remain in the area of generalities, we should be able to identify common ground.[3]

I should add, of course, that the general similarities between these two approaches should be self-evident in the sense that both are very much rooted in Keynes, or at least in their respective interpretations of Keynes's *General Theory*, although for proponents of the monetary circuit, Keynes's *Treatise on Money* is perhaps more central. From the start, therefore, they share similar intellectual roots. Indeed, as Gnos (2006, p. 87) writes, "today's French circuit school owes much to Keynes", and, as such, both approaches were keenly aware of the economics at Cambridge, certainly aided by the translation in

1942 of Keynes's *General Theory* by Jean de l'Argentaye, a French civil servant.

Moreover, and I would say unsurprisingly, it is no mere coincidence that Marc Lavoie is a leading voice of both approaches, which should make a comparison rather evident: a leading post-Keynesian, he was, as he says, "brought up in the tradition of the monetary circuit theory" (see Lavoie, 2012, p. 142). For the record, many have already commented on these similarities; for instance, Halevi and Taouil (2002) even refer to the "post-Keynesian Circuitistes", Berr and Monvoisin (2023) refer to Parguez's work as the "post-Keynesian circuit theory." So, clearly, the idea that there exists links between post-Keynesian and circuit theories is now widely accepted. As Lucarelli and Passarella (2012, p. 2) write, "the MTP presents a noteworthy degree of resemblance to (and consistency with) the current post-Keynesian economics." I myself wrote on this nexus (see Rochon, 1999a, 2003).

Another challenge for me is that I am not always certain where post-Keynesian economics begins and where the circuit approach ends, or indeed whether I consider myself a circuitist or a post-Keynesian *stricto sensu*. In this sense, my approach to macroeconomics was always "eclectic" (Lavoie, 2022, p. 44) – an expression I certainly embrace – so it is difficult to disentangle in my mind the various strands. Having learned post-Keynesian and heterodox economics in the mid-1980s from Marc Lavoie and Mario Seccareccia, it was natural for me to immediately see the similarities between the post-Keynesian approach, especially in its horizontalist form, and the ideas defended by the French circuitists. This was certainly helped by the fact that Alain Parguez was a regular visitor at the University of Ottawa in those years, with whom I had been in contact, and still very much so until his recent passing. My long walks with Alain, whether in New York, Paris, Toronto, or indeed in Kalamazoo where he visited me a few times, were always an exercise in weaving in and out of the circuit approach, peppered with references to Keynes, Kalecki, and Marx.

With respect to the eclecticism, I would argue that it is characteristic of a great many younger economists today, who are at ease borrowing from one approach or another. This is certainly what I see when I go to conferences. As Lavoie (2014, p. 42) writes, "Several young post-Keynesians feel at ease within all strands, taking the best elements from each." In this context, had this chapter been written even 20 years ago, it would have been very different to the current version.

In the first section of this chapter, I discuss what can be called the institutional rapprochement between the two schools, emphasizing the friendship between Alain Parguez, Marc Lavoie, and Mario Seccareccia. I also discuss Parguez's role in creating institutional links, mainly through the creation of the series *Monnaie et Production*, which he directed over a 12-year period, from 1984 to 1996. In this sense, this chapter focuses more on the French circuit authors. According to Lavoie (1990), it is in 1981 that Parguez started to see close links between the circuit approach and post-Keynesian economics.

In the second half of the chapter, I discuss the theoretical ideas that are shared by both approaches. This is not an exhaustive list, owing to space constraints. I will, however, list a handful of shared ideas or common ground.

A final note before we discuss the institutional history between circuit writers and post-Keynesians. There is a lot that this chapter does not do. In a way, it does not give a full account of all the protagonists involved. This is a Herculean task, and there is much more to this story than what is told here, which should at one point be undertaken properly.

THE EARLY INSTITUTIONAL LINKS BETWEEN POST-KEYNESIANS AND THE CIRCUIT APPROACH

The history of post-Keynesian economics has been well documented (see King, 2002; Lee, 2000; Rochon, 2023). As an institution, it emerged early in the 1970s at a number of meetings and sessions being organized at the American Economic Association annual meetings, starting in New Orleans, in 1971, through the efforts of Joan Robinson and Alfred Eichner. Moreover, as an intellectual body, it emerged in Joan Robinson's *Accumulation of Capital* (1956) – a book that contains all the essential elements of a positive and coherent post-Keynesian alternative to neoclassical theory.

The history of the theory of the monetary circuit, however, has been less well documented, and if it has, these articles are often published in French (for instance, see Poulon, 2018), thereby making them less accessible or less well known, yet it is a story that needs to be told because it is, in my opinion, an integral part of the history of heterodox economics, though King (2002) makes no mention of the theory of the monetary circuit in his *History of Post Keynesian Economics*. But given who is involved, I think it is an important missing piece of the post-Keynesian history puzzle.

In what follows, I offer but a glimpse of the early institutional attempts at bridging the circuit approach with the post-Keynesian school. It is impossible to give a full account, largely because not much has been written on this. Where I can, I indicate readings that give a fuller account of some events.

Let's begin with the term itself. Graziani (2003, p. 2) contends the term 'circuit' as used in the theory comes from the German: "The very term 'circuit', introduced in contemporary literature by French authors, reproduces the German *Kreislauf*, a term used by German writers to describe the circulation of money and of real goods", although the term also appears in the title of a 1903 book written by Johannsen, under the pseudonym J.J.O. Lah, *The Circuit of Money* (see, Graziani, 2003). Of course, one can read the important work of Marx and Wicksell for inspiration. In France, Gnos (2006) has argued that the very early ideas of circuit theory can be linked to 18th-century physiocrats, as found for instance in Francois Quesnay's *Tableau économique*.

But the modern revival of the circuit approach can be traced to both France, under Jacques Le Bourva (1962), Alain Parguez (1975, 1980),[4] Frédéric Poulon (1980, 1982), and Bernard Schmitt (1960); and Italy, in the writings of Augusto Graziani (1984) and Marcello Messori (see Bellofiore and Seccareccia, 1999). As Bellofiore (2019, p. 529) writes, "Augusto Graziani is, with Bernard Schmitt and Alain Parguez, one of the recognised founders of the contemporary version of the *theory of the monetary circuit*."

Bellofiore (2019) gives a brief account of the development of the Italian approach (see also Realfonzo, 2006; Lucarelli and Passarella, 2012) while Poulon (2018, p. 133) acknowledges that Parguez was "the undeniable discoverer" of the French circuit approach. Parguez's role in the forthcoming years in developing the ideas of the circuit and in forging close institutional links with post-Keynesians, as we will see below, will be crucial.

On that note, the close relationship and influence of circuit authors on post-Keynesian economics, and vice versa, is evident in many areas. Most specifically, the relationship between Alain Parguez, Marc Lavoie, and Mario Seccareccia, the latter two in Canada, was an essential link, especially once Parguez started visiting Ottawa on a regular basis (regularly over two decades), starting in the fall of 1981, when Lavoie introduced Parguez to Seccareccia. But there was also Parguez's presence in several Trieste Summer Schools (in the early 1980s; also attended by Jacques Henry and Mario Seccareccia in 1983 and by Marc Lavoie in 1984 where he first met Graziani), which provided him access, so to speak, to many post-Keynesians.[5]

Lavoie studied in Paris and met Parguez sometime in 1976–77, while attending a class at the Université Paris 1 (Panthéon-Sorbonne), given by Bernard Ducros, who was both Parguez's and Lavoie's doctoral supervisor (see Lavoie, 2003, for a discussion). When Ducros was unable to give his lecture, Parguez would step in and lecture in his stead. It is in this setting that Lavoie and Parguez first met, although it was a chance visit by Frédéric Poulon, in early 1976, in Quebec City, where he met Gilles Paquet, who was Lavoie's tutorial-supervisor, that convinced Lavoie to study at the Université Paris 1 for his graduate studies.[6]

But while in Paris under the influence of Ducros and Parguez, Lavoie was also very much interested in the ideas proposed by post-Keynesians, to which he had been introduced in the honours seminar offered by T.K. Rymes, and following his read of the famous Eichner and Kregel (1975) paper. He could see many similarities between the two approaches, as is evident in his early articles (see Lavoie, 1982, 1984, 1985; see also the discussion below). In that sense, from the very beginning of the emergence of post-Keynesian economics, starting with Eichner and Kregel (1975), there was a parallel and closely related approach emerging at the same time in Europe. And indeed, from the very beginning, I would argue through the friendship between Lavoie and Parguez, but involving others as well, that institutional links between the two approaches would develop less than a decade later.

This has been recognized by others as well. For instance, Gnos (2006, p. 87) writes, "French and Italian circuitist approaches have also inspired post-Keynesians outside Europe, especially in Canada." Graziani (2003, p. 4) reaches a similar conclusion: "Among the French and French-Canadian representatives of the circuit theory, Parguez and Lavoie are the two who move closest to the post-Keynesian approach." Lavoie himself argues that his early views were "spurred in part by the critiques of traditional theory by the French circuitists" (Lavoie, 2014, p. 183).

The story about the Italian approach, however, is not as clear. Bellofiore (2019, p. 540) writes that young Italians were influenced by the writings of post-Keynesians in the 1960s and 1970s: "the Italian young economists of the time were also exposed to the influence of Post-Keynesianism: both in the Cambridge (UK) variant, or in the US variant." This said, Bellofiore argues that Graziani developed his views on the circuit independently of the Anglo-Saxon influence.[7]

Perhaps an early first step of integrating post-Keynesian and circuit ideas was made at a conference held on 13 March 1981, at the University of Ottawa, hosted by Jacques Henry and Mario Seccareccia – a conference entitled "Keynes and Sraffa: recent questions in post-Keynesian economics."[8] At this conference, Lavoie (see Lavoie, 1982) presented a paper entitled "Les post-keynésiens et la monnaie endogène" ("Post-Keynesians and endogenous money"); while not a synthesis of post-Keynesian and circuit authors per se, the paper does cite authors from both approaches. In fact, in this article, Lavoie (1982, p. 216) suggests that post-Keynesians need to go further in their 'heretic' or nontraditional Anglo-Saxon views on money, by "finding inspiration in the work of advocates of endogenous money in France." This sentiment was somewhat echoed years later by Kregel, in his 1987 contribution to *Monnaie et Production*: "the circuit approach has done much to reawaken interest in Keynes's monetary theory of production and to extend it in new directions" (see Kregel, 1987, p. 11).

In France, the early and mid-1980s were a cauldron of activities aimed at bringing closer the partisans of the circuit approach and post-Keynesian economics. For instance, in 1981, Parguez (1981) noted that there existed similarities between the two approaches, referring specifically to the work of Shackle, Eichner, and, to a lesser degree, Davidson.

When Parguez arrived in Ottawa, in the fall of 1981, a close friendship developed between him, Lavoie, and Seccareccia. The following year, in 1982, Parguez published a special issue of *Economie Appliquée*,[9] entitled "La monnaie dans le circuit" (*Money in the circuit*), in which Lavoie published an article, as did Jacques Henry (also from the University of Ottawa), Sidney Weintraub, Jan Kregel, Richard Arena, and Frédéric Poulon. Already, through Parguez's efforts, we see a co-mingling of circuit and post-Keynesian authors and ideas, which will only grow over the following years.

This special issue, in a sense, can be considered "a prequel"[10] to the *Monnaie et Production* (Money and Production) series, which Parguez would begin editing the following year, the first issue of which would be published in 1984; Parguez would go on to publish ten special issues in *Économies et Sociétés*, between 1984 and 1996, with many of the issues containing a mix of circuit writers and post-Keynesians. Indeed, as Rochon and Seccareccia (2003, p. 6) write, this 1982 issue was "Alain's first try at editing a large number of papers, which gave him the impetus to start the *Monnaie et Production* series a couple of years later."

In 1983, Edwin Le Heron, along with Alain Barrère,[11] organized a conference at the Sorbonne in celebration of the centenary of Keynes's birth, from 12–15 September. The conference featured a number of circuit writers (Parguez, Poulon, and Schmitt, among others) as well as established post-Keynesians such as Nicholas Kaldor, Paul Davidson, Hyman Minsky, Sidney Weintraub, Robert Eisner, Jan Kregel, Edward Nell, Joseph Steindl, and Dudley Dillard.[12] This meeting resulted in the rather-thick book, *Keynes Aujourd'hui* (*Keynes Today*) with Economica, edited by Barrère (see Barrère, 1985). The book was reviewed, notably, by Lavoie (1985a).[13]

Meanwhile, the following year, in Nice, in 1984, an important conference took place under the guidance of Richard Arena and Augusto Graziani, that brought together a number of scholars, and resulted in a book edited by Arena and Graziani (1985). The main focus of that meeting was to put forward an alternative theory of money, but also to critically discuss various approaches to money, including the post-Keynesian and heterodox approaches. As the editors write, the meeting was about discussing the "necessary and profound renovation [rethinking] of contemporary monetary theory" (see Arena and Graziani, 1985, p. 5).

But in the introduction to this book, it is clear that they are very much aware of post-Keynesian economists. While the contributors were mostly circuit writers of various kinds (Arena, Bellofiore, Costabile, Graziani, Messori, and Parguez, among a few others), Jan Kregel attended.

Still, in 1984, an early paper to specifically look at the links between circuit authors and post-Keynesians would be, I believe, Lavoie (1984), in an article specifically entitled "Un modèle post-keynésien d'économie monétaire fondé sur la théorie du circuit" (*A post-Keynesian model of a monetary economy based on the theory of the circuit*), which was published in the inaugural issue of *Monnaie et Production*. That year, Graziani (1984) also published a now-famous paper on Keynes's finance motive in which there is a clear appreciation of a monetary circuit, while also quoting Paul Davidson and Kaldor–Trevithick.

In another article published that year, this time in English, in the (perhaps more accessible) *Journal of Economic Issues* (see Lavoie, 1984a), Lavoie writes about endogenous money by including in his analysis a key element of circuit theory, that is the idea of Le Bourva's credit divisor. The very long list of references contains well-known circuit and post-Keynesian authors.

Now turning to the publication of *Monnaie et Production*, there is no doubt that it was instrumental in furthering the development and exchange of ideas between post-Keynesians and circuit writers, as well as strengthening the institutional bonds.[14] *Monnaie et Production* was an annual supplement published by the journal *Économies et Sociétés*, which was one of two journals governed by the *l'Institut des Sciences Mathematiques et Économiques Appliquées* (ISMEA), which was created by François Perroux, in 1944. In 1982, Perroux stepped down from the ISMEA, which was now headed by Gérard de Bernis, long associated with the *Université de Grenoble*,[15] who created a number of series within the journal, including *Monnaie et Production*, for which he then asked Parguez to be editor.

According to Graziani (2003, p. 3), "So long as it was published, it was the only really international connection established between French followers of the circulation approach and their counterparts in Anglo-Saxon countries." This view is echoed by Lavoie (2003, p. 12) who writes that the series was "an outlet for the writings of both French- and English-speaking post-Keynesian and other heterodox economists." As a result, Parguez became the "champion of Keynesian economics in France" (Rochon and Seccareccia, 2003, p. 2).

In its very first issue, in April 1984, the links between circuit and post-Keynesian authors are evident. For instance, there were articles by Sheila Dow, Alain Parguez, Marc Lavoie, Mario Seccareccia, Gunnar Heinsohn and Otto Steiger, Jacques Henry, Jan Kregel, and Richard Arena. Graziani would publish an article in the series as early as 1985, on "Money, Interest and Public Spending."

Over those 12 years, other post-Keynesians would publish there as well, and the involvement of post-Keynesians would only grow. Among the authors, we find Victoria Chick and Stephen Rousseas in the 1986 issue, Augusto Graziani and John Hotson in 1987, Jane Knodell in 1988, Athanasios (Tom) Asimakopulos and Robert Guttmann in 1990, Philip Arestis, Tony Aspromourgos, Randall Wray, and Gerry Epstein in 1991, John Smithin, Cardim de Carvalho, Robert Eisner, and John Hotson in 1994, and Steve Keen, Todd Andresen, Paul Dalziel, Steve Pressman, Tom Palley, Peter Kriesler, and Joseph Halevi in 1996.[16]

Meanwhile, Lavoie would publish a paper in 1985 (see Lavoie, 1985), in a book edited by Marc Jarsulic; the paper was entitled "Credit and Money: The Dynamic Circuit, Overdraft Economics, and Post-Keynesian Economics." The main objective of the paper "was to show the similarities and differences between British and American post-Keynesian authors on one hand and French dissidents on the other – heterodox ones (the circuitists) and the orthodox ones (the *overdraft* economists)" (see Lavoie, 2020, p. xiv, emphasis in original).

The year *Monnaie et Production* ended, in 1996, *Money in Motion*, an important book edited by Ghislain Deleplace and Edward Nell, was published by Macmillan, largely influenced by and considered an extension of the Trieste conferences. In an important way, it could be seen as a 'second edition', so to speak, of the Arena book, published a decade before, with some of the same participants, but a great many new ones as well. This book was the result of a conference held in 1990 at the Jerome Levy Economics Institute, with the specific aim of bringing together post-Keynesians and circuit authors. Indeed, the book is subtitled *The Post-Keynesian and Circulation Approaches.*[17] It brings together 28 authors of all traditions and persuasions.

I will stop here. Undoubtedly there is more to tell, although from an institutional perspective, it is quite safe to say that today both approaches are well integrated. For instance, at various conferences and workshops, circuitists and post-Keynesians are well represented and interact on many levels.[18]

But, as I argued above, the role played by circuit writers in the history of post-Keynesian economics has to be told, as it is an integral part of that history. Bellofiore (2019) does this nicely, though the focus is on the Italian approach, headed by Graziani. In this chapter, I focused more on the role played by the French circuit school, headed by Parguez, and his eventual relationship with Marc Lavoie and Mario Seccareccia.

This story is very much personal, as a student of Lavoie and Seccareccia, and of Parguez in a way. Though close with Parguez, I developed a strong professional relationship with Claude Gnos and Sergio Rossi, proponents of the Schmittian circuit, which has not been explored here (although see Rossi (2006) for a description and summary).

THE INTELLECTUAL LINKS BETWEEN POST-KEYNESIANS AND CIRCUIT AUTHORS

As the previous section showed, attempts at summarizing the similarities between post-Keynesian economics and circuit authors have been ongoing for the better part of the last four decades. In terms of personal relationships, we can date the institutional rapprochement between the two approaches to the late 1970s or early 1980s.

In this section, I would now like to turn to the common ideas or vision between the two approaches, as both seek to depict the real world. This is not surprising as both approaches, as indicated above, are rooted in similar visions and interpretations of Keynes's, at least initially, *General Theory*.

While there are many common ideas, I will focus my attention on the following five: (i) the nature of the economic system; (ii) endogenous money; (iii) social classes and income distribution; (iv) effective demand; (v) uncertainty.

For those interested, I would recommend the following readings that develop the notions here. In particular, see Rochon (1999), Gnos (2006), and the introduction in Deleplace and Nell (1996).

Nature of the Economic System

In discussing the similarities between the two approaches regarding the nature of the economic system, three arguments come to mind. First, there is a clear rejection of equilibrium analysis by both approaches. In neoclassical economics, the system is said to be tending toward a stable and independent long-run equilibrium position, which acts as a centre of gravitation, provided there are no market imperfections impeding the economy's natural trajectory. In other words, the system can be said to be characterized by both forces of convergence and stability. Once in equilibrium, there are no incentives for the economy to move or to get out of equilibrium. This is why neoclassical theory must rely on shocks, both demand or supply shocks, to get the system out of equilibrium, at which point it is in *dis*equilibirum. Even this expression reveals the internal logic of neoclassical theory: the long-run equilibrium is the dominant sphere of analysis. Also, once out of equilibrium, the economy should gravitate toward a new and stable equilibrium; hence, given the flexibility of various prices, the system tends to reach equilibrium on its own.

Heterodox economists, post-Keynesians and circuit authors alike, however, see the economic system very differently. Accordingly, the system is best described as fragile and unstable, hence why the seeds of crises are internal to the economic system. There are no tendencies toward an equilibrium, neither in the short run nor the long run, or at least not one that is a centre of gravitation. Indeed, one could argue that a long-run position does not properly exist owing to the process of a moving economy, subject to many influences through time. Lavoie (1984a, p. 772) was very clear: post-Keynesians reject "any formulation of neoclassical general equilibrium."

In this sense, it is not unreasonable to assume that the economy might even move in the opposite direction than predicted as a result of uncertain events. As Deleplace and Nell (1996, p. 16) write, "the process of adjustment is not necessarily directed towards a prefigured position, because, as the movement takes place, the economy itself grows and changes. The adjustment may be path-dependent." These changes may move the economy in the opposite direction as a result of policy failures.

Second, both approaches reject the simultaneous determination of price and quantity, which is characteristic in neoclassical economics. Indeed, supply and demand analysis solves for market-clearing prices and quantities at the same time and, in fact, one could argue that they are determined by the same forces. Post-Keynesians and circuit writers, however, see the determination of prices and of output as separate, not only determined separately but also determined by different factors altogether. Prices are set by costs of production, while output is determined of aggregate demand.

Third, following from the above two arguments, both the post-Keynesian and the circuit approaches rely on what we can call the 'sequentiality of production' or the logic of production. While this is certainly explicit in circuit theory with its emphasis on the stages of production (Rochon, 1999), it is clearly evident in post-Keynesian economics. In other words, there can be no production before the hiring of workers; there can also be no production before bank credit is secured. Firms cannot collect revenues until goods are produced and sold. All this takes time (Deleplace and Nell, 1996).

Endogenous Money

Another common vision is the notion of endogenous money, that is "Production, employment, and investment cannot be adequately understood, or controlled, without an understanding of the monetary system" (Deleplace and Nell, 1996, p. 8). This is an obvious and easy core element. In fact, I would argue that certainly all heterodox traditions share at least some version of endogenous money. In this specific case, both post-Keynesians and circuit authors argue that because of the reversed causality between investment and saving, following Keynes, firms need access to credit to fund productive activities. It is this activity that leads to the creation of money. In other words, all would agree that "'money' is the by-product of a balance sheet operation of a third agent who, in modern parlance, can be dubbed a 'bank' ... the neoclassical scarcity principle can never be applied the creation of money" (Parguez and Seccareccia, 2000, p. 101, p. 106). This was recognized very early on by Robinson (1956) and later Kaldor (1970), but it was a feature in Eichner and Kregel as well. According to the authors (1975, p. 1309, fn. 39), "On the view presented here, that post-Keynesian theory deals with a monetized production economy in Keynes's sense, there can be no analysis of money separate from the analysis of the overall actions of the system." This is what Parguez (1996, p. 155) calls the "essentiality of money": "Money is the *sine qua non* of a capitalist economy, its existence condition."

Similarly, at the same time, Parguez (1975) was developing an anti-Hayekian theory of money that was not based on its scarcity. Graziani (2003) developed the idea of initial and financial finance, based on the very notion of endogenous money.

But the emphasis is slightly different, and they focus on different ends of the endogenous money story. In post-Keynesian economics, the emphasis is on the relationship between banks and the central bank. Yet, because of this relationship, it opens the door to a variety of theories of endogenous money, based on the stages of banking (as in Chick, 1986; published I might add in *Monnaie et Production*).

In contrast, for circuitists, the emphasis is clearly on the relationship between banks and borrowers: "The treatment of banks side by side with entrepreneurs and households still carries an air of originality" (Deleplace and Nell, 1996, p. 10). Here money is endogenous because firms need to borrow from banks to fund production needs and the purchase of capital goods. The emphasis is on the nature of money, not its relationship to a central bank: money is endogenous because of its very nature and because of 'logical necessity' of production. In other words, while in circuit theory money is endogenous regardless of the role of the central bank; in post-Keynesian theory, money is endogenous because of the role of the central bank.

Another difference is that while post-Keynesians anchor their views largely on Keynes's *General Theory* (indeed, still arguing whether Keynes had or assumed endogenous money within the book), circuit writers have not hesitated to go beyond Keynes and beyond the *General Theory*. As a result, they offer a richer context in which to analyse money.

Social Classes and Income Distribution

Embedded in the analysis of both approaches is the rejection of neoclassical theory's emphasis on methodological individualism in favour of a more classical approach resting on the existence of social classes or macro-groups (Graziani, 1990), either implicitly or explicitly. Indeed, as Arestis (1992, p. 101) reminds us, heterodox economics "is based on the premise that capitalism is a class-divided society." Lavoie (2014, p. 17) reaches the same conclusion: "In (nearly) all heterodox models there are social classes, workers, capitalists, entrepreneurs, bankers and rentiers."

This vision of society along class lines raises three important conclusions. First, it places income (and wealth) distribution at the core of the analysis, with a great many implications. Notably, functional distribution is given precedence, with much analysis done in terms of shares of income. Declining wage shares may carry important consequences for long-run growth. In turn, this has enabled many to construct macroeconomic models of growth that are either wage- or profit-led.

Second, it highlights the importance of power asymmetries. This is particularly important, for instance, in models that try to explain wage bargaining, or market power of firms, especially large, oligopolistic firms, or banks.

Third, this leads heterodox traditions, both circuitists and post-Keynesians alike, to view inflation as resting on the conflict over the distribution of income among these groups, notably between workers and capitalists. There is a clear rejection of demand-pull inflation in favour of inflation explained through costs of production, and more precisely through conflictual relationships between workers and firms. In fact, all inflation can be explained through conflict, at the national or international level of analysis.

Effective Demand

Another rather obvious argument common to both approaches is the notion of effective demand, around which there is considerable consensus and similar interpretations. In essence, both approaches view effective demand as the driving force of economic activity, certainly in the short run, and expectations of effective demand as dominating long-run considerations (more on the latter idea below). Indeed, as Lavoie (2014, p. 35) argues, "the assertion that the economy is demand-led both in the short and the long run is most likely a specific feature of post-Keynesianism."

In supporting the notion of effective and aggregate demand, heterodox authors specifically reject the very idea of Say's Law, which gives aggregate demand a passive role. Accordingly, for heterodox authors, it is supply that adapts to demand, certainly as it applies to oligopolistic markets. As demand grows, firms will respond by adjusting production. One immediate conclusion, therefore, is that it is output which adjusts to narrow the gap between supply and demand, and not prices.

But to be properly understood, the theory of effective demand must be well inserted within the framework of endogenous money: it is "tricky to disentangle these different notions" (Lavoie, 2014, p. 35), and the principle of effective demand "is best understood within the context of a macroeconomic explanation of a monetary production economy" (Lavoie, 2014, p. 82). This is what Kregel (1985, p. 133) called a "monetary theory of effective demand." The level of production and firms' ability to produce only depends on their ability to secure proper credit. Once firms have decided on their production levels, given expectations, it is the banks that will validate their production decisions. As Deleplace and Nell (1996, p. 5) wrote, "The theory of effective demand has to be rescued and reconstructed on a firmer foundation, one that takes monetary production as the starting point and recognizes the influences of class structure."

Uncertainty

In both approaches, the notion that we live in a world where the future is unknown is a central component, although it is treated differently. Davidson (1994) sees the notion of uncertainty as tied to the demand for money as liquidity, as a link between the present and the future, and its possible consequences for output and employment. In this sense, money binds the present and future, and acts as a "time machine": "Money is a 'time machine' that allows the transfer of purchasing power from the present to the future" (Fontana, 2000, p. 41).

For circuitists, however, uncertainty plays no role in this respect. As Deleplace and Nell (1996, p. 24) have stated, "no time relationships, no links between present and future, exist in the definition of money."

Rather, uncertainty enters the analysis in two ways. First, in entering firms' expectations of aggregate demand in the future, and how these expectations may influence their production decisions. As Parguez (1996, p. 159) writes, firms "bet on the short-run profits that should be both the outcome of their current sales and the proof banks need to support the rise in the effective capital value."

Second, uncertainty arises because banks also make bets on firms' abilities to reimburse their loans. In this sense, "The monetary circuit therefore pits the expectations of the firms against those of the banks. As long as the expectations of the banks are at least as optimistic as those of the firms, then credit will be given to firms, and production will begin" (Cottin-Euziol and Rochon, 2022, p. 3).

CONCLUSION

The history of post-Keynesian economics, both in terms of theoretical ideas and institutions, has a missing link, which only the influence of the theory of the monetary circuit can provide. In this essay, I tried to fill this gap by providing a glimpse of the institutional history of the theory of the monetary circuit, and how that is entangled with the development and history of post-Keynesian economics.

While there are some who are better suited to tell this story, I provide here an indication of the friendship and professional relationships between some scholars that may explain the story. Given the shared intellectual roots, it is no surprise that these relationships have only grown over the years. My only hope is that by telling a part of this story, many will find it of "great interest."

NOTES

1. The expression 'post-Keynesian' is used here with a hyphen, except in quotes where it appears without one.
2. I would like to thank Massimo Cingolani, Marc Lavoie, Edwin Le Heron, Wesley Marshall and Mario Seccareccia for comments. Of course, all errors remain mine alone.
3. For Lavoie (1996, 534), "Circuit theory ... constitutes the proper foundation to a non-orthodox monetary theory, which itself must be part of a larger non-orthodox research programme encompassing effective demand as well as value theory."
4. Note that while Parguez published his 1975 book in which there is an early version of a distinct Keynesian circuit of money (Parguez would use the expression 'circuit' in Parguez, 1982), Eichner and Kregel (1975) would also publish the first post-Keynesian journal article, in the *Journal of Economic Literature*. An interesting exercise would be to compare both writings and draw their similarities.
5. There is also no discussion of the Trieste Summer School in King (2002).
6. See Lavoie (2003) for a fuller account.
7. It should be noted that between 1975 and 1985, there were close links between Cambridge and the French Regulation School.
8. According to Le Heron, the story begins slightly before, around 1973, when Bernard Vallageas, who studied under Schmitt in Dijon, would come to Paris to give his presentation on circuit theory.
9. ISMEA published two journals, *Economie Appliquée* and *Économies et Sociétés*.
10. I owe this wording to Marc Lavoie, in an email, 14 March 2022.
11. Barrère published early on what may be considered the first Keynesian book in France. See Barrère (1952).
12. Thanks to Edwin Le Heron who shared this information in an email, dated 14 April 2023.
13. The French book was translated into English, as three separate volumes. See Barrère (1988; 1989; 1990).
14. It is worth mentioning that, in 1985, another close link was created when Eugenia Correa visited ISMEA, in Paris. Parguez and her would remain very close until his death.
15. The university has changed names over the years. It was once called the Université Pierre-Mendès-France.
16. A complete bibliographical list of articles can be found here: http://www.ismea .org/ISMEA/monnaieprod.html.
17. The fact the book was published at all was a monumental endeavour, which I undertook upon arriving at the New School in the fall of 1993. Within a few weeks of arriving, I asked Nell, who would become my supervisor, if he had a project for me to work on. He pointed to what I can only describe as a 'bunch of papers' on a table. The stack of paper was a mess, with most papers out of order. It took the better part of a year to get it in order.
18. Starting in 2002, I played my own small part by organizing a series of conferences, in Dijon (France), with Claude Gnos.

REFERENCES

Arena, R. and Graziani, A. (1985). *Production, Circulation et Monnaie*. Presses Universitaires de France: Paris.

Arestis, P. (1992). *The Post-Keynesian Approach to Economics*. Edward Elgar Publishing: Aldershot, UK and Brookfield, VT, USA.

Barrère, A. (1990). *Keynesian Economic Policies*. Macmillan: London.

Barrère, A. (1989). *Money, Credit and Prices in Keynesian Perspectives*. Macmillan: London.

Barrère, A. (1988). *The Foundations of Keynesian Analysis*. Macmillan: London.

Barrère, A. (1985). *Keynes Aujourd'hui: théories et politiques*. Economica: Paris.

Barrère, A. (1952). *Théorie économique et impulsion keynésienne*. Daloz: Paris.

Bellofiore, R. (2019). Augusto Graziani and the Marx–Schumpeter–Keynes 'Cycle of Money Capital': A Personal Look at the Early Italian Circuitism from an Insider. *Review of Political Economy*, *31* (4), 528–558.

Bellofiore, R. and Seccareccia, M. (1999). Monetary Circuit, in O'Hara, P.A. (ed.), *Encyclopedia of Political Economy*, (pp. 753–756) Routledge: London and New York.

Berr, E. and Monvoisin, V. (2023). Modern Post-Keynesian Approaches: Continuities and Ruptures with Monetary Circuit Theory. *Journal of Post Keynesian Economics*, *46* (2), 359–377.

Chick, V. (1986). The Evolution of the Banking System and the Theory of Saving, Investment and Interest. *Économies et Sociétés: Monnaie et Production*, *20* (8–9), 111–126.

Cottin-Euziol, E. and Rochon, L.-P. (2022). Monetary Circuit, in Vernengo, M. (ed.), *The New Palgrave Dictionary of Economics*, (pp. 1–8) Palgrave Macmillan: London,

Davidson, P. (2005). Responses to Lavoie, King, and Dow on What Post Keynesianism Is and Who Is a Post Keynesian. *Journal of Post Keynesian Economics, Spring*, *27* (3), 393–408.

Davidson, P. (2003–04). Setting the Record Straight on a History of Post Keynesian Economics. *Journal of Post Keynesian Economics, Winter*, *26* (2), 245–272.

Davidson, P. (1994). *Post Keynesian Macroeconomic Theory*. Edward Elgar Publishing: Cheltenham, UK and Brookfield, VT, USA.

Deleplace, G. and Nell, E. (1996). *Money in Motion: The Post-Keynesian and Circulation Approaches*. London: Macmillan.

Eichner, A.S. and Kregel, J.A. (1975). An Essay on Post-Keynesian Theory: A New Paradigm in Economics. *Journal of Economic Literature*, *13* (4), 1293–1311.

Fontana, G. (2000). Post Keynesians and Circuitists on Money and Uncertainty: An Attempt at Generality. *Journal of Post Keynesian Economics*, *23* (1), 27–48.

Gnos, C. (2006). French Circuit Theory, in Arestis, P. and M. Sawyer (eds), *A Handbook of Alternative Monetary Economics*, (pp. 87–104) Edward Elgar Publishing: Cheltenham, UK and Northampton, MA, USA.

Graziani, A. (2003). *The Monetary Theory of Production*. Cambridge University Press: Cambridge, UK.

Graziani, A. (1990). The Theory of the Monetary Circuit. *Économies et Sociétés: Monnaie et Production*, *7*, 7–36.

Graziani. A. (1985). Monnaie, Intérêt et Dépenses Publiques. *Économies et Sociétés*, *2*, August.

Graziani, A. (1984). The Debate on Keynes's Finance Motive. *Economic Notes*, *1* (1), 15–33.

Halevi, J. and Taouil, R. (2002). On a Post-Keynesian Stream from France and Italy: The *Circuit* Approach, in Arestis, P., M. Desai and S. Dow (eds), *Money, Macroeconomics and Keynes: Essays in Honour of Victoria Chick, Volume 1*, (pp. 91–102) Routledge: London.

Kaldor, N. (1970). The New Monetarism. *Lloyds Bank Review*, July, 1–7.

King, J.E. (2013). Post Keynesians and Others, in Lee, F.S. and M. Lavoie (eds), *In Defense of Post- Keynesian and Heterodox Economics: Responses to Their Critics*, (pp. 1–17) Routledge: London.

King, J.E. (2005). Unwarping the Record: A Reply to Paul Davidson. *Journal of Post Keynesian Economics*, Spring, *27* (3), 377–384.

King, J.E. (2002). *A History of Post Keynesian Economics since 1936*. Edward Elgar Publishing: Cheltenham, UK and Northampton, MA, USA.

Kregel, J.A. (1987). Shylock and Hamlet, or Are There Bulls and Bears in the Circuit? *Économies et Sociétés*, *9*, 11–22.

Kregel, J.A. (1985). Hamlet without the Prince: Cambridge Macroeconomics without Money. *American Economic Review: Papers and Proceedings*, May, *75* (2), 133–139.

Lavoie, M. (2022). *Post-Keynesian Economics: New Foundations*. Edward Elgar Publishing: Cheltenham, UK and Northampton, MA, USA.

Lavoie, M. (2020). *Post-Keynesian Monetary Theory: Selected Essays*. Edward Elgar Publishing: Cheltenham, UK and Northampton, MA, USA.

Lavoie, M. (2014). *Post-Keynesian Economics: New Foundations*. Edward Elgar Publishing: Cheltenham, UK and Northampton, MA, USA.

Lavoie, M. (2012). From Macroeconomics to Monetary Economics: Some Persistent Themes in the Theory Work of Wynne Godley, in Papadimitriou, D.B. and G. Zezza (eds), *Contributions in Stock-Flow Consistent Modeling: Essays in Honor of Wynne Godley*, (pp. 137–153) Macmillan: Basingstoke, UK.

Lavoie, M. (2005). Changing Definitions: A Comment on Davidson's Critique of King's *History of Post Keynesianism*. *Journal of Post Keynesian Economics*, Spring, *27* (3), 371–376.

Lavoie, M. (2003). The State, the Central Bank and the Monetary Circuit, in Rochon, L.-P. and M. Seccareccia (eds), *Monetary Economies of Production: Banking and Financial Circuits and the Role of the State. Essays in Honour of Alain Parguez*, (pp. 11–22) Edward Elgar Publishing: Cheltenham, UK and Northampton, MA, USA.

Lavoie, M. (1996). Monetary Policy in an Economy with Endogenous Credit Money, in Deleplace, G. and E. Nell (eds), *Money in Motion: The Circulation and Post-Keynesian Approaches*, (pp. 532–545) Macmillan: London.

Lavoie, M. (1990). Le Circuit dans la Pensée Post-Keynésienne Américaine. *Économie*, *6*, 105–118.

Lavoie, M. (1987). Monnaie et production: une synthèse de la théorie du circuit. *Économies et Sociétés*, *20* (9), 65–101.

Lavoie, M. (1985). Credit and Money: The Dynamic Circuit, Overdraft Economics, and Post-Keynesian Economics, in Jarsulic, M. (ed.), *Money and Macro Policy*, (pp. 63–84) Kluwer: Hingham.

Lavoie, M. (1985a). Keynes aujourd'hui: théories et politiques ALAIN BARRÈRE (éditeur). Economica, Paris, 1985, 610 pp., index. *L'Actualité économique*, *September*, *61* (3), 402–405.

Lavoie, M. (1984). Un modèle post-keynésien d'économie monétaire fondé sur la théorie du circuit. *Économies et Sociétés, April, 59* (1), 233–258.

Lavoie, M. (1984a). The Endogenous Credit Flow and the Post Keynesian Theory of Money. *Journal of Economic Issues, 18* (3), 771–797.

Lavoie, M. (1982). Les post-keynésiens et la monnaie endogène. *L'Actualité économique, January–June, 58* (1–2), 191–222.

Le Bourva, J. (1962). Création de la monnaie et multiplicateur de credit. *Revue Économique, Janvier, 13* (1), 29–52.

Lee, F.S. (2000). The Organizational History of Post Keynesian Economics in America, 1971–1995. *Journal of Post Keynesian Economics, 23* (1), 141–162.

Lucarelli, S. and Passarella, M.V. (2012). *New Research Perspectives in the Monetary Theory of Production*. Bergamo University Press: Bergamo.

Parguez, A. (1996). Beyond Scarcity: A Reappraisal of the Theory of the Monetary Circuit, in Deleplace, G. and E. Nell (eds), *Money in Motion: The Circulation and Post-Keynesian Approaches*, (pp. 155–199) Macmillan: London.

Parguez, A. (1982). La monnaie dans le circuit. *Economie Appliquée, 35* (3), 231–265.

Parguez, A. (1981). Keynes et la Révolution. *Cahiers d'économie Politique, 6*, 171–187.

Parguez, A. (1980). Profit, épargne, investissement: Eléments pour une théorie monétaire du profit. *Economie Appliquée, 33* (2), 425–455.

Parguez, A. (1975). *Monnaie et Macroéconomie: Théorie de la Monnaie en Déséquilibre*. Economica: Paris.

Parguez, A. and Seccareccia, M. (2000). The Credit Theory of Money: The Monetary Circuit Approach, in Smithin, J. (ed.), *What Is Money?*, (pp. 101–123) Routledge: London.

Passarella, M.V. (2014). Financialization and the Monetary Circuit: A Macro-Accounting Approach. *Review of Political Economy, 26* (1), 128–148.

Poulon, F. (2018). Le Circuit Keynésien: Unde, ubi et quo, in Berr, E., V. Monvoisin and J.-F. Ponsot (eds), *L'économie post-keynésienne: histoire, théories et politiques*, (pp. 127–144) Editions du Seuil: Paris.

Poulon, F. (1982). *Macroéconomie Approfondie. Équilibre, Déséquilibre, Circuit*. Cujas: Paris.

Poulon, F. (1980), Graphe, Crise et Circuit Keynésien. *Revue d'économie politique, 69* (2), 371–409.

Realfonzo, R. (2006). The Italian Circuitist Approach, in Arestis, P. and M. Sawyer (eds), *A Handbook of Alternative Monetary Economics*, (pp. 105–120) Edward Elgar Publishing: Cheltenham, UK and Northampton, MA, USA.

Robinson, J. (1956). *The Accumulation of Capital*. Palgrave: London.

Rochon, L.-P. (2023). The Historical and Institutional Roots of Post-Keynesian Economics. *Review of Political Economy, 35* (1), 6–27.

Rochon, L.-P. (2003). Money and Endogenous Money: Post-Keynesian and Circulation Approaches, in Rochon, L.-P. and S. Rossi (eds), *Modern Theories of Money*, (pp. 115–141) Edward Elgar Publishing: Cheltenham, UK and Northampton, MA, USA.

Rochon, L.-P. (1999). *Credit, Money and Production: An Alternative Post-Keynesian Approach*. Edward Elgar Publishing: Cheltenham, UK and Northampton, MA, USA.

Rochon, L.-P. (1999a). The Creation and Circulation of Endogenous Money: A Circuit Dynamique Approach. *Journal of Economic Issues, 33* (1), 1–21.

Rochon, L.-P. and Rossi, S. (2013). Endogenous Money: The Evolutionary versus Revolutionary Views. *Review of Keynesian Economics, Summer, 1* (2), 210–229.

Rochon, L.-P. and Seccareccia, M. (2003). Alain Parguez's Contribution to Political Economy, in Rochon, L.-P. and M. Seccareccia (eds), *Monetary Economies of Production: Banking and Financial Circuits and the Role of the State. Essays in Honour of Alain Parguez*, (pp. 1–7) Edward Elgar Publishing: Cheltenham, UK and Northampton, MA, USA.

Rossi, S. (2006). The Theory of Money Emissions, in Arestis, P. and M. Sawyer (eds), *A Handbook of Alternative Monetary Economics*, (pp. 121–138) Edward Elgar Publishing: Cheltenham, UK and Northampton, MA, USA.

Rousseas, S. (1996). The Spheres of Industrial and Financial Circulation Revisited, and Their Implications for Post Keynesian Economic Policy, in Deleplace, G. and E. Nell (eds), *Money in Motion: The Post-Keynesian and Circulation Approaches*, (pp. 672–683) Macmillan: London.

Schmitt, B. (1960). *La formation du pouvoir d'achat*. Sirey: Paris.

4. The contribution of Modern Monetary Theory to heterodox economics

Philip Armstrong

INTRODUCTION

This chapter begins by briefly examining the nature of heterodoxy in economics and the extent to which it may be viewed as purely oppositional to orthodoxy (however defined) or whether schools made up of economists who self-define as heterodox make – or have the potential to make – worthwhile contributions to the discipline (Mearman et al., 2019; Armstrong, 2018, 2020a, 2020b). This is followed by a consideration of the nature of a "heterodox community" or even if there are grounds to believe that a stronger unifying dynamic exists which might underpin a "heterodox paradigm" or disciplinary matrix which, in turn, would enable heterodox scholars of different schools to contribute jointly to the development of economic knowledge.

The analysis then turns to the distinguishing features of Modern Monetary Theory (MMT) and the nature of its unique contribution to economic theory. The range of attitudes of heterodox scholars to their fellow economists working in other heterodox schools is examined, with a particular focus upon attitudes to MMT and whether opposition – where it occurs – can be justified.

The chapter supports the view that the insights provided by MMT form the basis of the case for the acceptance of Modern Monetary Theorists as members of a heterodox community and, looking further, claims that the advocates of MMT would have significant potential to add to the development of economic knowledge as contributors to a heterodox paradigm should such a structure be accepted as both feasible and potentially useful (Armstrong, 2020b).

NATURE OF HETERODOXY – COMPROMISE OR CONFLICT

It could be argued heterodox merely means "not orthodox"[1] but heterodox scholars unsurprisingly contend there is more to heterodoxy than that. Mearman (2011, pp. 482–483) argues that a definition of "not orthodox" is:

> rather unsatisfactory because it appears to undersell heterodox economics, which in its traditional composite elements, such as Marxism and Keynesianism, would appear to be more than merely critique. Both Marxism and Keynesianism, for example, contain constructive programmes of economic theory… economic method, logic, ontology, politics, ethics… which differ from those espoused by mainstream economics…

Lee (2010) contends that the different groups that collectively form the heterodox community have each produced meaningful criticisms of mainstream economics and their separate criticisms form complementary elements of an overall critique of both the methodology and technical apparatus of mainstream economics. O'Hara (2002, p. 611) specifies the groups or communities that might be considered heterodox; he first highlights the particular focus and insights provided by heterodox economists as a whole as "an emphasis on ethics, morals and justice situated in an institutional setting", before pointing out the specific contributions of each school.

Mearman (2011) distinguishes between two opposing views, described as "splitters" and "lumpers". Splitters approach heterodoxy with the aim of breaking up a possible whole into parts in order to facilitate analysis. They may be characterised as having their own approach – or even paradigm – and may focus intensely on a text (or group of texts) by a single author such as Marx or Keynes. Given science is a social activity, in their actual practice they spend the majority of their time engaging with economists of the same school. The internal communication within such an approach would be expected to be extensive as the members of the group use the same concepts, effectively "speaking the same language". Refinements of their own theories are effectively prioritised. The negative aspect to such a structuring of heterodoxy is the increase in the number of approaches and the corresponding increase in difficulty in general inter-paradigm communication. Dow (2018) argues that as science is a community-based activity, limiting the number of paradigms is a practical necessity.

In contrast, lumpers look for shared foundations in order to support their desire to discover a commonality which might lead to fruitful work and enhance the chances of meaningful knowledge coming to light (Armstrong, 2018, 2020b). It might be argued that some groups have sufficient common ground to be considered in a collective sense at least for the purpose of some forms of analysis. This is not to say that differences do not exist, or even that they are unimportant, only that sufficient commonality exists for heterodox groups to combine their approaches and insights so as to yield fruitful results. Other groups may be considered as being so different that working in close cooperation is neither feasible nor desirable and the sense of "otherness" needs to be maintained. It is argued here that the essential ontology underpinning mainstream or neoclassical economics is such that it could not and should not be synthesised with heterodoxy[2] but a desire to associate and share ideas would seem reasonable in the case of heterodox groups which possess a common ontological structure but aim to uncover different aspects of economic reality. In this case different heterodox schools might be considered as distinct but complementary elements capable of operating within the same paradigm or "disciplinary matrix".

The argument presented here supports the contention that by founding their theorising upon a realist social ontology (specifically critical realism, Armstrong, 2020a, 2020b), such a common ontological structure might be developed. Critical realism provides a potential underlabouring[3] of hetero-dox schools and a potential unifying force (Lawson, 1997, 2003; Lee, 2010; Armstrong, 2018, 2020a, 2020b; Potts and Armstrong, 2020). Lee (2010, p. 9) notes that critical realism is associated with particular heterodox approaches.[4] Those very heterodox groups that accept the need for an "ontological turn", explicitly utilise a layered ontology and embrace pluralism[5] might successfully coexist within one community studying economics and, importantly, interact in such a way as to encourage progress by fostering the advancement of knowl-edge of real economic mechanisms and structures. Such a community, using a range of substantive theories all of which are "underlaboured" by critical realism, would have sufficient common ground to engage in wide-ranging and meaningful internal communication. For lumpers, then, commensurability and communication between heterodox groups are implicitly more highly valued than is the case for the splitters. In their day-to-day practice they might be expected to engage in a higher proportion of intergroup debate than their colleagues in the former group.

Mearman (2011, p. 503) finds evidence which supports both camps. He notes that the "empirical evidence here supports either urge: it suggests consid-erable heterogeneity in that little structure can be found within the community of self-identified heterodox economists. However, in other ways, there are reasons to lump: there is a shared dislike of the mainstream; and concepts such as history are almost universally held". The research in Armstrong (2020b) supports the contention that no strong dynamic for change is present within economics. The majority of heterodox economists interviewed[6] consider that although significant complementarity exists between heterodox economists working in different schools its extent is too small (and the disagreements too great) to make the development of an integrated disciplinary matrix a realistic prospect: "although the results… suggest that the replacement of the hegemonic neoclassical paradigm – although unlikely in the foreseeable future – is nevertheless possible, support for a heterodox paradigm as the basis for the development of meaningful economic knowledge (in opposition to the mainstream approach) was not strongly expressed" (Armstrong, 2020b, p. 233, parentheses in the original). The majority of interviewees "believe the looser concept of the 'community' represents the highest level of integration that they would support or even envisage" (Armstrong, 2020b, p. 233).

THE DISTINGUISHING POINTS OF MMT

Theories of Money

Modern Monetary Theorists support credit and state theories of money[7] (Wray, 1998, 2004) and reject both the Austrian and the Marxist versions of origin-of-money stories based upon a conception of money as a "creature of commodities". MMT stands in opposition to the Austrian school's contention that money arose as a cost-saving development of barter, contending that such a view is not drawn from a consideration of actual history but rather from a conjectural history[8] (Dowd, 2000; Armstrong, 2015). For the Austrian school (and neoclassical economists), this advocacy of a conjectural history follows from – and provides support for – their individualist ethics (Armstrong, 2015). From an Austrian perspective, arguing that money developed as a "natural" response to changing circumstances by individuals maximising expected utility (Menger, 1892) necessarily means a foundational role for the state is denied. Instead, the state is characterised as a later – detrimental – influence on the system, expropriating private sector money to serve its own purposes.

The Marxist commodity variant of the origin-of-money story (Lapavitsas, 2003, 2005) is richer than the orthodox money-from-barter myth, being founded upon the contention that it is intercommunity trade that leads to the development of a "universal equivalent" which eventually permeates and monetises the previously nonmonetary economies involved in the trading. Lapavitsas and Aguila (2020, p. 6, emphasis added) argue that money "*emerges* at point of… *contact*" between nonmonetary societies. However, not only does such a claim receive no empirical support (and is, therefore, best categorised as another form of conjectural history), importantly it is also inconsistent with Marx's advocacy of historical materialism (Chapman, 1980; Armstrong, 2022).

Innes's presentation (1913, 1914) of the credit theory provides a powerful critique of orthodox theory concerning the ontology of money. For Innes, the nature of money springs from credit and debt relationships. Innes defines money as credit,

> Credit is the purchasing power so often mentioned in economic works as being one of the principal attributes of money, and... Money, then, is credit and nothing but credit. A's money is B's debt to him, and when B pays his debt, A's money disappears. This is the whole theory of money. (Innes, 1913, p. 392)

Innes (1914, p. 160) defines state money as credit, "Every time a coin or certificate is issued... A credit on the public treasury is opened, a public debt incurred". Innes recognises that a debt to the state or tax liability can be paid by the return of the government's own debt instrument; in other words, there exists "the right of the holder of the credit (the creditor) to hand back to the issuer of the debt (the debtor) the latter's acknowledgement or obligation, when the former becomes debtor and the latter creditor" (Innes, 1914, p. 160, parentheses in the original).

According to the State Theory of Money (Knapp, 1924), rather than springing from a process involving individuals searching for the most efficient way of reducing the costs of barter, it is the state that decides on the unit of account and the "money things" that are to be used in settlement of debts to the authorities – taxes – denominated in this unit. The imposition of the tax liability comes first, followed by the spending of the currency which is required to settle it. Logically and practically the emission of state money is anterior to its collection. The significance of the power of the state is noted by Knapp, "Within a state the validity of the kinds of money is not a trade phenomenon but rests on authority" (Knapp, 1924, p. 217).

Furthermore, it is possible to utilise a structure based upon the relationship between the credit theory of Innes and the state theory developed by Knapp. Smithin (2018, pp. 194–195) contends that the study of money and monetary issues should follow a four stage "schema" beginning with a realist social ontology,[9] followed by economic sociology, monetary macroeconomics and, finally, political economy. Applying this structure allows us to see credit theory as foundational and forming part of the first stage, seeking to explain the ontology of money itself or what money *is*. The state theory then applies to the second stratum; the economic sociology which explains what form of credit is acceptable in payment of debt in the specific society in which we live[10] (Armstrong and Siddiqui, 2019).

The MMT Money Story

The importance of sequence is stressed in the MMT money story.[11] It begins with a powerful stakeholder, more commonly the state, desiring to provision itself by transferring resources from the private sector to itself (Mosler, 2020). The government first levies a tax liability on its population and determines the means by which that liability can be satisfied, for example, US dollars or UK pounds. The existence of the tax obligation creates willing private sector sellers of goods and services who require the state currency to pay their tax bill. The state can spend its currency to buy the goods and services available for sale. The state always spends by the issue of new money and is conceptualised as a currency-issuer.[12] Once the non-government sector has acquired state money it can pay its taxes and, in addition, it may well be the case that the private sector wishes to save state currency and so will offer sufficient goods and services for sale to the state in order to satisfy this demand. From this perspective, government deficit spending, or spending in excess of tax obligations, simply provides the state money which the non-government sector wishes to save.

Consistent with the credit theory of money, MMT conceptualises the state money held as saving by the non-government as a tax credit (Mosler, 2020). It will remain as saving until used to pay taxes. Alternatively, the state may offer the non-government sector the opportunity to buy interest-bearing state debt. Such a purchase is best conceptualised as an asset swap as will become apparent below. In addition, given MMT recognises the importance of sequence, it stands in opposition to politically imposed rules (Armstrong, 2020c) such as debt ceilings, prohibition of direct sales of public sector debt to a nation's central bank (CB) and the necessity for a national treasury to maintain a positive overnight balance at its own CB.[13] Such rules may have had a function under previous monetary regimes[14] but are best conceptualised as voluntary constraints for a government issuing its own fiat currency under floating exchange rates (Armstrong, 2015, 2020c).

The Central Bank and the Banking System

Critics often argue that MMT neglects the private money circuit and fails to consider the relationship between private banks and the CB, but such accusations are not justified and follow from a failure to consider the literature (Armstrong, 2020b). The role of a CB is described by Mosler and Armstrong (2019, p. 1) as an "operator of a spreadsheet which includes a transactions account for each member bank, generally called a 'reserve account' that records balances generally called 'reserves'". They continue,

> the CB also keeps accounts for the Treasury and for foreign CBs. The CB marks balances in the various accounts up and down, credits and debits – on instructions from those entities with accounts. Furthermore, the state sets the operating procedures for the CB and the banking system, including regulations regarding overdrafts (negative

balances), which are accounted for as loans from the CB. The CB itself neither has, nor does not have, funds. Rather, it acts as the "scorekeeper" for the members, crediting and debiting their accounts as per their instructions, and accounting for what it does with debits and credits in the CB accounts... Mosler and Armstrong (2019, pp. 1–2, parentheses in the original)

When considering the underlying operational reality of the monetary system, MMT supports the contention that although CBs may have a measure of discretion when acting as the state's agent, for example in the setting of the policy rates, CBs should not be conceptualised as institutions independently of the state. If allowed to act independently, a CB could, literally, outbid any private bidder for all the goods and services available in domestic currency – a situation which no society could accept – and therefore CBs *must* work closely with national treasuries as a matter of course. Indeed, Mosler and Armstrong (2019, pp. 1–2) note that CBs "are created, regulated, and supervised by the state to serve public purpose, with all profits credited to the state".[15]

Mosler and Armstrong (2019, p. 3, parentheses in the original) note "the state's CB is the only source of reserves for that currency. Reserve balances are created when the CB credits member reserve accounts. And as a monopolist (single supplier) of reserves to the banking system, the CB is necessarily the 'price setter'". Looking deeper, the CB has price-setting power for two rates. The first is called the own rate,[16] which is how that item exchanges for itself. For a currency, the own rate is called the interest rate[17] (Mosler and Armstrong, 2019, p. 3). Although in the UK and US, for example, the CB sets the overnight rate and allows "market forces" to determine the long-term rate structure, the insights of MMT show that the state, via its CB, could directly set the entire term structure of risk-free rates, or put another way, the CB could control the shape of the yield curve. This would require the CB to stand by to purchase unlimited quantities of government debt at a price consistent with its interest rate ceiling target at each maturity level and sell securities to support its lower boundary (Mosler, 2012; Mosler and Armstrong, 2019).

When considering banks, MMT recognises that banks are agents of the CB, granted the privilege of creating money in the form of bank deposits, denominated in state currency, subject to strict regulatory requirements. MMT rejects the idea that it is acceptable to model banks as acting as pure intermediaries which simply take money from a source or sources and lend the money to others. Banks do not take deposits and then lend them out, indeed, banks may make loans without the possession of prior deposits (or reserves). Banks take a position in assets by granting credit to borrowers and at the same time accepting liabilities upon themselves (put another way, banks buy a customer's loan note and pay for it with their own liability). A bank customer who is granted a loan gains a bank deposit (a liability to the bank) and at the same time the bank acquires an asset (the loan). Assuming the loan is spent, and the receiver of the credit holds an account in a different bank, the lending bank will find that initially its balance sheet shrinks, i.e. it loses the deposit and reserves. However, once the loan is repaid (with interest), the reserves are replenished (with additional reserves equivalent to the interest) on the asset side. On its liability side the interest payment has boosted the bank's net worth. Provided the borrower repays the debt in full the bank makes a profit on the transaction. It is clear from this mechanism that "loans create deposits" not the other way round (Armstrong, 2015).

From an MMT perspective, loans simultaneously "create" both deposits (and any required reserves) as a point of logic and a matter of accounting. Importantly, the concept of CB "accommodation" has no applicability, as any bank's reserve requirement remaining on settlement day is, in fact, booked as a loan from the CB as an "overdraft". Mosler (quoted in Armstrong, 2015) notes,

> The only way the central bank could "not accommodate" would be to prevent the check or interbank transfer from occurring in the first place, which is beyond impractical and even moot in the case of deposit insurance where the government guarantees clearing of client checks written against insured deposits. Therefore, the central bank requires banks to have sufficient equity capital and sets asset and liquidity standards required of banks so that it can prudently allow "daylight over-drafts" of member bank clearing accounts in the normal course of business.

Misconceptions abound concerning the balance sheet changes associated with government spending and the payment of taxes.[18] MMT provides general clarity absent in alternative approaches. Importantly, it shows that bank deposit money cannot be used to *directly* settle a tax liability. When the government spends, it credits a bank account, at the same time adding reserves to the account holder's bank's reserve account at the CB. When taxes are paid, reserves are removed from the banking system. It may appear that a private individual can pay their tax bill using bank money, however, on further reflection, this view can be seen as a mischaracterisation of the actual process involved. If a private sector individual or institution pays taxes by means of a cheque the relevant bank deposit falls by the amount of the payment, but the settlement of the tax liability occurs when the taxpayer's bank's reserve account at the CB is debited by the same amount. It is the transfer of bank reserves from the taxpayer's bank's reserve account to the treasury account that settles the tax bill. As MMT stresses, a reserve add (government spending or lending) must precede a reserve drain (tax payment or bond sales).

MMT, the Price Level and Inflation

MMT's approach to the determination of the price level and the nature and causes of inflation is arguably the most controversial aspect of its contribution to theory. The insights set out by MMT's founding thinker, Warren Mosler, are the most novel and have not yet been fully embraced by all the key MMT advocates. Nevertheless, it is argued here that they are a key element of MMT. Mosler (2023, p. 87) argues that "MMT… is currently the only school of economic thought that… specifically identifies and models both the source of the price level and the dynamics behind changes in the price level…" MMT goes beyond the Post-Keynesian approach; the advocates of MMT accept that institutional structure and market power influence the size of the mark-up (or margin) and thus the level of prices but, significantly, according to MMT, *the price level is ultimately a function of the prices the government pays when it spends* (Mosler, 2020, 2012; Wray, 1998). As mentioned above, given the government is the sole supplier of the state money required by the non-government sector to settle their tax liabilities, it necessarily sets the terms of exchange for goods and services.

Looking deeper, Mosler (2023, p. 89) argues there are *two separate dynamics* underpinning the determination of the price level.

> The first is the introduction of absolute value of the state's numeraire, which takes place by the prices the state pays when it spends. Moreover, the only information with regard to absolute value as measured in units of the state's currency is the information transmitted by state spending. Therefore, all nominal prices can necessarily be traced back to prices the state pays when spending its currency.

Put another way, the value of a unit state money is determined by what is required to obtain it.

Mosler further argues, "The second dynamic is the transmission of this information by markets allocating by price as they express indifference levels between buyers and sellers, and all in the context of the state's institutional structure" and concludes that "The price level, therefore, consists of prices dictated by government spending policy along with all other prices subsequently derived by market forces operating within government institutional structure" (see Mosler, 2023, p. 89).

MMT's approach to inflation is characterised by a recognition that if an economy is to be described as suffering from inflation, a sustained, general rise in the level of prices is required and that a simple rise in price index is not sufficient to merit the term "inflation" (Armstrong, 2015).

Modern Monetary Theorists stand in opposition to advocates of the quantity theory of money and MMT's insights into the operational reality of the monetary system show that inflation is not the result of increases in the *quantity* of spending (or increases in the money supply) per se, rather it is about the *prices paid by the government*.

> The value of the currency is defined by what a given amount of it can buy. So, for example, if the government increases purchases at current prices, regardless of the quantity of money spent, that additional (price constrained) spending has not driven up prices, and the value of the currency has not been altered. However, if the government instead pays more for the same items purchased, the value of the currency, by definition, has become lower, as it takes more of it to buy the same quantity than was previously the case. (Armstrong and Mosler, 2020, p. 4, parentheses in the original)

As long as goods and services are offered for sale at current prices the state can increase its purchases at those prices, but if the state competes with the private sector at full employment by continuously raising the prices it is willing to pay, this represents a corresponding continuous reduction of the value of money, defined as inflation. MMT further recognises that continuous price increases of goods and services can have multiple causes and commonly occur when significant unemployment and spare capacity exist (Fulwiler et al., 2019). Given the predominance of oligopoly as a market structure, businesses are able to utilise their market power both to pass on costs and to raise profit margins. In addition, asset price rises, for example in property markets, facilitated by the endogeneity of state-guaranteed bank finance,[19] supply restrictions or bottlenecks (as has been apparent during the Covid pandemic), and a supportive tax structure that works to elevate demand can all lead to upward pressure on prices. It is important to stress again that to be described as "inflation" the resulting price rises would need to exhibit a perpetuating dynamic, with higher prices being paid by the government, for the fall in the value of money to be sustained, e.g. during the so-called wage–price spirals (of the type seen in the 1970s), workers and capitalists were both strong enough to battle each other in an attempt to maintain their share of real income in the face of cost shocks (such as oil price rises). In this case, the government effectively ratified the resulting price rises by raising the prices it paid accordingly.[20]

Modern Monetary Theorists reject traditional monetary policy as a means to combat inflation. MMT denies that monetary policy works in the way suggested by central bankers who believe raising rates reduces inflationary pressures by reducing aggregate demand, via a primary channel of private sector lending, where higher rates discourage lending and lower rates support lending (Armstrong, 2019). Mosler (quoted in Armstrong, 2019) argues that "CBs… assume that the propensities to consume out of interest income differ between borrowers and savers, such that when rates rise, for example, borrowers cut back on their deficit spending to a greater extent than savers increase their spending… therefore, central bankers conclude, higher rates are contractionary and lower rates expansionary."

However, given *the state is a net payer of interest to the economy*, higher rates are adding interest income to the economy and lower rates are removing interest income from the economy.

> With debt to GDP ratios often approximating 100% of GDP, the interest added or subtracted by this channel is likely to dwarf the effect of the differing propensities between private sector borrowers and savers. Lower rates may help borrowers to service loans and qualify for new loans, but lower net income works against new borrowers' income levels and the general ability to service loans in the economy. (Armstrong, 2019)

Mosler (quoted in Armstrong, 2019), cites corroboratory evidence from recent experience of Japan, the US and the eurozone, and concludes that, "higher rates are in fact an expansionary force rather than the contractionary force assumed by central bankers. That is, global central bankers have it backwards – they are easing when they believe they are tightening and tightening when they believe they are easing".[21]

Contrary to how it is often portrayed, MMT does not recommend "after-the-fact" tax changes as a means to control inflation. Fulwiler et al. (2019, emphasis added) note, with respect to the US,

> When MMT says that a major role of taxes is to help offset demand rather than generate revenue, we are recognising that taxes are a critical part of a whole suite of potential demand offsets… [but] when we do advocate using tax increases to address inflationary pressure, we are not suggesting that Congress attempt to raise taxes in real time after inflation has already emerged. Indeed, our approach is precisely intended to avoid a situation in which Congress merely spends without paying attention to inflation dynamics until it is too late. Thus, we argue varying tax rates and other inflation offsets should be included in the budgeting process *from the outset*.

Furthermore, given its recognition of the existence of multiple causes of inflation within the existing institutional structure, MMT naturally supports the contention that different policy approaches may be required in different circumstances, for example, employing policies directly targeted at improving the robustness and flexibility of supply chains and tackling excessive profit-making by oligopoly firms by strategic price controls (Weber, 2021).

MMT's recognition that the prices paid by government set the complete backdrop for market prices provides a key insight informing the design of counter-inflation policy. In theory, if the government reduces the prices it is prepared to pay, initially private firms may seek alternative private buyers but if the government maintains low price offers over a sustained period, thereby reducing government spending, this causes private incomes to fall, reducing demand, ultimately forcing private sellers to accept the state's lower offers to avoid defaulting on tax liabilities. However, in practice, if such a policy was introduced into a market economy it would be highly disruptive (Wray, 1998, pp. 170–174). Mosler (2010, p. 114) argues that the government fixing a buying price for all goods and services would be a "completely impractical way to keep prices from going up", and instead supports the policy of setting just one price and then "market forces adjust all other prices to reflect relative values". Given the foundational importance of the price of labour, MMT thus supports the introduction of a permanent buffer stock of employed labour as its *primary* anti-inflationary policy (Armstrong, 2023).

Support of a Job Guarantee (JG) – which its advocates argue is likely to be much more effective in promoting price stability than the current policy of using the unemployed as a buffer stock (Mitchell, 2010, 2011) – is a key aspect of MMT. Under a JG scheme, the state stands by to offer any unemployed person ready, willing and able to work a job at a fixed wage; the introduction of a JG scheme would effectively reduce "unemployment", as defined, to zero; anyone who is either unwilling or unable to accept a job is not included as "unemployed". There is no element of compulsion involved, the scheme is entirely voluntary. Its use is consistent with the simultaneous pursuit of both price stability and full employment and its function as a price anchor reduces (but does not eliminate) price volatility in the system (Tcherneva, 2020; Armstrong, 2020b).

The JG wage effectively provides a wage floor for both private and public sector non-JG jobs (Armstrong, 2020b), so private sector employers would be required to offer workers compensation competitive with JG rates of pay. The JG job pool would effectively become an employed labour buffer stock (Wray, 1998; Mosler and Silipo, 2016) which enlarges in times of recession and reduces in times of boom. In worsening economic conditions private sector workers would move into the JG job pool and in improving conditions private sector employers might offer pay rates in excess of the JG wage in order to attract additional workers from the pool (or other benefits which make private sector employment more attractive).

Periodically, the JG wage might be increased ultimately requiring firms to increase compensation to retain their employees and attempt to cover the extra costs by a combination of productivity rises, reduced profit margins and higher product prices. However, even if a one-off price rise followed the increase in the JG, this would not constitute "inflation" unless it generated a wage–price spiral, a situation that should by no means be expected. Indeed, the "price anchor" role of JG policy would be critical and should be expected to result in enhanced wage stability by setting a well-publicised wage for a buffer stock of employed labour which might be used as an alternative source of supply of workers by private employers when faced with increased wage demands.

MMT and Trade

From an MMT perspective, exports are real costs as they require giving something up that could have been consumed at home (there is a domestic opportunity cost), whereas imports are real benefits as they involve other nations giving something up that they could have consumed (there is a foreign opportunity cost). Given a nation's ability to consume goods and services is based upon what it can produce domestically plus what it can import, it follows that a country should aim to fully employ its available labour force and maximise output (subject, of course, to the demands of ecological sustainability) and that the addition of net imports "means that a nation gets to enjoy a higher material living standard by consuming more goods and services than it produces for foreign consumption" (Mitchell, 2018).[22] MMT recognises that the existence of a current account deficit (CAD) is de facto evidence that foreigners have positive net savings desires for financial assets denominated in domestic currency. As long as such desires exist, a nation can run a CAD and there is no "imbalance" in the sense described by orthodoxy. Both the net importing nation and the overseas holders of net financial assets are able to satisfy their consumption and net savings desires, respectively (Mosler, 2010).

Furthermore, MMT recognises that if a nation is real resource poor, then even if it operates at full employment it may be unable to produce all the goods and services it requires to enable its population to flourish and if no overseas positive net savings desire for its financial assets exists, it would be required to export goods and services to obtain the necessary foreign exchange. Since exports are the real cost of the imports, if a nation lacks sufficient real resources to export it may be unable to import the essential products, such as food and energy, it requires. In this case, international support would be required (Siddiqui and Armstrong, 2018). MMT recognises the real burden that would follow from incurring debts denominated in foreign currency and Modern Monetary Theorists have advocated strongly for the development of multinational mechanisms designed to facilitate the transfer of real resources from the global north to the global south (Mitchell, 2023).

ATTITUDES TO MMT INSIDE AND OUTSIDE HETERODOXY

Although MMT has been part of economics discourse since the early 1990s (Mosler, 1993), until comparatively recently the majority of mainstream economists seemed unaware of its existence (Armstrong, 2020a). Indeed, outside a small group of heterodox economists – predominantly Post-Keynesians – knowledge of MMT was very limited in the economics academy. However, first the global financial crisis and second, the global Covid pandemic gave impetus to the blossoming of interest in MMT. Although, as might have been expected and in line with a Kuhnian view of science,[23] the mainstream orthodoxy responded to contradictory evidence by producing ad hoc modifications to established theory and there was an effective "circling of wagons" around orthodoxy, the obvious failure of mainstream economics to explain real-world events or offer effective policy remedies contributed to the motivation of heterodox thinkers to look to MMT as a potential contributor to economic knowledge (Armstrong, 2020a).

Part of this orthodox defence involved first ignoring possible alternatives and where that became increasingly difficult engaging with them by initially attempting to ridicule them and then by mischaracterisation (Armstrong, 2023). MMT has suffered greatly from both of these approaches (Armstrong, 2018, 2020a, 2023). Mainstream economists, especially those of elevated status, have tended not to engage with MMT directly,[24] leaving most of the work to others, usually journalists in the mainstream media.[25] A relatively recent development in the financial media has been to make minor concessions to MMT, in an attempt to reduce its significance, respond to it in a cursory way and move on in the hope that in the future it can be ignored again (Davies, 2019; Armstrong, 2019, 2023).

The relationships between heterodox schools can be both complex and evolving, for example that between Marxists and Keynesians remains highly problematic[26] (Joseph interviewed in Armstrong, 2020a, pp. 343–344). The more serious commentaries upon and critiques of MMT have come from outside the mainstream, from Marxists (Lapavitsas and Aguila, 2020) and, in particular, Post-Keynesians (see, for example, Fullbrook and Morgan, 2020). Of the early major MMT thinkers, Warren Mosler, Bill Mitchell and Randy Wray, only Wray might be described as coming from a Post-Keynesian tradition (Mosler comes to MMT from finance and Mitchell from a Marx/Kalecki background). Commonalities between MMT and Post-Keynesians can be readily identified (Rochon, 2020, p. 338) but there are also a number of differences (Rochon, 2020; Sawyer, 2020, 2007, 2003).

To summarise the attitude of the Post-Keynesian community to MMT is no easy task.[27] At one end of the scale, Lavoie has given due credit to MMT, pointing to both its new theoretical insights and its impact (Lavoie, 2011, 2020, pp. 227–228), however, in stark contrast, Palley argues that the claims of MMT are either simplistic or flawed (Palley, 2014, 2015a, 2015b). Armstrong (2020b) also notes that support for MMT certainly exists within Post-Keynesianism but argues that Post-Keynesians tend to downplay the significance of MMT, considering the key insights of MMT are already present in Post-Keynesianism, and mistakenly "focus on the idea that MMT advocates over-stress the role of the state in the money creation process to the neglect of private money creation" Armstrong (2020b, p. 157). From an MMT perspective, Post-Keynesian critique of treasury/CB consolidation is misplaced (see "The Central Bank and the Banking System" above) and Post-Keynesians fail to recognise MMT's insights into trade (see "MMT and Trade" above). Furthermore, only a small minority of the heterodox economists, including Post-Keynesians,[28] support MMT's advocacy of a JG or appreciate MMT's insights into the balance sheet effects of government spending on the CBs and the private banking system (Armstrong, 2020b).[29]

From an MMT perspective, the critiques emanating from within Post-Keynesianism fail to stand up to serious scrutiny and can be mainly attributed to a lack of understanding of the actual extant institutional arrangements which underpin the operation of the monetary system and a failure on the part of critics to come to terms with the actual content of MMT, as opposed to how it is often mistakenly portrayed (Armstrong, 2020b). MMT's distinctive focus on the operational reality of monetary systems has enabled it to provide rigorous explanations of the real causal mechanisms at work under fixed and floating exchange rate regimes and if it is accepted that the insights following from MMT are both highly significant and different from both mainstream economics and other heterodox schools, it would seem entirely reasonable to suggest that MMT ought to be a legitimate part of a heterodox community.[30]

Dow (2018, p. 21) argues "...the onus is on each economist to engage in debate about the relative merits of the different approaches, being able to defend her chosen approach, but also able to understand enough about alternative approaches to engage in more-or-less effective communication." With respect to the disputes between heterodox economists (for example, between Marxists and Keynesians/Post-Keynesians and between Post-Keynesians and advocates of MMT), clearly defending and elaborating their own theories is vital (this in itself poses no problems and, indeed, may lead to enhanced knowledge), but it needs to be carried out in a scholarly and respectful way if it is to facilitate the development of economic knowledge. The individual identity of a particular group need not be compromised and rigorous debate, of course, could and should continue, but I suggest that ill-constructed critiques of MMT based upon a lack of understanding of what MMT is actually saying (as has been the case both inside and outside heterodoxy) is likely to hamper the development of the discipline.

CONCLUSION

In this chapter, the argument presented supports the contention that heterodox schools are distinct, but nevertheless hold things in common, meaning that potential exists for effective collaboration. Debate within and between hetero-dox schools is beneficial, but rejection of a school based upon lack of knowl-edge of that school is not. A range of approaches enhances the opportunity for the development of economic knowledge, and pluralism in all its forms should be supported. However, the idea that "anything goes" is rejected as the number of coexisting paradigms must be limited in number given that scientific prac-tice, in this case economics, is a social enterprise. A paradigm should not be conceptualised as a conscious construction; the boundaries of a paradigm are permeable and flexible (Dow, 2018), rather, it is a socially determined struc-ture underlying a mode of scientific behaviour.

The "taxes drive money approach" which underlies MMT enables it to provide insights absent from other heterodox schools, in particular, the expla-nation of the real causal mechanisms at work in monetary systems which operate under different exchange rate regimes. Thus, MMT should be accepted as a legitimate school within a heterodox community and – looking forwards – have a role within a heterodox paradigm which can be effectively "underla-boured" by critical realism (Armstrong, 2018, 2020b).

In the case of heterodox economics, a shared ontological vision provides the basis of just such a constitution. Heterodox groups such as Marxists, Post-Keynesians and Modern Monetary Theorists have enough potential to operate within what might be regarded, from this perspective, as a single paradigm while maintaining their own identity – via the differing emphases they place on specific aspects of economic theory. However, currently at least, the differences between heterodox economists are apparently too marked for a heterodox paradigm to function effectively and produce meaningful knowl-edge so it seems that the introduction of a more pluralist economics education may constitute a prerequisite for its future development (Armstrong, 2020b).

POSTSCRIPT

This chapter was written with the aim of situating MMT within heterodoxy by outlining its key insights. It was not written as a defence against MMT's critics (see Armstrong 2020b, 2023). In due course, in conjunction with my fellow Associates at the Gower Initiative for Modern Money Studies, I will respond to the criticisms set out in the chapter, 'MMT: The good, the bad and the ugly'. The response will be published on the Gower Initiative website at gimms.org.uk.

ACKNOWLEDGEMENTS

The author would like to thank Warren Mosler, Marc Lavoie and Mark Epstein for their helpful comments. All mistakes remain my own.

NOTES

1. The two terms, "orthodox" and "mainstream" are often used interchangeably when discussing economics, however Jamie Morgan (Armstrong, 2020a, pp. 399–400) puts forward a convincing case that they should be distinguished from each other.
2. Mainstream economists follow a formal deductivist method, founded upon methodological individualism, making their approach incompatible with heterodox scholars who embrace a realist social ontology (Potts and Armstrong, 2020, pp. 63–69).
3. A philosophical basis for social theorising in economics can be provided by means of a critical realist "underlabouring" but social ontology "is never a substitute" for such theorising (Lawson, 2003, p. 53).
4. A detailed analysis of the nature of realist social ontology (and critical realism (CR)) is outside the scope of this chapter, however I note here that numerous scholars have written in favour of the contention that a range of schools might be underlaboured by CR (Armstrong, 2020b).
5. Dow (2018) discusses the different forms that pluralism might take (Armstrong, 2018, pp. 29–31).
6. Armstrong (2020a, 2020b) conducts a qualitative research programme based on semi-structured interviews of leading economists who self-identify as heterodox from a range of schools, including Post-Keynesians, Institutionalists, Marxists, Sraffians and Modern Monetary Theorists.
7. MMT is consistent with chartalism and, indeed, Modern Monetary Theorists have been referred to as "neochartalists" (Wray, 1998, 2014).
8. "A conjectural history provides a benchmark to assess the world we live in, but it is important to appreciate that it is *not* meant to provide an accurate description of how the world actually evolved. The conjectural history is a useful myth, and it is no criticism of a conjectural history to say that the world failed to evolve in the way it postulates" (Dowd, 2000, p. 139, emphasis in original).
9. For a discussion of the relevance of realist social ontology to economics see Armstrong (2020a, 2020b).
10. Evidence in support of credit and state theories can be found in numerous sources from authors working in a wide range of disciplines including economists (Wray, 2004; Keynes, 1930), sociologists (Ingham, 1996, 2004), economic historians (Polanyi, 1944/1957), anthropologists (Graeber, 2011: Humphrey and Hugh-Jones, 1992) and scholars of law (Desan, 2014).
11. Armstrong (2020b) discusses the antecedents of MMT.
12. Armstrong (2019) notes that, for a nation with its own sovereign currency under floating exchange rates, MMT conceptualises a state as a currency-issuer which is never revenue constrained in its own currency and rejects the mainstream concept of a government budget constraint (GBC) (Mitchell, 2011). The GBC conceptualises the government as a currency-user, which might finance its spending by taxation, borrowing (debt issuance) and "printing money". Only under a gold standard or fixed exchange rate regime is a state required to act as currency-user, with spending offset by taxation or borrowing (Mosler, 1993; Armstrong, 2015).
13. Debt ceilings, such as those imposed in the US, are a potential political limit on the level of state debt, rather than a monetary one. Preventing CBs from buying

state debt directly from the government follows from a residual belief in monetarism – that direct CB purchases "monetise" state debt and are therefore inflationary. In reality, the government always spends by the issue of new money, adding reserves to the system. The state has no operational need to sell debt and if it chooses to do so by selling it to the non-government sector, it merely changes the composition of non-government sector risk-free assets (Armstrong, 2020c).

Another self-imposed constraint is the requirement for treasuries to hold a positive balance at their own CB before spending. Such rules run contrary to the logic inherent in MMT, that government spending or lending must precede taxation or state borrowing. Meeting this requirement simply requires a particular sequence of transactions involving the CB and the treasury which, once completed, results in the government spending as set up in its budget and the private sector holding more government securities than previously. Thus, the rule is shown to have no meaningful impact (Wray, 2012, pp. 105–109).

14.   CBs and commercial banks are reserve constrained by design under a gold standard or fixed exchange rate systems. Under such regimes, government debt sales are required to compete with the option to convert to gold (or foreign currency) at a fixed rate and in these circumstances interest rates are "market determined" (Mosler, 1993; Armstrong, 2015, 2020b).

15.   MMT is characterised by an appreciation of this status of CBs. This view is consistent with MMT's support of CB and treasury "consolidation" as a pedagogical tool in the teaching of monetary macroeconomics. MMT does not deny that a study of actual operational relationship between treasuries and CBs (including the various political rules in place at given points in time) is not important, far from it (Berkeley et al., 2021), but, nevertheless, stresses that the status of monopoly-issuer of the currency lies with the state and the CB carries out policy as directed by the state (Mitchell, 2016; Lavoie, 2020, pp. 223–226).

16.   The second is the rate state money exchanges against goods and services (discussed in the next section).

17.   The payment of interest on credit balances on accounts at the CB is a political decision and operationally required under the current system. "In practice, policy rates above 0% are supported by the CB paying interest on reserves, or by the CB maintaining additional accounts, called securities accounts, on behalf of the Treasury. Such accounts are more commonly known as Treasury bills, notes, and bonds. Securities accounts are interest-bearing alternatives to reserve accounts and function to support a term structure of rates above 0%" (Mosler and Armstrong, 2019, p. 3).

18.   With respect to the UK, Berkeley et al. (2021) describe in detail the financial operations of the UK government and the accounts and structure of the UK Exchequer. They also provide a summary of their research in Berkeley et al. (2023).

19.   The conceptualisation of banks as agents of the CB (noted above) underlies MMT's support for banking regulation (Mosler, 2012). Mosler (2010, pp. 113–114) notes that the price level is not only a function of the prices paid by the state but also of the collateral demanded when the state-controlled bank (its CB) lends. Mosler thus stresses the need to maintain strict bank regulation, with respect to collateral and capital requirements, in order to prevent the inherent endogeneity of money creation in the banking system leading to excessive lending which, in turn, would lead to upward pressure on prices.

20.   From an MMT viewpoint, a policy of wage indexation (commonly introduced during periods characterised by "wage–price spirals") is necessarily inflationary as it leads to automatic increases in government wage offers and thus perpetuates price rises.

21.   For example, in March 2021, the UK Office of Budget Responsibility provided an example of the fiscal effect of an interest rate rise, "… if short- and long-term interest rates were both 1 percentage point higher than the rates used in our forecast – a level that would still be very low by historical standards – it would increase debt interest spending by £20.8 billion (0.8 per cent of GDP) in 2025–26. To put this into context, it is roughly equivalent to two-thirds of the medium-term fiscal tightening announced by the Chancellor in this Budget".

22.   This approach forms part of a "base case" argument and, for example, MMT advocates accept there may be valid strategic reasons why nations might choose to support domestic production rather than rely on imports.

23.   See Kuhn (2012/1962).

24.   Wren-Lewis (2016a, 2016b) is one of relatively few New Keynesian economists to actively engage with MMT, however his failure to correctly conceptualise and distinguish between the different operational realities applying under fixed and floating exchange rate systems leads to ill-constructed critique.
      It is also possible that there is change in the air as the growing profile of MMT seems to be encouraging an increasing number of mainstream economists to engage with it, for example Drumetz and Pfister (2021), Portes (2019).

25.   Such poorly constructed critiques are common, see, for example, Davies (2019), Schulze (2020), Das (2021). Articles in the financial press often mischaracterise MMT and fail to stand up to even limited scrutiny, the lack of adequate understanding of monetary operations on the part of the authors being readily apparent (Armstrong, 2019). Such a lack of understanding is also evident when politicians comment on MMT (Reynolds, 2019).

26.   Howard and King (1992) discuss the divisions between so-called "Keynesian sympathisers" and "anti-Keynesian Marxists". Apparently, Marxists have their counterparts within Post-Keynesianism with respect to MMT, which may be termed "anti-MMT Post-Keynesians" (see Fullbrook and Morgan, 2020).

27.   For example, Watts (2016, p. 3) points to Post-Keynesian support for MMT but also notes that many Post-Keynesians "do not subscribe to functional finance principles and/or are hostile to a Job Guarantee" (Juniper et al., 2014–15).

28.   Armstrong (2020a, 2020b) investigates the awareness of and attitudes to MMT in the economics profession.

29.   The disputes between MMT and Post-Keynesians over "details" might be described by the term "narcissism of small differences" (Freud, 1930; Mongiovi, in Armstrong, 2020b, p. 716).

30.   Similarly, MMT should be part of any future heterodox paradigm (Armstrong, 2020b).

REFERENCES

Armstrong, P. (2023). "Tombstone for a Tombstone": Dealing with the "bad science" behind mainstream criticism of MMT. *The Gower Initiative of Modern Money Studies*, January 28. https://gimms.org.uk/2023/01/28/tombstone-for-a-tombstone/. Accessed 01/05/2023.

Armstrong, P. (2022). A Modern Monetary Theory advocate's response to "Modern Monetary Theory on money, sovereignty, and policy: A Marxist critique with reference to the Eurozone and Greece" by Costas Lapavitsas and Nicolás Aguila (2020). *The Japanese Political Economy, 48* (1), 49–66.

Armstrong, P. (2020a). *Can Heterodox Economics Make a Difference: Conversations with Key Thinkers.* Edward Elgar Publishing, Cheltenham, UK and Northampton, MA, USA.

Armstrong, P. (2020b). Modern Monetary Theory and its relationship to heterodox economics. Solent University. https://ssudl.solent.ac.uk/id/eprint/4127/. Accessed 15/12/2021.

Armstrong, P. (2020c). An MMT perspective on macroeconomic policy space. In Fullbrook, E. and Morgan, J. (Eds) *Modern Monetary Theory and Its Critics*, pp. 67–96. Real World Economics Books, Bristol.

Armstrong, P. (2019). A simple MMT advocate's response to the Gavyn Davies article "What you need to know about modern monetary theory". *The Gower Initiative of Modern Money Studies*, May 27. https://gimms.org.uk/2019/05/27/phil-armstrong-gavyn-davies-response/. Accessed 15/11/2021.

Armstrong, P. (2018). Modern Monetary Theory and a heterodox alternative paradigm. *The Gower Initiative of Modern Money Studies*, December 26. https://gimms.org.uk/2018/12/26/mmt-heterodox-alternative-paradigm/. Accessed 15/11/2021.

Armstrong, P. (2015). Heterodox Views of Money and Modern Monetary Theory. *moslereconomics.com.* https://moslereconomics.com/wp-content/uploads/2007/12/Money-and-MMT.pdf. Accessed 15/11/2021.

Armstong, P. and Mosler, M. (2020). Weimar Republic Hyperinflation through a Modern Monetary Theory Lens. *The Gower Initiative for Modern Money Studies.* https://gimms.org.uk/2020/11/14/weimar-republic-hyperinflation-through-a-modern-monetary-theory-lens/.

Armstrong, P. and Siddiqui, K. (2019). The case for the ontology of money as credit: Money as bearer or basis of "value". *Real World Economics Review, 90, December*, 98–118.

Berkeley, A., Tye, R. and Wilson, N. (2023). An accounting model of the UK Exchequer. In Wray, L.R. and the Gower Initiative for Modern Money (Eds) *Modern Monetary Theory: Key Insights, Leading Thinkers*, pp. 1–40. Edward Elgar Publishing, Cheltenham, UK and Northampton, MA, USA.

Berkeley, A., Tye, R. and Wilson, N. (2021). An accounting model of the UK Exchequer 2nd edition. *The Gower Initiative of Modern Money Studies*, February 21. https://gimms.org.uk/2021/02/21/an-accounting-model-of-the-uk-exchequer/. Accessed 15/12/2021.

Chapman, A. (1980). Barter as a universal mode of exchange. *L'Homme, 20* (3), 33–83.

Das, S. (2021). Spending without taxing: Now we're all guinea pigs in an endless money experiment. *The Guardian*, December 10. https://www.theguardian.com/commentisfree/2021/dec/10/spending-without-taxing-now-were-all-guinea-pigs-in-an-endless-money-experiment. Accessed 15/12/2021.

Davies, G. (2019). What you need to know about Modern Monetary Theory. *Financial Times.* https://www.ft.com/content/744f4fc4-6762-11e9-9adc-98bf1d35a056. Accessed 15/11/2021.

Desan, C. (2014). *Making Money: Coin, Currency, and the Coming of Capitalism.* Oxford University Press, Oxford.

Dow, S. (2018). Pluralist economics: Is it scientific? In Decker, S., Elsner, W. and Flechtner, S. (Eds) *Advancing Pluralism in Teaching Economics: International Perspectives on a Textbook Science*, pp. 13–30. Routledge, London.

Dowd, K. (2000). The invisible hand and the evolution of the monetary system. In Smithin, J. (Ed.) *What Is Money?* pp. 139–141. Routledge, Abingdon.

Drumetz, F. and Pfister, D. (2021). The Meaning of MMT. *Banque de France*, Working Paper Series no. 833. https://publications.banque-france.fr/en/meaning-mmt. Accessed 15/12/2021.

Freud, S. (1930). *Civilisation and Its Discontents*. Internationaler Psychoanalytischer Verlag Wien, Wien.

Fullbrook, E. and Morgan, K. (Eds) (2020). *Modern Monetary Theory and its Critics*. Real World Economics Review Books, Bristol.

Fulwiler, S., Grey, R. and Tankus, N. (2019). An MMT response on what causes inflation. *FT Alphaville*, March 1. https://www.ft.com/content/539618f8-b88c-3125-8031-cf46ca197c64. Accessed 15/12/2021.

Graeber, D. (2011). *Debt: The First 5000 Years*. Melville House, New York.

Howard, M. and King, J.E. (1992). *A History of Marxian Economics, Volume 2, 1929–1990*. Princeton University Press, Princeton.

Humphrey, C. and Hugh-Jones, S. (Eds) (1992). *Barter, Exchange and Value: An Anthropological Approach*. Cambridge University Press, Cambridge.

Ingham, G. (2004). *The Nature of Money*. Polity/Blackwell, Oxford.

Ingham, G. (1996). Money is a social relation. *Review of Social Economy, 54* (4), 507–529.

Innes, A.M. (1914). The Credit Theory of Money. *Banking Law Journal, 31, January*, 151–168.

Innes, A.M. (1913). What is money? *Banking Law Journal, May*, 377–408.

Juniper, J., Sharpe, T.P. and Watts, M.J. (2014–15). Modern Monetary Theory: Contributions and critics. *Journal of Post Keynesian Economics, 37* (2), 281–307.

Keynes, J.M. (1930). *A Treatise on Money*, 2 vols. Harcourt and Brace, New York.

Knapp, G.F. (1924/1973). *The State Theory of Money*. Augustus M. Kelley, New York.

Kuhn, T. (2012/1962). *The Structure of Scientific Revolutions.* University of Chicago Press, Chicago.

Lapavitsas, C. (2005). The Emergence of Money in Commodity Exchange, Or Money as the Monopolist of the Ability to Buy. *SOAS, Department of Economics*, Working Paper no. 126. https://www.soas.ac.uk/sites/default/files/2022-10/economics-wp126.pdf. Accessed 15/11/2021.

Lapavitsas, C. (2003). Money as a universal equivalent and its origin in commodity exchange. https://www.soas.ac.uk/sites/default/files/2022-10/economics-wp130.pdf. Accessed 15/11/2021.

Lapavitsas, C. and Aguila, N. (2020). Modern Monetary Theory on money, sovereignty, and policy: A Marxist critique with reference to the Eurozone and Greece. *The Japanese Political Economy, 46* (4). https://doi.org/10.1080/2329194X.2020.1855593. Accessed 15/11/2021.

Lavoie, M. (2020). Modern Monetary Theory and Post-Keynesian Economics. In Fullbrook, E. and Morgan, J. (Eds) *Modern Monetary Theory and Its Critics*, pp. 207–232. Real World Economics Books, Bristol.

Lavoie, M. (2011). The monetary and fiscal nexus of neo-chartalism: A friendly critical look. http://www.boeckler.de/pdf/v_2011_10_27_lavoie.pdf. Accessed 15/11/2021.

Lawson, T. (2003). *Reorienting Economics*. Routledge, London.

Lawson, T. (1997). *Economics and Reality*. Routledge, London.

Lee, F. (2010). *A History of Heterodox Economics.* Routledge, Abingdon.

Mearman, A. (2011). Who do heterodox economists think they are? *American Journal of Economics and Sociology, 70* (2), 480–510.

Mearman, A., Berger, S. and Guizzo, D. (2019). *What Is Heterodox Economics?: Conversations with Leading Economists.* Routledge, Abingdon.

Menger, C. (1892). On the origin of money. *Economic Journal, 2* (6), 239–255 (trans. Caroline A. Foley).

Mitchell, W. (2023). The MMT perspective on international trade and finance. In Wray, L.R. and the Gower Initiative for Modern Money (Eds) *Modern Monetary Theory: Key Insights, Leading Thinkers*, pp. 94–124. Edward Elgar Publishing, Cheltenham, UK and Northampton, MA, USA.

Mitchell, W. (2018). Trade and finance mysteries – part 1. May 8. https://billmitchell .org/blog/?p=39282. Accessed 24/01/2022.

Mitchell, W. (2016). Modern Monetary Theory – what's new about it? August 22. https://billmitchell.org/blog/?p=39282. Accessed 24/01/2022.

Mitchell, W. (2011). Austerity proponents should adopt a job guarantee. https:// billmitchell.org/blog/?p=14208. Accessed 29/09/2023.

Mitchell, W (2010). Whatever – its either employment or unemployment buffer stocks. December 30. https://billmitchell.org/blog/?p=17564. Accessed 24/01/2022.

Mosler, W. (2023). A framework for the analysis of the price level and inflation. In Wray, L.R. and the Gower Initiative for Modern Money (Eds) *Modern Monetary Theory: Key Insights, Leading Thinkers*, pp. 87–93. Edward Elgar Publishing, Cheltenham, UK and Northampton, MA, USA.

Mosler, W. (2020). MMT white paper. https://moslereconomics.com/mmt-white-paper/ . Accessed 15/11/2021.

Mosler, W. (2012). Proposals for the Banking System, the FDIC, the Fed, and the Treasury. In Rochon, L-P. and Olawoye, S.Y. (Eds) *Monetary Policy and Central Banking*, chapter 4. Edward Elgar Publishing, Cheltenham, UK and Northampton, MA, USA.

Mosler, W. (2010). *The 7 Deadly Innocent Frauds of Economic Policy.* Valance, US Virgin Islands.

Mosler, W. (1993). Soft currency economics. https://moslereconomics.com/mandatory -readings/soft-currency-economics/. Accessed 1/12/2023.

Mosler, W. and Armstrong, P. (2019). A discussion of central bank operations and interest rate policy. *The Gower Initiative of Modern Money Studies*, February 24. https://gimms.org.uk/wp-content/uploads/2019/02/Central-Bank-Interest-Rate -Policy-Mosler-Armstrong.pdf. Accessed 15/11/2021.

Mosler, W. and Silipo, D. (2016). Maximising Price Stability in a Monetary Economy. *Levy Economics Institute*, Working Paper no. 864, April.

O'Hara, P. (2002). The role of institutions and the current crisis of capitalism: A reply to Howard Sherman and John Henry. *Review of Social Economy, 60* (4), 609–618.

Palley, T. (2015a). Money, fiscal policy, and interest rates: A critique of Modern Monetary Theory. *Review of Political Economy, 27* (1), 1–23.

Palley, T. (2015b). The critics of Modern Money Theory (MMT) are right. *Review of Political Economy, 27* (1), 45–61.

Palley, T. (2014). Modern Monetary Theory (MMT): The Emperor still has no clothes. http://www.thomaspalley.com/?p=393.

Polanyi, K. (1944/1957). *The Great Transformation.* The Beacon Press, Boston, MA.

Portes, J. (2019). Nonsense economics: The rise of Modern Monetary Theory. *Prospect Magazine*, January 30. https://www.prospectmagazine.co.uk/ideas/economics/42224/nonsense-economics-the-rise-of-modern-monetary-theory. Accessed 15/11/2021.

Potts, N. and Armstrong, P. (2020). What Marx and Kalecki/Post-Keynesians do not share, and why this is not a barrier to their learning from each other to their mutual advantage. In Hermann, A. and Mouatt, S. (Eds) *Contemporary Issues in Heterodox Economics*, pp. 63–84. Routledge, Abingdon.

Reynolds, J. (2019). Why Labour doesn't support Modern Monetary Theory. Labour List, June 4. https://labourlist.org/2019/06/why-labour-doesnt-support-modern-monetary-theory/. Accessed 15/11/2021.

Rochon, L-P. (2020). MMT and TINA. In Fullbrook, E. and Morgan, J. (Eds) *Modern Monetary Theory and Its Critics*, pp. 332–352. Real World Economics Books, Bristol.

Sawyer, M. (2020). Modern Monetary Theory: Is there any added value? In Fullbrook, E. and Morgan, J. (Eds) *Modern Monetary Theory and Its Critics*, pp. 353–379. Real World Economics Books, Bristol.

Sawyer, M. (2007). Seeking to reformulate macroeconomic policies. https://www.boeckler.de/pdf/v_2007_10_26_Sawyer.pdf. Accessed 15/11/2021.

Sawyer, M. (2003). Employer of last resort: Could it deliver full employment and price stability? *Journal of Economic Issues*, 37 (4), 881–909.

Schulze, G. (2020). Modern Monetary Theory is not the answer. *Forbes*, March 2. https://www.forbes.com/sites/georgeschultze/2020/03/02/modern-monetary-theory-is-not-the-answer/?sh=2810f8cf5088. Accessed 15/11/2021.

Siddiqui, K. and Armstrong, P. (2018). Capital control reconsidered: Financial policies in developing countries/financialization and economic policy. *International Review of Applied Economics*, 32 (6), 713–731.

Smithin, J. (2018). *Rethinking the Theory of Money, Credit, and Macroeconomics: A New Statement for the Twenty-First Century*. Lexington, Washington D.C.

Tcherneva, P. (2020). *The Case for the Job Guarantee*. Polity, Cambridge.

Watts, M. (2016). Fiscal Policy and the Post-Keynesians. Paper presented at the AHE annual conference. Glasgow, Scotland, July.

Weber, I. (2021). Could strategic price controls help to fight inflation? *The Guardian*, December 21. https://www.theguardian.com/business/commentisfree/2021/dec/29/inflation-price-controls-time-we-use-it. Accessed 26/01/2022.

Wray, L.R. (2014). From the State Theory of Money to Modern Money Theory: An Alternative to Economic Orthodoxy. *Levy Institute*, Working Paper no. 792. https://www.econstor.eu/bitstream/10419/110046/1/780086651.pdf. Accessed 15/11/2021.

Wray, L.R. (2012). *Modern Monetary Theory*. Palgrave Macmillan, Basingstoke.

Wray, L.R. (2004). *Credit and State Theories of Money*. Edward Elgar Publishing, Cheltenham, UK and Northampton, MA, USA.

Wray, L.R. (1998). *Understanding Modern Money*. Edward Elgar Publishing, Cheltenham, UK and Lyme, NH, USA.

Wren-Lewis, S. (2016a). MMT: Not so modern. https://mainlymacro.blogspot.com.au/2016/03/mmt-not-so-modern.html. Accessed 15/11/2021.

Wren-Lewis, S. (2016b). MMT and mainstream macro. https://mainlymacro.blogspot.com.au/2016/03/mmt-and-mainstream-macro.html. Accessed 15/11/2021.

5. Modern Monetary Theory: the good, the bad and the ugly

Marc Lavoie

INTRODUCTION

I first wrote about Modern Monetary Theory, or Modern Money Theory (MMT), previously labelled *neo-chartalism*, when I reviewed (Lavoie, 1999) Randy Wray's book (1998). This led me to later distinguish between what I called *the neo-chartalist* view and *the post-chartalist* view while explaining the basics of monetary creation with the help of T-accounts (Lavoie, 2003). In the *neo-chartalist* case, the central bank purchases the securities issued by the government, and later sells back most of these securities to the private sector; in the *post-chartalist* case, commercial banks purchase these securities and then sell some of these to the central bank, in order to acquire cash and the required reserves, a case which I had partially described in an earlier book (Lavoie, 1992, pp. 166–9). It took me another ten years to gather my thoughts on the subject, letting others express their views on the arrival of this new school of thought, when I wrote a long 'friendly critique' back in 2011, which was published in 2013 (Lavoie, 2013). I was asked to revisit MMT twice, as part of a symposium (Lavoie, 2019) and then in a key lecture on MMT and the eurozone (Lavoie, 2022b). I should also point out that for a few years I benefited from research money provided by Warren Mosler, who many consider as the godfather of MMT, through the support of the UMKC (University of Missouri-Kansas City) Center for Full Employment and Price Stability. And I have often been invited to make presentations to the graduate students of the University of Missouri in Kansas City and to lecture at the Minsky Summer School of the Levy Economics Institute – two of the main centres of MMT thinking. All this to say, as Wray (2012, p. xiii) notes, that, despite not being part of the MMT group, I am among those outsiders who 'have also contributed to the development of the theory', while being then, and still today, critical of certain aspects of MMT.

I have recently written, in reference to Stigler and Ricardo's theory of value, that I agree with 93 per cent of MMT. Much of what I will say here will be devoted to the remaining 7 per cent, but that should not deter readers from recognizing that MMT is part of the Institutionalist branch of post-Keynesian economics, as also argued by Reynold Nesiba (2013), and that whatever critiques one can make of MMT it is certainly more correct than mainstream economics. Bill Mitchell, a founder of MMT, identifies MMT's defining characteristics and key advantage as its 'detailed analysis of institutions and how they actually operate', adding that MMT was 'developed on observing real-world institutions', in particular the 'institutional characteristics' of various currency systems (Mitchell in Armstrong, 2020, p. 153).

In this chapter I will not exactly follow the outline provided by its title. I will start by discussing the ugly side of MMT, then its good side, that is, its contributions to fiscal policy and macroeconomics, and will finish with discussing the bad, that is, the aspects of MMT which in my opinion should be questioned or amended. This last section of the chapter will thus cover (part of) the 7 per cent which I mentioned above. In so doing, I will try as best as I can to go beyond what I have written in previous papers on the topic. A broad balanced review of the various earlier critiques addressed to MMT, which is certainly worth reading, is provided by Nesiba (2013).

THE UGLY

While getting much attention on social media, MMT has been subjected to a barrage of critiques, both from fellow post-Keynesians and from mainstream economists. Some are well informed, mostly those from heterodox economists, others rarely so. It is not always easy to keep one's cool, when told that 'MMT is a mix of old and new, the old is correct and well understood, while the new is substantially wrong' (Palley, 2015b, p. 46), or when it is charged that 'what's right is not new, what's new is not right, and what's left is too simplistic' (Buiter and Mann, 2019, p. 1). It is sometimes argued that 'professional jealousy' is the main driver of heterodox critics (Wray in Armstrong, 2020, p. 289) with some resenting the success of MMT in drawing attention (Potts in Armstrong, 2020, p. 432). Louis-Philippe Rochon (2019, p. 159) has argued that 'MMTers themselves must accept part of the blame for fanning the flames of some of their critics, by either refusing to directly answer pertinent or valid criticism, or by engaging in their own discrediting behaviour, dismissing critics, in an often cult-like behaviour', with Steve Keen (in Armstrong, 2020, p. 363) adding that 'there are also a lot of people who just find them arrogant and difficult to deal with'. MMT authors have been defending their ideas and claims for 25 years, so there must be some lassitude in attempting to justify their main claims or to correct false perceptions about their theories.

Still, in a recent symposium, where various MMT and post-Keynesian authors were given the opportunity to respond to two well-documented critiques of MMT, their authors, Drumetz and Pfister (2023, p. 79), complained that they were subjected to derogatory or insulting remarks such as: 'the authors do not understand that…; the authors make the hysterical claim that…; if the authors had read the MMT literature more thoroughly…; a paper which is littered with factual errors and misrepresentations; [the authors] repeatedly make claims which are unsustainable; the article falsely represents MMT as…'. Ironically, they had earlier complained that MMT authors often accused 'those who do not share their ideas of being incompetent' (Drumetz and Pfister, 2021, p. 21). Similar sentences can be found in a recent MMT rebuttal to the critique made by two Marxian economists:

> their approach fails to stand up to scrutiny; [their arguments] are both theoretically hollow and not consistent with the evidence; the authors mischaracterize MMT, due at least in part to their paying insufficient attention to the MMT literature; their failure to understand operational reality in the eurozone at anything other than a superficial level. (Armstrong, 2022, pp. 49–50, 56)

Phil Armstrong's chapter in this book (Chapter 4, p. 62) asserts that:

> the critiques emanating from within Post-Keynesianism fail to stand up to serious scrutiny and can be mainly attributed to a lack of understanding of the actual extant institutional arrangements which underpin the operation of the monetary system and a failure on the part of critics to come to terms with the actual content of MMT, as opposed to how it is often mistakenly portrayed.

In his book of interviews, Armstrong concluded that the critiques of post-Keynesians are 'misguided and based upon an inaccurate understanding of the nature of money … and a failure to correctly conceptualise the operational reality of monetary systems' (Armstrong, 2020, p. 453).

There is nothing new in the tone of these critiques. I complained ten years ago about the unscholarly vigour with which some MMT authors responded to criticism, as well as 'the aggressive reaction against critics by some non-academic supporters of neo-chartalism', such that some post-Keynesians preferred to avoid any debate on the topic (Lavoie, 2013, p. 7).

This brings to the fore the notion that MMT, in contrast perhaps to most economic theories, is being discussed intensely both by academics in university circles and by activists on blogs and the Internet. John Quiggin identifies (2020, p. 528) two versions of MMT. One is an 'academic' version, which details all sorts of restrictions to the general validity of the theory; the other is what Quiggin called *popular* or *vulgar* MMT, 'in which the statement "taxes don't finance public expenditures" is interpreted to mean that government can increase spending as much as they like'. I made a somewhat similar distinction ten years ago, pointing out that, as recognized by MMT authors themselves, there exist two MMT strands, the so-called *specific* or *academic* one, which described in minute detail the specific operational and legal procedures involved in the monetary and fiscal nexus, and the so-called *general* strand, which relied on the consolidation of the balance sheets of the government and of the central bank, and which is at the heart of the arguments that can be found in the blogosphere or in the bestseller book of Stephanie Kelton (2020). The presence of these two strands creates a lot of confusion, as MMT authors reverse back to the specific or academic version whenever the oversimplified *general* or *vulgar* version is being attacked, thus creating the criticism that the goalposts are constantly moving.

One annoying feature of MMT authors is their propensity to make believe that they were the first economists to make crucial points about monetary economics. I have given several examples in a previous paper (Lavoie, 2019, pp. 102–3). The worse example is that of Bill Mitchell (2019) when he claimed that 'MMT economists were the first in the modern era to point out that loans create deposits, not the other way around', thus leaving aside the whole post-Keynesian literature of the 1970s and 1980s associated with Jacques Le Bourva, Nicholas Kaldor, Tony Cramp, Joan Robinson, Alfred Eichner and Basil Moore, as well as many others.

Another example is the claim that in the past post-Keynesians failed to put fiscal policy to the fore and neglected the issue of crowding out, thus implying that MMT works were a great improvement on that front. It is easy to find several post-Keynesian works that very explicitly rejected crowding out and advocated a dominant fiscal policy, as in Nell (1988), Fazzari (1994–95) and James Galbraith (1994–95), not to speak of the numerous articles jointly written by Philip Arestis and Malcolm Sawyer.

In addition, despite MMT authors having initially clearly indicated their tight links with post-Keynesian economics (Lavoie, 2013, pp. 5–7), some give the impression that MMT came from nowhere, except as some type of modern revival of Keynes and of Lerner's functional finance, creating on its own all sorts of novel economic theories that question the mainstream view based on a vertical Phillips curve and a supply-led economy. This is most strongly asserted by Bill Mitchell (in Armstrong, 2020, p. 163), who claims that MMT authors have 'built a body of work that's an identifiable school of thought', whereas 'in the Post-Keynesian world, there is no real coherent macroeconomics' (p. 152). His colleague and co-author Martin Watts (in Armstrong, 2020, p. 282) is much more generous, pointing out that MMT includes 'a lot of Post-Keynesian insights over a number of years concerning the monetary system, credit creating, quantity theory of money and the money multiplier not being valid'.

Scholars interviewed by Phil Armstrong (2020) essentially believe that MMT is a variant within post-Keynesian economics. Armstrong (2020, p. 17) himself argues that that MMT 'is an important development in Post-Keynesianism'. He adds: 'I don't see any inconsistency with Post-Keynesianism. I just think MMT adds insights and pushes them into the foreground' (p. 21). This is also the view of James Juniper (in Armstrong, 2020, p. 125), according to whom MMT 'is a recognisable school within Post-Keynesianism'. Similarly, for Geoffrey Harcourt (in Armstrong, 2020, p. 116), MMT 'still got an underlying Post-Keynesian basis, but they have a unique twist on it', while for Anwar Shaikh (in Armstrong, 2020, p. 256), 'MMT is Post-Keynesian economics of a particular sort'. More straightforwardly, Andrew Kliman (in Armstrong, 2020, p. 138) thinks 'of MMT as Post-Keynesian', which is also the view of both Malcolm Sawyer (in Armstrong, 2020, p. 229) and Engelbert Stockhammer (in Armstrong, 2020, p. 272), the former saying that MMT authors 'operate within the general Post-Keynesian world' while the latter maintains that MMT 'is part of Post-Keynesianism'. Victoria Chick (in Armstrong, 2020, p. 24) takes a stern view, arguing that MMT 'is a minor gloss on something which is already well known'!

THE GOOD

Rhetoric and Economic Policies

The first obvious good thing is that MMT's visibility has induced many noneconomists to get interested in the arcane subject of monetary economics. The desire of MMT authors to speak to nonacademic audiences has sparked phenomenal activity via blogs and social media. Their efforts have convinced several business journalists and financial advisors to reconsider their views of conventional wisdom, question mainstream austerity fears of public deficits and debt, and reconsider how interest rates get set. Several articles have appeared in magazines and influential newspapers, such as the *Washington Post* or the *New York Times*, trying to explain to their readers the main claims of MMT and how they contradict the received view. As a consequence, government officials, central bankers as well as well-known mainstream economists, have been forced to provide an opinion about MMT and its policy recommendations. Along with several others, Engelbert Stockhammer (in Armstrong, 2020, p. 272) is impressed by how MMT advocates 'have demonstrated that you can reach unanticipated audiences and also become politically effective'. This political effectiveness is also pointed out by Palley (2015a, p. 21), when he says that in situations of high unemployment, which many countries have faced for many years, 'MMT makes a valuable contribution as part of the rhetoric advocating expansionary fiscal policy'.

Rochon (2019) points out that mainstream economists and the advocates of TINA (There Is No Alternative) once had an easy task, using simple rhetoric to compare governments with prudent households that avoid unsustainable debt levels and burdens on the next generation who may face rising tax rates in an attempt to balance the budget or reimburse the debt. The denials previously offered by old Keynesians or post-Keynesians, based as they were on complicated stories, could not make a dent on TINA. To this, the simple MMT polemical response has been that the government is not akin to a household and that 'sovereign currency issuing governments, with flexible exchange rates and without foreign currency debt, are financially unconstrained' (Palley, 2020, p. 473). And as Palley (in Armstrong, 2020, p. 187) further recognizes, despite being one of its most ferocious critics, MMT is 'a progressive polemic that counters the austerity polemic of the right-wing'.

It must be said that recent events have made it easier to convey the MMT message. After all, the actions of several Western governments during the Covid-19 pandemic, especially in 2020, appeared to come directly from the MMT bluebook. Extraordinary income-support programmes were created for those unable to attend work, with households receiving more aggregate disposable income than before the pandemic; governments issued huge amounts of securities, most of which were quickly purchased by their central bank, which thus accumulated large amounts of government deposits before these were eventually transferred to the banking accounts of firms and households. All in all, short-term and long-term interest rates on government debt were brought down to or kept at zero or nearly zero, despite the huge government deficits. While government officials or central bankers were denying that they were now following the prescriptions of MMT, it was difficult for them to explain in which way these policies and their results differed from those advocated by MMT economists. The case of Japan with its large deficits and zero interest rates could not be considered an exception anymore.

MMT authors have certainly been influential in spreading the view among both their heterodox and orthodox colleagues that, at least within certain circumstances and institutional frameworks, the decisions of central governments to raise public expenditures and public deficits were not constrained by financial considerations. Unfortunately, the rising inflation rates of 2022, essentially due to supply-chain problems, the war against Ukraine and the rise of commodity prices, have given apparent ammunition to those US senators who predicted in 2019 that MMT posed a threat to the economy of the United States, as 'the implementation of Modern Monetary Theory would lead to higher deficits and higher inflation'.[1]

MMT is not only on the map as an alternative to TINA, it has induced a revival in the study of heterodox macroeconomics. Several students have told me or colleagues that they came to study post-Keynesian economics because they first heard of MMT on social media. In their desire to know more about MMT, they discovered that heterodox schools exist and that post-Keynesian economics in particular was in the background of MMT. One drawback of MMT today is that, besides the use of T-accounts and Godley's three-balance identity – the fundamental identity – its authors rarely provide any formalized account of their theories. Students seduced by MMT but who favour formalization are thus enticed to move towards post-Keynesian economics, which thus benefits from the exposure that MMT gets on social media and in the press.

But besides this and the success that MMT has encountered on the policy front, what is the good side of MMT? What are its contributions to economics in general and to monetary policy more specifically?

Economic Theory

MMT is usually recognized as having contributed to our understanding of specific theoretical issues. First, MMT authors have certainly helped to combat the mainstream view on the origins of money, based on commodity money as an improvement over barter. Their opposing views have resurrected Knapp's chartalist approach and Innes's credit approach to money. Second, the core of MMT and its proposals for the creation of job guarantee programmes, also called the state as an employer of last resort or buffer-stock employment programmes, have contributed to improved countercyclical macroeconomic policy. Of particular note is spatial Keynesianism, that is, geographically targeted government support, focussing on job creation where it is most needed. Another important contribution of MMT has been the revival of Abba Lerner's functional finance approach, which plays such an important role when dealing with fiscal policy and challenging the mainstream view of sound finance. One might also argue that MMT authors have contributed to generalize the knowledge and usefulness of Godley's three-balance identity, which, along with functional finance, helps to understand that public debt is not necessarily an evil. As a general statement, one can also argue that MMT authors have been quite active in combatting dubious alternative heterodox proposals such as 100 per cent reserve requirements.

There is one aspect of MMT that constitutes a clear advance in post-Keynesian monetary theory. As Sawyer (in Armstrong, 2020, p. 230) rightly notes, in the past, post-Keynesians associated with the monetary circuit approach were mostly concerned with the relationship between nonfinancial firms and the banks, while Cambridge post-Keynesians such as Kaldor and American post-Keynesians such as Basil Moore studied the relationship between commercial banks and the central bank. MMT authors have brought to the fore an analysis of the relationship between the government, its deficits and its central bank, as well as going into the details of the clearing and settlement system of a monetary economy.[2] As Mosler says in his white paper, 'MMT began as a description of Federal Reserve Bank monetary operations, which are best thought of as debits and credits to accounts as kept by banks, businesses and individuals' (in Armstrong, 2020, p. 461). The inquiries of MMT authors have allowed post-Keynesians to better understand the importance of autonomous liquidity factors, in particular the impact of government expenditure or of collected taxes on the reserves of the banking system, and the alternative ways in which government expenditures could be financed (Bell, 2000).[3] This analysis allows us to understand that if there are excess reserves in the system there is nothing that commercial banks as a group can do to get rid of them, something not always well understood by some post-Keynesians, as reported by Fiebiger (2016). While this analysis can be said to have been first formulated by Mosler (1994), the works and blogs of several MMT scholars such as Bell-Kelton, Forstater, Fullwiler, Tcherneva, Tymoigne, Watts and Mitchell have gained both popular and academic recognition.

Further, Wray (1998, 2012) explains that whenever the government spends it issues a cheque or an electronic payment that goes through the clearing and settlement system. This means that the recipient of the payment gets a deposit in some banking institution, while the bank sees an increase in its deposits (its reserves) at the central bank. There is thus an autonomous increase in the amount of liquidity in the overnight interbank market. Similarly, when the government collects taxes from an agent, the payment goes through the clearing and settlement system, so that there is a decrease in the bank deposits of the agent while the agent's bank observes a decrease in its reserves at the central bank. This is another example of an autonomous factor. Note that the funds are not destroyed: while banks have less deposits at the central bank, the government now has a larger amount of deposits at the central bank (not part, however, of the definition of central bank money), which can now be used to fund more expenditures. A surprising feature, at least from the point of view of those that have been brought up in the tradition of the loanable funds approach or of the IS/LM (investment-saving/liquidity preference-money supply) model, is that, all else equal, a government deficit funded from its account at the central bank tends to lower the overnight interest rate.

THE BAD

We now reach the 7 per cent that I mentioned in the introduction. These 7 per cent in fact represent what ought to be considered as amendments to the main MMT story or doubts about it. Many of these issues depend on the discrepancies between the *general* and the *specific* approaches, or between the *academic* and *popular* versions of MMT. Most of these amendments or critiques have been made already 20 years ago, so MMT authors may feel that they provided rebuttals for these critiques a long time ago. The fact that someone might disagree with an MMT proposition or with the relevance of an assumption made by an MMT scholar does not mean that the critic lacks understanding of monetary operational details or of the MMT literature. It may mean instead that the critic has a different interpretation of the operational details outlined by MMT authors and that the critic is aware of the existence of operational features in monetary systems which are different from those usually discussed by MMT authors – the US system. I start with the core claim of MMT, that the government does not need to tax or to borrow in order to spend, and will then move on to subsidiary issues that have given rise to critiques in the past.

Neither Taxes nor Bonds Finance Government Spending

MMT authors make two nearly identical statements that need to be disentangled. The first one is that MMT 'views taxation not as funding spending in a functional sense…. Taxes don't fund spending, it's just recapturing what they've already spent' (Armstrong, 2020, p. 17), the argument being that there is a causal priority of government spending over taxation. Now, as Chick (in Armstrong, 2020, p. 17), responded 'this is a parallel assertion to Keynes's assertion that investment precedes saving. It's exactly the same principle'. When asked about the logic of the statement that the government needs to spend before it can collect back taxes, Harcourt (in Armstrong, 2020, p. 115) reacted in just the same way: 'Well, that's just Keynes. It's that investment creates saving, its just another version of that'. Chick (pp. 20–21) continues, however, by saying that 'I don't think it's that important. It adds this one point, which Post-Keynesians should have thought of making, but didn't'. As Malcolm Sawyer (in Armstrong, 2020, pp. 221–2) points out, drawing on the analysis of the theory of the monetary circuit à la Alain Parguez and Augusto Graziani as MMT authors also have done, one can make a distinction between *initial* finance at the start of the circuit and *final* funding at the end of the circuit, and say that taxes provide final funding for government spending at the end of the circuit. So, there is no controversy here. Or if there is, it is only due to a problem of terminology.

But there is a second statement, apparently only slightly different from the first, which one often hears from MMT advocates, which is that 'the US government does not have to borrow in order to spend' (Kliman in Armstrong, 2020, p. 138). An earlier statement can be attributed to Wray (1998, p. 78): 'The Treasury spends before and without regard to either previous receipt of taxes or prior bond sales'. This is an entirely different ball game. In the *general* or *popular* version, this is justified by the consolidation assumption, where the central bank and the Treasury are considered as a single consolidated unit. MMT authors base most of their popular arguments and slogans on this assumption that the central bank and the government (the Treasury) are or ought to be considered as one and the same institution. However, when Armstrong (2020) asked about this assumption in his interviews, nearly all scholars informed about this controversy were adamant that consolidation was improper and would lead to misleading conclusions and a mistaken under-standing of the operational reality of monetary economics and of government spending.[4] MMT authors on the other hand argue that critics are misled by the presence of self-imposed constraints and fooled by the smoke and mirror operations that these entail.

The purpose of MMT, according to Bill Mitchell (2021), is 'to understand the actual way in which the central banks, commercial banks and treasuries interact rather than specifying how we might want them to act in some stylised fictional world and then inferring things from that fiction as if it applies to the world we live in'. The *general* or *vulgar* version, for popular consumption, describes the world as Mitchell and other MMT advocates would like it to be or as it might have been at some point in the past (without self-imposed con-straints), not as it is now.[5] There is thus some irony in making use of consolida-tion, as it leaves aside the crucial issue of initial finance. MMT authors like to make the distinction between currency users and currency issuers, with the US government being claimed to be a currency issuer. But as Chick (in Armstrong, 2020, p. 18) sharply noted, at least under current arrangements, 'The Treasury doesn't emit money. The Fed does emit money'. Leaving aside consolidation, just like firms or households need to borrow from banks, the government (the Treasury) needs to borrow from financial institutions or from the central bank in order to acquire funds in its banking account. As in the private sector with investment, there has to be a stage of initial finance when the government wishes to spend. A statement to the effect that the government does not need to tax or to borrow in order to spend is thus misleading, at least in my opinion.

Going Through North American Specifics

Of course, MMT advocates have gone through the specifics and have avoided consolidation when doing scholarly work. The easiest way out is to assume that the central bank always buys government bonds on the primary market and figure out what happens to bank reserves from then on. This is what I have called the *neo-chartalist* case (Lavoie, 2013). But we do know that central banks are often prohibited from purchasing bonds on the primary market (except when rolling over previously issued securities), which means that the story has to be more complicated. The specific case described by a number of MMT authors is that government bonds have first to be sold to primary dealers. We are then told that the proceeds of the sales are being repatriated to the gov-ernment account at the central bank (Wray, 2012, pp. 103–4). This means that the banking system will end up with a deficit amount of reserves, which the central bank will be obliged to provide in order to achieve its overnight interest rate target. This leads to the modified claim that 'the US government and its agents [presumably including the central bank], from inception, necessarily spend (*or lend*) first, only then can taxes be paid or US Treasury securities purchased' (Mosler in Armstrong, 2020, p. 462, my emphasis). So now the story is that 'it's impossible to pay tax unless there's been some spending or lending' (Armstrong, 2020, p. 184). The story is that for taxes or newly issued bond purchases to be paid and settled, banks must first have access to reserves: these will be obtained either when the government spends from its central bank account, or when the central bank provides overdrafts to the banking system (the latter sometimes being confusingly incorporated within public spending by some MMT authors).

But even this modified *neo-chartalist* story can be misleading. First, under current circumstances, as a consequence of past quantitative easing policies, banks are flushed with excess reserves and hence are under a floor system; they don't need to take advances from the central bank when their customers are paying their taxes and the funds are being transferred to the central bank (Fiebiger, 2016, p. 599). Second, until the 2008 global financial crisis, the US government held a large share of its proceeds from bond issues in various bank accounts, the so-called *Treasury tax and loans* accounts. This is noted by various MMT scholars (Tymoigne, 2020, p. 52). This meant that most paid taxes were simply transferred from the account of taxpayers at commercial banks to the *Treasury tax and loans* accounts of the government at various commercial banks. Similarly, when primary dealers did purchase newly issued government securities, there would be no reduction in the total amount of reserves in the banking system. While the payment would be immediately credited to the government account at the Fed, since the Fed acted as the fiscal agent of the Treasury, the proceeds would quickly be moved towards the *Treasury tax and loan* accounts, so as to neutralize their impact on the amount of reserves in the banking system, thus limiting any need for lending or repo (repurchase agreement) operation.

What is ironic is that, starting with Bell (2000), MMT advocates have themselves described in great detail the functioning of these *Treasury tax and loans* accounts, emphasizing the required coordination between the government (the Treasury) and the central bank to avoid overly large fluctuations in the amount of reserves in the banking system. In fact, this necessary coordination is sometimes used as an argument in favour of the consolidation assumption. In the case of the United States, until very recently, the coordination thus occurred through the existence of these *tax and loan* accounts at commercial banks, so that federal tax payments only involved payments between banks, with transfers of reserves occurring mostly inside the private banking system. Symmetrically, whenever the government would spend, commercial banks would get a call and funds would be transferred from the *tax and loans* account of the Treasury towards its account at the Fed so as to keep constant the amount of government deposits at the central bank and thus minimize the impact on the overall amount of reserves. Thus, at least in the US case, either because of the floor system with excess reserves, or because of the presence of *tax and loans* accounts, the claim that there has to be government spending or central bank lending to allow the banks of taxpayers and of primary dealers to settle payment does not hold. The funds used for government spending come from bonds which have been previously sold to the private sector![6] In addition, other countries may have other coordination mechanisms.

Take the Canadian case (before Covid-19). I have provided an analysis of the Canadian monetary and payment system in a number of papers, showing that the simplicity of the Canadian system, with its zero-reserve framework, perfectly illuminates the accuracy of the post-Keynesian approach (Lavoie, 2005, 2019). An additional feature of the Canadian system is that clearing is not done on the books of the central bank, as happens in most financial systems. Clearing occurs on the books of a private clearing house, run by the Canadian Bankers Association; only the settlement of the payments that have not been compensated throughout the day at the clearing house, notably through overnight market loans, occurs on the books of the central bank.

As long as transactions do not involve the central bank, on its own or as the financial agent of the government, the amount of reserves (now called settlement balances in Canada) will not change and will remain at zero. Note that there is no relationship whatsoever between economic activity, the amount of tax payments and the amount of bank deposits on one hand, and bank reserves on the other, since bank reserves at the end of each day are virtually zero. Monetary systems where there are no compulsory reserve requirements are a perfect case for the argument that the purpose of reserves is not to constrain the creation of bank loans and that central banks act essentially in a defensive manner. When payments involve the account of the central bank at the clearing house, the positive (negative) balances of the central bank at the clearing house will exactly balance the negative (positive) balances of the overall banking system. By the end of the day, if collected taxes exceed payments by the government out of its account at the central bank, the monetary authorities will need to remove its positive balances at the clearing house, and thus provide extra balances to the banking sector, so as to bring the deficit balances of the private sector at the clearing house back to zero.

Thus, in the Canadian system, banks do not need to hold reserves to compensate for the tax payments that are being made to the government; it is the central bank that will move government deposits towards the banks (through an auction) before the end of the day to ensure that banks are not in a negative position at the clearing house; banks are not forced to take advances from the central bank in order to settle tax payments. In both Canada and the United States, at least before quantitative easing took over, to avoid fluctuations in the overall size of reserves and hence to achieve the target overnight rate, from a quantitative point of view, transfers of government deposits were the main tool, whereas open-market operations or repo operations were only a subsidiary tool.

Going Through Foreign Specifics

Finally, we may deal with another institutional set-up, different from the US one or the Canadian one, based on a so-called overdraft system, where the central bank cannot make outright purchases of government bonds, neither on the primary nor on secondary financial markets, as developed in Lavoie (2022b). This was the case of the eurozone before 2010 and it is the case of Chile, for instance, and it is a configuration promoted by the IMF. We may call this the *anti-chartalist* case. The bonds must all be bought by banks or dealers. If the government holds its funds at commercial banks, there is no loss of reserves when the bonds are being purchased. If the government holds the proceeds of the bond sales at the central bank, then the central bank must provide advances to the financial sector for settlement to happen. Such a central bank controls the overnight rate – it is a ceiling system as banks are *in the Bank* – but it has no control whatsoever on the long-term bond rate if financial institutions decline to purchase the newly issued bonds or refuse to roll over existing stocks of bonds. The central bank is still a *lender of last resort to the banks*, but it is not a *purchaser of last resort to the government*, in contrast to the Canadian and US cases.

The main claim of MMT is that countries with a *sovereign currency* cannot default and hence the level of the deficit or that of the public debt is irrelevant. The standard definition of a sovereign currency (Wray, 2019) is that the government runs a floating exchange rate, it chooses a currency that becomes the money of account, it imposes taxes in the chosen currency, it issues securities in its own currency and it issues securities denominated in the home currency. The *anti-chartalist* case defined above corresponds to all these conditions, as long as we recognize, as Chick did in the interview previously mentioned, that it is the central bank and not the Treasury that issues currency. Still, in this *anti-chartalist* case, the government may default, since there is nothing that the central bank can do if banks and other financial institutions decline to purchase or roll over the bonds issued by the government. The government is at the mercy of financial markets. Operational reality and self-imposed constraints do matter. One cannot always rely on the consolidated *general* or *vulgar* framework.

While it must be granted that the United States and several other advanced economies cannot default for the reasons outlined by MMT authors, several post-Keynesian authors with ties with semi-industrialized countries have underlined that the five conditions outlined by Wray are unlikely to be sufficient to avoid default or a financial crisis. External constraints do limit monetary sovereignty, irrespective of the chosen exchange rate regime, as Kregel (2020) points out. Running a flexible exchange rate regime will not alleviate the problems faced by these countries when having large deficits in an attempt to achieve full employment (Vergnhanini and De Conti, 2017; Bonizzi et al., 2019; Epstein, 2019, ch. 3; Prates, 2020; Vernengo and Pérez Caldentey, 2020). The main argument is that these countries have a currency which is low in the hierarchy of currencies, so that their exchange rate is more liable to fluctuations. A depreciation induced by a trade deficit resulting from a public deficit is likely to be accompanied by rising inflation, due to a high pass-through coefficient, and hence to falling real wages and a recession. Furthermore, while the government may issue its debt in the domestic currency, this is not necessarily the case of the private sector which needs foreign currency to import needed commodities, and hence currency depreciation will induce a rising debt burden for the private sector and hurt economic activity. In addition, if some portion of the public debt denominated in the home currency is held by non-residents, they may decide to sell the bonds to resident banks and trade the proceeds to obtain dollars, thus putting further downward pressure on the home currency.

CONCLUSION

In this chapter I have tried to show why MMT is still a controversial topic, not only among mainstream economists, but also among heterodox economists and, in particular, among post-Keynesian economists. At first sight this controversy and its occasional acrimonious debates are surprising since post-Keynesians share a considerable amount of common ground with MMT scholars, in particular the belief that fiscal policy can be more powerful than monetary policy to fight unemployment, the theories of money endogeneity and interest rate determination, the rejection of any argument based on the money multiplier or the fractional-reserve banking system, sharing as well the lessons that can be drawn from great economists of the past such as Keynes, Kalecki, Minsky and Godley. Despite this, or perhaps because of this common ground, there have been several articles by post-Keynesians questioning MMT. I have done this here, to a large extent, by making use of the instructive and revealing interviews conducted by Phil Armstrong – the author of the alternative chapter on MMT.

The bulk of the debate, as shown in the previous section, turns around the interpretation of the operational reality relating government expenditures to its financing, as well as its relationship with the central bank and commercial banks. MMT authors conclude from their description of these relationships that it is best to amalgamate the Treasury and the central bank into one entity to apprehend correctly the underlying reality and thus avoid the smoke and mirrors brought about by formal prohibitions and other self-inflicted constraints. Other post-Keynesians, observing the same institutions, reject this consolidation, believing instead that it cannot be generalized to all monetary set-ups and that consolidation obstructs our comprehension of the political economy of the fiscal and monetary nexus. Some paradoxical MMT statements might thus be misleading, or they may be misinterpreted by orthodox authors.[7] Some of the features that MMT authors consider to be MMT insights might thus be correct only under very strict circumstances.

There are many other MMT proposals that are open to debate, whatever MMT advocates may think of their validity. To conclude, I can provide a brief list of them. MMT authors often claim that a currency has value only because it must be used to pay taxes – chartal money; but this seems to overly minimize the importance and role of confidence and credibility for the worth of a currency, notwithstanding the existence of competing currencies. MMT authors believe that the target nominal overnight rate always ought to be set at 0 per cent; but this seems to minimize the possibility of financial instability and asset inflation. MMT authors advocate the creation of a government employment of last resort (ELR); but isn't there a risk that such a programme may induce the government to gradually let go well-paid unionized jobs within the public sector? MMT authors consider that the ELR programme is an integral part of MMT because it can always be financed since there is no financial constraint on a central government and because they believe that since the government can set the ELR wage rate it will be able to control wage inflation and price inflation, thus simultaneously achieving full employment and low inflation; but isn't this an oversimplified view of the wage bargaining process in industrial relations, and doesn't this omit price inflation caused by external factors, such as the rise in the cost of imported intermediary commodities or the impact of exchange rate depreciation?

Yet, despite this, it remains that MMT has opened up the range of fiscal policies and has provided a useful *argumentaire* against the standard claim that the government is running out of money and hence can't financially afford this or that government programme.

NOTES

1. US government (2019). https://www.govinfo.gov/content/pkg/BILLS-116sres182is/pdf/BILLS-116sres182is.pdf.
2. However, as recalled in Lavoie (2013, pp. 11–12), Cambridge authors such as Joan Robinson and also Godley and Cripps understood these relationships.
3. Changes in official foreign exchange reserves are another autonomous liquidity factor, which central banks must take care of in order to achieve their target interest rate, as explained in post-Keynesian economics through the *compensation thesis* (Lavoie, 1992, pp. 189–92; Lavoie, 2022a).
4. Chick (p. 18), Goodhart (p. 106), Reis (pp. 207–8), Semmler (p. 241), Shaikh (pp. 257–8), Stockhammer (p. 269), Dow (p. 307), Keen (p. 361) and Smithin (p. 447) all give a clear no answer to consolidation. Palley (pp. 185–6) and Sawyer (p. 227) give a 'horses for courses' answer. Only Potts (p. 431), Armstrong's supervisor, gives a clear yes answer.
5. Kregel (1988) reminds us that in the past some central banks were created so as to provide an 'unoffchokable' amount of funds to the Treasury, so that in some sense they could be considered as a single institution. But, at the time, these central banks were faced with gold convertibility, so that at some point they would decline to act as the initial purchaser of government debt. In modern times Kregel says, the central bank is 'divorced' from the Treasury.
6. See Fiebiger (2016) for a list of the differences between the standard MMT story and the post-Keynesian story essentially based on the above.
7. For instance, a survey was organized in 2019 asking economists whether the following statement, attributed to MMT, was correct: 'Countries that borrow in their own currency should not worry about government deficits because they can always create money to finance their debt' (https://en.wikipedia.org/wiki/Modern_Monetary_Theory). MMT authors claim that *printing money* is not what they mean, recognizing however that their terminology can be confusing (Fullwiler, 2020). Saying that the vertical component of central bank money *leverages* the horizontal component of bank money is another useless MMT misuse of terms (Lavoie, 2013, p. 8).

REFERENCES

Armstrong, P. (2020). *Can Heterodox Economics Make a Difference? Conversations with Key Thinkers*. Edward Elgar, Cheltenham, UK and Northampton, MA, USA.
Armstrong, P. (2022). A modern monetary theory advocate's response to 'modern monetary theory on money, sovereignty, and policy: A Marxist critique with reference to the Eurozone and Greece' by Costas Lapavitsas and Nicolás Aguila (2020). *The Japanese Political Economy*, *48* (1), 49–66.
Bell, S. (2000). Do taxes and bonds finance government spending? *Journal of Economic Issues*, *34* (3), 603–620.
Bonizzi, B., A. Kaltenbrunner and J. Michell (2019). Monetary sovereignty is a spectrum: Modern monetary theory and developing countries. *Real-World Economics Review*, *89* (October), 46–61.
Buiter, W. and C.L. Mann (2019). Modern Monetary Theory (MMT): What's right is not new, what's new is not right, and what's left is too simplistic. Citi GPS.

Drumetz, F. and C. Pfister (2021). *The meaning of MMT*. Banque de France working paper. https://publications.banque-france.fr/sites/default/files/medias/documents/wp833_0.pdf.

Drumetz, F. and C. Pfister (2023). It takes two to tango: A reply to our MMT critics. *European Journal of Economics and Economic Policies: Intervention*, *20* (1), 78–89.

Epstein, G.A. (2019). *What's Wrong with Modern Money Theory? A Policy Critique*. Springer Nature, Cham.

Fazzari, F.M. (1994–95). Why doubt the effectiveness of Keynesian fiscal policy? *Journal of Post Keynesian Economics*, *17* (2), 231–248.

Fiebiger, B. (2016). Fiscal policy, monetary policy and the mechanics of modern clearing and settlement systems. *Review of Political Economy*, *28* (4), 590–608.

Fullwiler, S. (2020). When the interest rate on the national debt is a policy variable (and 'printing money' does not apply). *Public Budgeting and Finance*, *40* (3), 72–94.

Galbraith, J.K. (1994–95). John Maynard Nosferatu. *Journal of Post Keynesian Economics*, *17* (2), 249–260.

Kelton, S. (2020). *The Deficit Myth: Modern Monetary Theory and the Birth of the People's Economy*. Public Affairs, New York.

Kregel, J.A. (1988). Central bank monetary control and financial structure: Some general considerations. In Jossa, B. and Panico, C. (Eds). *Teorie Monetarie e Banche Centrali* (pp. 30–45). Liguori, Naples.

Kregel, J.A. (2020). External debt matters: What are the limits to monetary sovereignty? *Japanese Political Economy*, *46* (4), 287–299.

Lavoie, M. (1992). *Foundations of Post-Keynesian Economic Analysis*. Edward Elgar Publishing, Aldershot, UK and Brookfield, VT, USA.

Lavoie, M. (1999). Book Review: Understanding Modern Money. *Eastern Economic Journal*, *25* (3), Summer, 370–372.

Lavoie, M. (2003). A primer on endogenous credit-money. In Rochon, L.-P. and Rossi, S. (Eds). *Modern Theories of Money: The Nature and Role of Money in Capitalist Economies* (pp. 506–543). Edward Elgar Publishing, Cheltenham, UK and Northampton, MA, USA.

Lavoie, M. (2005). Monetary base endogeneity and the new procedures of the Canadian and American monetary systems. *Journal of Post Keynesian Economics*, *27* (4), Summer, 689–709.

Lavoie, M. (2013). The monetary and fiscal nexus of neo-chartalism: A friendly critique. *Journal of Economic Issues*, *47* (1), 1–32.

Lavoie, M. (2019). Modern monetary theory and post-Keynesian economics. *Real-World Economics Review*, *89* (October), 97–108.

Lavoie, M. (2022a). *Post-Keynesian Economics: New Foundations*, second edition. Edward Elgar Publishing, Cheltenham, UK and Northampton, MA, USA.

Lavoie, M. (2022b). MMT, sovereign currencies and the Eurozone. *Review of Political Economy*, *34* (4), 633–646.

Mitchell, W.F. (2019). Paying interest on excess reserves is not constrained by scarcity. *William Mitchell – Modern Monetary Theory*. http://bilbo.economicoutlook.net/blog/?m=20190716.

Mitchell, W.F. (2021). MMT economists do not seek to enumerate how many angels can dance on the head of a pin. *William Mitchell – Modern Monetary Theory*. http://bilbo.economicoutlook.net/blog/?p=48613.

Mosler, W. (1994). Soft currency economics. http://mosiereconomics.com/mandatory-readings/soft-currency-economics/.

Nell, E.J. (1988). *Prosperity and Public Spending: Transformational Growth and the Role of Government*. Unwin Hyman, Boston.

Nesiba, R.F. (2013). Do Institutionalists and post-Keynesians share a common approach to Modern Monetary Theory (MMT)? *European Journal of Economics and Economic Policies: Intervention, 10* (1), 44–60.

Palley, T.I. (2015a). Money, fiscal policy, and interest rates: A critique of Modern Monetary Theory. *Review of Political Economy, 27* (1), 1–24.

Palley, T.I. (2015b). The critics of Modern Money Theory (MMT) are right. *Review of Political Economy, 27* (1), 45–61.

Palley, T.I. (2020). What's wrong with Modern Money Theory: Macro and political economic restraints on deficit-financed fiscal policy. *Review of Keynesian Economics, 8* (4), 472–493.

Prates, D. (2020). Beyond Modern Money Theory: A Post-Keynesian approach to the currency hierarchy, monetary sovereignty, and policy space. *Review of Political Economy, 8* (4), 494–511.

Quiggin, J. (2020). Book review of *Macroeconomics* by Mitchell, Wray and Watts. *Economic Record, 96* (315), December, 528–530.

Rochon, L.-P. (2019). MMT and TINA. *Real-World Economics Review, 89* (1), 156–166.

Tymoigne, E. (2020). Monetary sovereignty: Nature, implementation, and implications. *Public Budgeting and Finance, 40* (3), 49–71.

Vergnhanini, R. and B. De Conti (2017). Modern Monetary Theory: A criticism from the periphery. *Brazilian Keynesian Review, 3* (2), 16–31.

Vernengo, M. and E. Pérez Caldentey (2020). Modern Money Theory (MMT) in the Tropics: Functional finance in developing countries. *Challenge, 63* (6), 332–348.

Wray, L.R. (1998). *Understanding Modern Money*. Edward Elgar Publishing, Cheltenham, UK and Lyme, NH, USA.

Wray, L.R. (2012). *Modern Money Theory: A Primer on Macroeconomics for Sovereign Monetary Systems*. Palgrave Macmillan, Basingstoke.

Wray, L.R. (2019). Alternative paths to modern money theory. *Real-World Economics Review, 89* (October), 5–22.

6. Identity, risk, and financial capitalism: a post Keynesian research agenda on racial and gender stratification in the U.S.

Melanie G. Long

INTRODUCTION

Despite areas of progress, the U.S. economy is characterized by a range of gender and racial disparities.[1] In fact, the disruptions caused by the COVID-19 pandemic demonstrated that social stratification[2] not only persists but may have worsened in certain dimensions. Even among essential workers in the U.S., the employment costs of the downturn in 2020 were disproportionately felt by black and Hispanic women. Hundreds of thousands of women left the workforce when schools went online. From housing security to health, the crisis had differential effects by race and gender.

In this sense, the COVID-19 pandemic was a story of unevenly distributed risk—economic and otherwise. Post Keynesian economics offers unique analytical tools for studying how agents cope with risk, the role of financial markets, and the macroeconomic implications of both distribution and uncertainty. This moment thus offers an opportune time to ask how post Keynesian research can inform and be informed by an understanding of racial and gender inequality.

This question is certainly not a new one. In a 2010 *Cambridge Journal of Economics* symposium on post Keynesian and feminist economics, Irene van Staveren commented that the "routes followed by each tradition run parallel or even cross" and examined the "fruitful mutual engagements" possible via a synthesis of these schools of thought (van Staveren, 2010, p. 1140). Twelve years later, these mutual engagements have developed in some areas while lagging in others.

In this chapter, I motivate and trace out potential starting points for a post Keynesian research agenda on the links between identity and financial capitalism, drawing on insights from feminist and stratification economics. The combination of existing racial and gender inequities, financialization, and the individualization of risk in the U.S. is likely to shape distribution and macroeconomic outcomes in ways that a class-based analysis alone would miss. I argue that these links should be investigated through additional empirical work on disparities in credit markets and wealth accumulation as well as their implications for the effects of macroeconomic policy.

THEORETICAL AREAS OF CONSENSUS AND EXISTING WORK

There have been multiple calls for greater collaboration between heterodox schools of thought working on dimensions of inequality other than class. In addition to feminist economics, the insights of stratification economics on racial discrimination have been applied to understanding financial crises (Seguino, 2019). The interested reader can find detailed reviews of each school of thought in previous work (e.g., see Agenjo-Calderón and Gálvez-Muñoz, 2019; Chelwa, Hamilton, and Stewart, 2022). In the following section, I instead briefly summarize theoretical starting points that are common in these fields and shared with post Keynesian economics.

Group Identity and Social Embeddedness

Heterodox economists studying social stratification generally argue that identity is not simply an exogenous, static characteristic of individuals. Gender has been described by researchers in feminist traditions as a "performance" that others do or do not recognize in specific contexts (Danby, 2012) and as a social categorization that is partly imposed but can also be "renegotiated" and "manage[d]" (Folbre, 2021, p. 45). Similarly, stratification economists Chewla, Hamilton, and Stewart (2022) argue that individuals select a specific "identity profile composition" (p. 379). Such profiles include group identities such as "Whiteness," which can be "invested in" or "divested from" depending on the returns to that identity (p. 380). Barriers, which may change over time, constrain the extent to which subjugated groups can adopt a dominant identity (p. 381).

These conceptions of identity imply that agents are "socially embedded," a notion shared with post Keynesian economics (van Staveren, 2010, p. 1126). Gender and race have meaning in a particular cultural, temporal, and economic context and shape access to resources. Class serves a similar function in post Keynesian and Kaleckian models. While the starting point for neoclassical models is to posit a singular "household" that owns the factors of production and engages in production, post Keynesianism assumes that these groups are fundamentally different in their opportunities to save, produce, and obtain desired outcomes in social conflicts.

If race and gender are similar in nature to class identifiers, then identity can play an equally valid role in macroeconomic research. Identity can be seen as another structural aspect of an economy or society, serving to create and recreate groups subject to different institutional rules.

Market and Non-Market Power

Feminist and stratification economists replace a narrow definition of discrimination with a broader notion that emphasizes power as a source of group disparities. This contrasts with the neoclassical tradition following Becker (1957), in which discrimination has been modeled as stemming either from an arbitrary bias (taste-based discrimination) or from productivity expectations (statistical discrimination). Discrimination is therefore a residual: any wage or employment differential that cannot be explained once all individual employee qualifications are controlled for may be attributable to discrimination.

The neoclassical framing of discrimination treats labor market characteristics as exogenous rather than as the potential product of prior processes, which may include instances of discrimination, institutions that exclude certain groups, or gaps in bargaining power (Figart, 1997). For instance, the argument that gender wage gaps attributable to women having lower labor force attachment are not discriminatory in nature ignores the possibility that women's engagement in care work may result from household bargaining, where women are likely to have less power.[3]

Neoclassical theories of discrimination also suggest that many forms of discrimination will be competed away under perfectly competitive labor market conditions. Stratification economists turn this reasoning on its head. Far from being a costly bias, investing in discrimination can be rational as a means for dominant groups to maintain power (Darity Jr, Hamilton, and Stewart, 2015). Discrimination is its own form of competition, but often occurs prior to market exchange. The dominant group shapes institutions and rules to limit the opportunities of subaltern groups to gain access to the credentials or resources needed to compete in labor markets (Chelwa, Hamilton, and Stewart, 2022).

This holistic approach to competition and discrimination aligns with the post Keynesian focus on power. Market power exists in most markets and allows firms to engage in markup pricing. Kaleckian models draw from Marx and suggest that the functional distribution of income depends on workers' bargaining power in labor markets. The notion of discrimination as competition suggests that firms develop and exert power in ways that a focus on market power might miss. It also points to the importance of disaggregating "workers' bargaining power," which is far from monolithic. Not only does bargaining power vary by race and gender, but it is co-created with gendered conflict. For instance, Seguino and Braunstein (2019) present evidence that women in developing economies are systematically crowded out of scarce "good jobs" with high pay, reducing overall worker bargaining power and the labor share of income.

Distribution and Growth

Finally, feminist economists have argued for widening the scope of economics to include unpaid caregiving activities, which is missed in measures of market output (Agenjo-Calderón and Gálvez-Muñoz, 2019; Folbre, 2006). Women globally continue to bear a disproportionate share of childcare, eldercare, and household work responsibilities. Estimates based on the opportunity costs of women's time suggest that unpaid care would have a market value equal to 9.0% of global GDP, and as high as 40% of GDP in some countries (ILO, 2018).[4]

Care occurs both within and beyond individual households. In the U.S., informal support networks supplement increasingly scarce state safety nets (Domínguez and Watkins, 2003). For instance, Banks (2020) examines the extensive "unpaid collective work" that black women carry out within communities. A wide range of work is done outside of markets to meet people's needs, prompting feminist economists to call economics the study of "social provisioning" (Agenjo-Calderón and Gálvez-Muñoz, 2019).

Care is also a macroeconomic issue—a nexus where issues of distribution, production, and growth meet, much as they do in post Keynesian growth models. Women's contributions to unpaid care reflect and reproduce gender wage gaps by creating systematic differences in labor force participation. As with any investment in human capacities, care is also critical to maintaining the productivity of labor and the rate of economic growth.

A feminist structuralist macroeconomic literature based on these connections between distribution and growth emerged in the 1990s and has seen significant growth in recent years (Grown, Elson, and Cagatay, 2000). These models generally adopt a Kaleckian starting point, positing gender as a group membership analogous to class. Blecker and Seguino's (2002) germinal work in this field models a two-sector open economy where women disproportionately work in a labor-intensive export manufacturing sector and men are represented in the non-tradable sector and capital-intensive manufacturing. The model demonstrates a tension between wage equity and growth in semi-industrial export-oriented economies, one that can be relieved in some cases through exchange rate depreciation or improvements to women's bargaining power.

A later body of work introduces social reproduction explicitly into the Kaleckian model (Braunstein, van Staveren, and Tavani, 2011; Braunstein,

Bouhia, and Seguino, 2020). Agents in this model put time and market commodities into care provisioning, including individuals within households and governments (e.g., through the public provisioning of care services). The extent to which individuals are motivated to provide care is described as the economy's "caring spirits" and leads to two regimes on the demand side: care-led regimes where higher wages promote economic activity via investments in human capacities and inequality-led regimes where higher wages reduce capitalist investment.

On the supply side, the resources needed for social reproduction—time and paid commodities—create a potential trade-off. Higher female labor force participation may lead to a net reduction in the provisioning of caring labor due to women's time constraints, inequitable sharing of care responsibilities, and wages that are too low to fund paid substitutes. The authors call this a "low-road" regime and the inverse a "high-road" regime. An economy that combines the high-road and care-led regimes is likely to see higher wages for women support both growth and social reproduction, while increased wages for women generate volatile or lower growth in low-road and/or inequality-led economies.[5]

Feminist structural macroeconomic models offer many points of departure for further post Keynesian theoretical and empirical work. Importantly, the models summarized above belie the potential view that "macroeconomic aggregates... [are] above the earthy complications of social relations" (Braunstein, van Staveren, and Tavani, 2011, p. 6). They demonstrate that (gendered) social provisioning impacts both distribution and aggregate macroeconomic outcomes.

RACE, GENDER, AND RISK

These themes—social embeddedness, power, and distribution—remain important links between post Keynesianism and identity-focused heterodox schools of thought. Multiple reviews of recent developments in post Keynesianism have pointed to the potential for examining racial and gender inequality (King, 2015; Hein, 2017).

In fact, a post Keynesian lens may be uniquely suited to understanding the current moment, given the paradigm's micro- and macroeconomic insights on uncertainty and crisis. A series of risks were realized in the U.S. in 2020 and the years that followed: economic risks, health risks, environmental risks, and others, all of which were subject to significant uncertainty. By many metrics, minoritized communities and women within those communities were most vulnerable to these risks. The pandemic demonstrated both the uneven distribution of vulnerability and the ways in which this distribution is becoming more uneven, even as some economic disparities appear to be closing.

In labor markets, for instance, gaps in unemployment and labor force participation rates have shrunk since the 1980s. However, marginalized groups remain engaged in relatively precarious forms of work. An analysis of Current Population Survey data from 1995 to 2017 found that women, particularly those with children, and black and Hispanic workers are overrepresented in work that is "uncertain, unprotected, and/or economically insecure," which the authors link to the declining role of employment relations where employees could expect internal mobility, job security, and benefits (Albelda, Bell-Pasht, and Konstantinidis, 2020, p. 544).

In their study of the finances of U.S. households, Morduch and Schneider (2017) term this the "Great Job Shift" and connect it to "just-in-time" scheduling, greater income volatility, and greater vulnerability to macroeconomic shocks. They also note that industries such as retail and restaurants where these types of jobs are prevalent disproportionately employ black and Latina women. An accounting of these shifts focusing on class alone ignores the role of class in shaping bargaining power, as noted above. To the extent that institutions and discrimination keep black and Latina women from access to other opportunities, these shifts within market economies towards more precarious employment will inherently be racialized and gendered.

Care obligations also contribute to work uncertainty. With an aging U.S. population and continued shortages in paid care workers (who themselves tend to be black, Hispanic, and immigrant women in economically insecure jobs), women continue to carry out a greater share of eldercare. Meanwhile, black and Hispanic women have higher average fertility rates than white women in the U.S. Children and adult dependents generate yet additional types of risk—such as unexpected health challenges and the resulting financial and time costs—that can cascade into job loss and housing insecurity.

The roots of many of these labor market developments are much older, but they became simultaneously relevant during the COVID-19 pandemic. The respiratory virus had the most severe effects in communities of color due in part to the prevalence of workers of color in service industries and in occupations with limited power to secure safe workplace environments. Unemployment rates also spiked for black and Hispanic women, followed by major decreases in labor force participation rates for women with children as schools and childcare centers closed. Women's labor force participation rate fell by nearly half a percentage point between August and September 2020 (56.1% to 55.7%), while men's dropped by 0.1 percentage points (67.6% to 67.5%).

Meanwhile, these labor market developments interacted with other gendered and racialized sources of risk. Housing insecurity disproportionately rose for many of these same groups during the pandemic (Park, 2021). Low levels of liquid assets were found to explain part of this differential, particularly among households that experienced job loss (Grinstein-Weiss, Chun, and Jabbari, 2022). Aggregated indicators showing a rise in savings during the pandemic miss heterogeneity by race and ethnicity.

The impact of the pandemic on those holding student debt is not yet clear. Undertaking higher education is a risky but increasingly necessary endeavor and one that 54% of U.S. students at public institutions must borrow to fund (NCES, 2022). The returns to college are not guaranteed, particularly for those graduating into a recession and/or facing discrimination. Black women are among the fastest growing group of college students, must borrow the most to attend, and face the greatest risk of debt default after graduating (Addo, Houle, and Simon, 2016; American Association of University Women, 2017). The pause on federal student debt repayments has kept delinquency rates low for now but is expected to be discontinued in January 2023. Rising interest rates and a cooling job market are likely to impact borrowers next year.

Other federal, state, and local policies such as expanded unemployment benefits and economic impact payments curbed some of the worst economic effects of the pandemic. However, these policies were imperfect in their reach, as discussed in more detail below. The crisis foreshadows a future of increasingly severe volatility, as the likelihood of pandemics and other noneconomic risks such as extreme weather events are only expected to rise.

ADVANCING A POST KEYNESIAN SOCIAL STRATIFICATION RESEARCH AGENDA

Feminist macroeconomists have called the COVID-19 pandemic a moment to rethink and broaden the scope of the field. Heintz, Staab, and Turquet (2021) describe it as the culmination of three "interlocking crises"—care crises, environmental crises, and macroeconomic crises—with distributional consequences by gender and class. As the feminist structuralist literature shows, attention to non-market processes deepens the explanatory power of post Keynesian growth models, and the same can be said for understanding the COVID-19-induced crisis.

The analysis above suggests that we can broaden this argument even further to go beyond moments of crisis. Households' uneven exposure to and resources for coping with risk will continue to create new, and often financialized, dynamics at both the micro and macro levels that should be part of a post Keynesian research agenda.

The ways that households respond to risk are areas where a post Keynesian analysis can be valuable. Whereas risk is certain and purely probabilistic in neoclassical models, post Keynesians, particularly those in the fundamentalist post Keynesian tradition such as G.L.S. Shackle and Hyman Minsky, have highlighted that many economic risks can at best be imperfectly assessed.

Uncertainty implies that future economic outcomes are not only unknown, but their probabilities are unknowable. Agents can only act on their beliefs about the future and their confidence that those beliefs are correct.

Households facing an increasingly complicated and significant set of risks find a range of ways to cope with them. Many of these are specifically gendered or depend on the institutions to which a social group has or does not have access. They often intersect with financial markets as well. Households are increasingly reliant on debt and/or assets to engage in endeavors such as higher education or to serve as buffers against income and expenditure shocks. This borrowing (or its inaccessibility, in some cases) in turn interacts with existing areas of inequality, with consequences both for distribution and macroeconomic outcomes. It is to our understanding of this risk–stratification–finance nexus that an expansion of empirical post Keynesian work can contribute. I outline here three possible areas of such work: financial exclusion, wealth inequality, and policy implications.

Credit Markets and Financial Exclusion

The modeling of credit markets is critical for understanding "finance-dominated capitalism" (Hein, 2017). As alluded to above, fixed money contracts backed by legal enforcement offer a way for economic activity to occur in the face of uncertainty. Banks lend firms the funds needed to finance production with the confidence that the terms of the contract will be met independent of the firm's specific outcomes (Davidson, 1991). However, there may be limits to this willingness to lend to the extent that rising firm leverage implies rising risk (Kalecki, 1937).

These microeconomic observations in turn have macroeconomic implications. For instance, the post Keynesian claim that money is endogenous is premised on how credit markets operate. Banks' willingness to accommodate increased demand for loans was at the core of the structuralist–horizontalist debate (Lavoie, 1996). Credit may also serve an expansionary role when wages are stagnant. A growing literature has examined the dynamics of debt-financed consumption in the U.S. and elsewhere (Hein, 2017). As consumer finance was made increasingly available and housing prices rose in the years leading up to the 2008 Financial Crisis, households were able to maintain higher consumption levels than incomes alone would predict, albeit with rising debt-to-income ratios. The resulting "debt-led private demand boom" (Hein, 2017, p. 151) proved to be highly volatile in the long run, as Minsky (1982) predicted. Rising rates of leverage during expansions will eventually put some firms in unsustainable financing situations where current receipts cannot cover current obligations. The result will be an increasingly fragile system and, upon its collapse, a credit crunch and widespread debt deflation.

The post Keynesian tradition thus offers a rich lens for understanding credit markets and their relationship to both microeconomic and macroeconomic risk. Yet the stratified nature of U.S. credit markets has often gone underexamined in post Keynesian work. The proportion of "unbanked" households in the U.S.—those without a saving or checking account—has fallen in recent years and as of 2019 was at 5.4% (FDIC, 2020). This figure hides sizable heterogeneity in financial exclusion by race and ethnicity. Nearly 14% of black households and 12% of Hispanic households reporting being unbanked in the same year. Shifts in the banking industry and deregulation during the 1980s prompted banks to systematically abandon predominantly black and Hispanic communities (Dymski, 2009). Other causes of financial exclusion include limited access to bank branches, overdraft fees that punish those with volatile incomes, and concerns about privacy or documentation.

Financial exclusion incurs real long-term costs. Unbanked households have fewer opportunities to develop a credit history, since utility or rent payments are not reported in credit scores. Along with potentially costly fringe financial services such as check-cashing outlets or title lenders (Rhine, Greene, and Toussaint-Comeau, 2006), informal borrowing from friends and family is commonly used by the financially excluded, particularly women of color, as a means of coping with unexpected expenses (Long, 2020). Although informal support is a valuable tool for coping with emergencies, it is weak to economy-wide shocks. Empirical work suggests that it may also contribute to the racial wealth gap between black and white households (e.g., see Chiteji and Hamilton, 2002).

Predatory forms of credit market *inclusion* are present as well, sometimes called "hyperinclusion" (Dymski, Hernandez, and Mohanty, 2013). Women and minoritized groups are disproportionately represented among debtors in the U.S. Women and people of color were disproportionately likely to receive subprime loans during the lead-up to the 2008 Financial Crisis (Fishbein and Woodall, 2006), and brokers specifically targeted older black women on fixed incomes for loans (Wyly and Ponder, 2011).[6] Single female-headed households accounted for a major part of the increase in mortgage debt among lower-income U.S. households during the crisis and experienced faster increases in leverage than other groups (Long, 2018). Notably, the increase in lending to women and minoritized groups did not result in lasting wealth accumulation (Weller and Hanks, 2018). The links between education, housing, and indebtedness, particularly for black women, speak to the role that debt plays in coping with social reproduction responsibilities and the risks they entail.

How can post Keynesian work inform and be informed by existing research on these credit market inequities? As the dynamics above suggest, the narrative of the 2008 Financial Crisis is incomplete without attention to gender and race. Minsky's Financial Instability Hypothesis predicted that financial innovation would play a role in precipitating instability like that seen in the financial crisis (Carter, 1989). Yet innovations surrounding mortgage-backed securities would have had much more limited impact in the economy without access to an unsaturated market—a group of prospective and previously excluded borrowers to whom risky loans could be offered. The 2008 Minsky moment was in this sense not just a story of class or income. It interacted with race and historical inequalities in the housing markets of predominantly black communities (Dymski, 2009). It required the existence of a group of potential borrowers who could be exploited due to their vulnerability for the bubble to become as large as it did.

Moreover, the likelihood and magnitude of a crisis depends on who is impacted. In the case of speculative debt bubbles, which groups are seeing debt-to-income ratios or leverage grow more quickly? Extending the Minskian model from firms to households suggests that if hyperinclusion pushes households into the category of "Ponzi finance," then an increase in interest rates, a decline in income, or an increase in expenditures can be enough to trigger a default. This possibility returns to the question of how risk is distributed, as discussed earlier. Single female-headed households, particularly those with dependents, are among those who experienced disproportionate growth in mortgage debt in 2008 (Long, 2018) while also being exposed to more economic risk in that they have lower levels of wealth, more precarious employment, and greater care responsibilities (Albelda, Bell-Pasht, and Konstantinidis, 2020; Weller and Tolson, 2017).

Credit rationing by race and gender can also shape economic activity outside of crises. *Ceteris paribus*, tighter credit constraints depress investment and thereby aggregate demand. If lender discrimination reduces the supply of credit for minoritized groups, for instance, economic activity in that area is likely to be depressed as well. Attention to financing barriers facing communities of color is therefore an important step towards informing regional or local development applications of post Keynesian theory. Some researchers have advocated for more work in this area, noting persistent regional disparities in income within national economies (Dymski and Kaltenbrunner, 2021; Mitchell and Juniper, 2007; Petach, 2021).

Dymski and Aldana (2014) offer one example of empirical work in the post Keynesian tradition on credit rationing by race and ethnicity. The authors examine how the racial composition of metropolitan areas correlates with lending patterns by race and ethnicity. The results point to a "racial u-curve" that the authors theorize using concepts from stratification economics. The extent of discrimination appears to increase in areas where black and Hispanic residents make up a moderately large proportion of the population, then subsides again. Predominantly white lenders may see these applicants as an increasing threat as the proportion rises, up to a turning point where discrimination becomes unfeasible or costly. The authors conclude by calling for more work that "explore[s] the links between social divides that matter for economic outcomes... and Post Keynesian concepts such as uncertainty, sufficiency of aggregate demand, endogenous money, and power" (p. 89).

Wealth Inequality

While distribution has long been a focus of post Keynesian work, a focus on the wealth distribution specifically has emerged more recently (Hein, 2017). High-profile work such as that of Piketty (2014) has brought increased attention to the particularly extensive inequality in wealth within high-income economies and the potential for this inequality to worsen depending on the returns that accrue to capital. Work such as that by Onaran, Stockhammer, and Grafl (2011) and Stockhammer and Wildauer (2016) has examined whether household assets impact consumption and thus should factor into macroeconomic consumption functions.

By some measures, the wealth distribution in the U.S. is more starkly unequal by race and ethnicity than by socioeconomic status. For example, among white households, those with a household head with less than a high school degree have 18.2% of the wealth on average of those with postgraduate education. Yet among those with a high school degree, black households have only 5.6% of the wealth of a similarly educated white household (Darity et al., 2018). In the aggregate, black households' net worth is only 15 cents for every dollar of wealth held by white households (Bhutta et al., 2020).

The U.S. racial wealth gap is not explained by differences in educational attainment, income, or employment status (Darity et al., 2018). In this sense, an analysis of class divisions or aggregate distributional outcomes is insufficient to understand the racial wealth gap. A lens that is attentive to the racialized dimensions of financial markets is necessary. The relative availability and cost of credit and financial services shapes households' ability to accumulate wealth (Fitzpatrick, 2015). A history of discriminatory mortgage lending and financial exclusion has contributed to residential segregation and lower housing prices in black communities (Dymski, 2009; Fishback et al., Forthcoming). Yet a gap remains even conditional on homeownership (Darity et al., 2018), suggesting that discrimination and other structural barriers play an important role as well.

There is also evidence of wealth inequality by gender. The feminization of poverty, particularly among single women with dependents, means that women are less likely to have sufficient income to save. Unless borrowing translates into sustainable gains in assets, net worth is eroded by greater indebtedness, which can be driven by care responsibilities and the previously noted targeting of predatory lenders. Inequities in bargaining power by gender within opposite-sex couples may influence women's access to assets in dual-headed households. Work using the SCF (Survey of Consumer Finances) suggests that married or cohabiting women with lower bargaining power are less likely to hold saving accounts under their name, putting their control over assets at risk if the household were to dissolve (Klawitter and Fletschner, 2011).

The macroeconomic dynamics of the COVID-19 pandemic combined with existing inequities to expand wealth gaps. The wealth share of the top 1% increased over the first year of the pandemic in the U.S. due to an increase in the rate of return for the wealthiest households (Kartashova and Zhou, 2021). Large rebounds in stock and business equity values later in 2020 and in early 2021 (relative to smaller increases in housing values) explain these differentials. The result was more than just a widening class gap between capitalists and workers, whose primary wealth is their home. The racial gap in returns to wealth also widened, driven by differences in the types of wealth held and by the higher average interest rate paid on debt by black households.

These gaps in net worth matter because the magnitude of a household's assets and debts relative to their income represent resources (or constraints) for responding to unexpected shocks. Liquid assets provide a buffer to income loss, while costlier debt is more vulnerable to default. In this way, net worth should be part of post Keynesian work on the fragility of the economic system. As a source of nonlabor income, wealth is also critical to understanding distributional dynamics in the economy. Racial and gender wealth gaps can reproduce other forms of inequality over time as wealth is passed on and accumulated across generations.

In fact, recent empirical work on returns to wealth in the *Journal of Post Keynesian Economics* illustrates why post Keynesian work on wealth stratification matters. Ederer, Mayerhofer, and Rehm (2021) find evidence that the rate of returns to wealth differ between the "asset-poor," "middle-class home owners," and "capitalists" using European data (p. 296). The authors note that if capitalists have access to greater returns to wealth than workers, the result is a potentially "explosive" increase in inequality per Piketty's (2014) argument. Such shifts in the wealth distribution could in turn impact growth or its stability through multiple channels, including the risk of falling growth rates if the wealthy have a lower marginal propensity to consume out of wealth.

A similar research question can be asked in the context of the racial wealth gap, with a similar rationale. Petach and Tavani (2021) apply the rates of return series used by Ederer, Mayerhofer, and Rehm (2021) to U.S household-level data from the U.S. SCF. Their results indicate that as much as 14% of the racial wealth gap may be attributable to a gap in the returns to wealth across black and white households. This differential is not explained by time preferences, employment or income, types of assets held, or behavioral factors. The authors suggest Hamilton and Darity's (2010) baby bonds proposal as a partial solution. By granting federal bonds to individuals at birth based on household wealth, both the racial wealth gap and the gap in returns could be directly reduced, since growth rates on bonds would be guaranteed.

While primarily couching their argument in equity terms, Petach and Tavani suggest that the baby bonds proposal offers efficiency gains as well. Black households may have higher savings rates on average to compensate for lower rates of return. If true, addressing the gap in the rate of returns has the potential to increase consumption and economic activity per a post Keynesian frame-work. More broadly, low wealth holdings and/or high indebtedness among large portions of the population worsen the potential for instability and slow growth and should thus be of inherent interest to post Keynesian researchers. Falling net worth can prompt declines in firm investment as entrepreneurs predict lower long-term demand among consumers repaying debt and limit future financing options for borrowers as their debt-to-leverage ratios increase (Weller and Karakilic, 2022). In other words, when households' buffers to economic risk are low, macroeconomic volatility can be expected to increase.

Macroeconomic Policy Implications

The evidence examined above points to two stylized facts about racial and gender stratification in the U.S. economy. First, vulnerability to shocks—as measured by the magnitude of the risks faced and the (in)ability to cope with those shocks—is generally greater for female-headed and for black and Hispanic households. Second, various forms of racial and gender inequality in the financial system influence and interact with the vulnerability described above.

Given these observations, what are the implications for post Keynesian economic policy recommendations? There is a growing literature in the field examining questions such as whether economies are wage- or profit-led, with corresponding policy implications (Hein, 2017). However, there are fewer examples of empirical post Keynesian studies that directly examine how these policies, once put into practice, interact with racial and gender inequality. Do certain demand-management policies in turn influence the racial and gender gaps discussed above? And do they remain effective in their demand-management role given those existing inequities?

Related to the first question, there is an emerging empirical literature on the effects of monetary policy on the aggregate income distribution that can provide a framework for additional work (Kappes, 2023). There are multiple channels theoretically linking monetary policy to distribution, including port-folio effects (via changes in the relative value of assets held by households across the income distribution), employment and wage effects, and capital earnings or debt burden effects. Due in part to variability in the geography studied, econometric techniques applied, and method used to measure inequality, the results vary widely across studies.

This analysis can be extended beyond the personal income distribution to study social stratification. A priori, the income effects of contractionary policy are likely to be disproportionately adverse for women and minorities. Interest rate hikes redistribute income from debtors to savers, with marginalized groups being disproportionately present among the former. The precarity of black and Hispanic women's employment also suggests that monetary tightening will result in greater employment losses for these groups. Wealth effects are less clear. Contractionary policy reduces home and stock values, which are disproportionately held by white men and dual-headed households, but the previous evidence on differential rates of return suggests that white households may be able to magnify gains and mitigate losses relative to other groups.

Several studies find evidence that contractionary monetary policy most adversely impacts women's unemployment rates in developing economies (Braunstein and Heintz, 2008) and black men's and women's unemployment rates in the U.S. (Carpenter and Rodgers, 2004; Seguino and Heintz, 2012; Thorbecke, 2001). Others find no evidence of gendered labor market impacts (Takhtamanova and Sierminska, 2009; Zavodny and Zha, 2000) or find that racial differentials in the impacts are small (Bartscher et al., 2022). Only one paper has assessed how portfolio composition effects specifically might impact racial wealth inequality, concluding that expansionary monetary policy reduces the gap (Bartscher et al., 2022). The gaps in this literature regarding unconventional monetary policy and wealth suggest that there is considerable room for additional research.

These issues are particularly relevant post-pandemic, with the Federal Reserve engaging in a series of aggressive rate hikes in 2022 to stem inflation. Debate has focused largely on how aggressively the central bank should engage in contractionary policy to dial in inflation without prompting a recession. There has been little attention paid to the distributional consequences, including the impacts on the financial fragility of households holding debt with rising interest rates.

Fiscal policy and redistributive programs are also liable to have racial or gender biases that should be part of post Keynesian policy analysis. As with monetary policy, inequitable access to credit markets, financial services, and labor markets means that certain policy transmission channels are less likely to benefit marginalized groups. Policy-induced improvements in employment opportunities may be diminished for black or Hispanic workers in the face of discrimination. Conversely, policies that reduce effective demand may lead to heightened competition for good jobs and the crowding out of minoritized groups. Policies that focus on employment as a means of meeting needs or that primarily reward paid work (e.g., Social Security) reflect what Elson and Cagatay (2000) call a "male breadwinner bias" by excluding women, who are more likely to take time out of the labor force.

Moreover, the legislation that operationalizes fiscal policy may be written in ways that purposefully render some social groups ineligible. During the COVID-19 pandemic, both existing safety nets and emergency relief programs (Economic Impact Payments through the CARES Act and the extended Child Tax Credit) left out unauthorized immigrants and restricted or delayed access for legal immigrants living with unauthorized immigrant family members (Gelatt, Capps, and Fix, 2021). Similarly, the implementation of work requirements in 1990s welfare reform in the U.S. penalized single caregivers—disproportionately women of color. When programs are crafted in ways that systematically leave out marginalized groups, the distributional and macroeconomic impacts of said policies change.

Finally, insufficient outreach and stigmatization means that eligible households may not sign up for programs. Millions of additional households that would have been eligible for pandemic relief funds or the extended Child Tax Credit never received benefits. These households generally did not file taxes because their annual income fell below the threshold for filing. While they were eligible for benefits, receiving said benefits would require signing up at the IRS website and many did not. Only 29% of low- and moderate-income households surveyed were aware of the Child Tax Credit (Hamilton et al., 2021). Other barriers to signing up included limited internet access and language barriers on the IRS website. The result was that the reach of this program fell far short of its poverty-reducing potential (Pressman and Haywood Scott III, Forthcoming).

Even among those who did apply, benefits were delayed by weeks or longer among the unbanked (Holtzblatt and Karpmann, 2020). Checks or prepaid debit cards had to be mailed to these households and were sometimes lost. Moreover, households without checking accounts then had to pay check-cashing costs or fees to use debit cards for payments such as rent. To the extent that those in poverty or facing the barriers described above are more likely to be single women with dependents and people of color in the U.S., these gaps in coverage have direct implications for social stratification.

These issues mean that fiscal and monetary policies that are theoretically in line with post Keynesian theory may in practice worsen social stratification. Moreover, they are less likely to be effective if their reach is diluted. In their analysis of racialized credit rationing, Dymski and Aldana (2014) argue that "demand management policies [in the U.S.] are increasingly ineffective because they do not take into account these inequalities in the structure of market opportunities" (p. 71). The areas of empirical work recommended above can help post Keynesians develop more nuanced policy recommendations to generate inclusive growth, such as the example of baby bonds discussed previously or child allowance policies that support those caring for dependents.

CONCLUSION

Social stratification by race and gender is as salient a factor as class distinctions in shaping a range of economic outcomes in the U.S. The persistence of a racial wealth gap across socioeconomic groups and the gendered division of labor between paid market work and unpaid care work speak to this, as does the economic marginalization of trans and nonbinary people. Such stylized facts suggest that any theoretical paradigm that studies the consequences of distributional shifts—as post Keynesianism has a history of doing—should be attentive to racial and gender inequality.

Racial and gender inequality also interacts with financial capitalism in ways that generate economy-wide impacts. Short-term stability and long-term growth are jeopardized when marginalized groups have chronically precarious financial health and are subject to predatory lending practices. As the COVID-19 crisis has illustrated, even an economic system that is seemingly healthy by a metric such as GDP can be highly vulnerable to shocks, particularly when many households have limited means of coping with those shocks.

However, identity merits the attention of post Keynesians not only because of its clear macroeconomic implications. The field should also address racial and gender inequality as matters of inherent economic justice. Keynes's own legacy in this regard is complicated. He supported eugenics, which has racist underpinnings and is incompatible with a comprehensive notion of justice (Macciò, 2016). Yet the final chapter of the *General Theory* argues that distribution does inherently matter, calling the "arbitrary and inequitable distribution of income and wealth" one of the "outstanding faults of the economic society" (Keynes, 1936 as cited in Macciò, 2016, p. 720).

As the post Keynesian research agenda continues to evolve, it should acknowledge previously underexamined distributional conflicts and pursue inclusive growth in a broader sense. It should include work that complements and is informed by other heterodox traditions working on stratification by race, gender, caste, sexuality, and other dimensions of identity. The result will be a richer post Keynesianism, both in its normative aims and in its explanatory power.

NOTES

1.   Of course, racial and gender disparities are meaningful elsewhere around the world, and, conversely, other dimensions of identity also matter for economic

outcomes in the U.S. The scope of this chapter is necessarily limited, and the focus is based on my own areas of research. However, the recommendations for expanding post Keynesian analysis apply in many ways to these other contexts as well.

2. Following work from sociology and stratification economics, I use "social stratification" henceforth to refer to both racial and gender stratification. Chelwa, Hamilton, and Stewart (2022) define stratification as "a variety of mechanisms that can generate inequality" and refer to the related sociological concept wherein "intergroup differences [are] the outcome of group contestations beyond contestations at the individual level" (p. 378).

3. Recent work seeking to empirically define "systemic discrimination" makes progress towards broadening mainstream definitions of discrimination (Bohren, Hull, and Imas, 2022).

4. The opportunity cost method as applied in these estimates is arguably a conservative method for valuing unpaid care. The ILO (2018) report uses the hourly minimum wage as their measure of opportunity cost. Other methods such as the "specialized substitute" approach would yield higher estimates (Benería, 1999).

5. For a more extensive review of the extant literature in the feminist macroeconomic tradition, refer to Braunstein, Sequino, and Altringer (2021).

6. More recent work continues to find evidence of unexplained racial gaps in mortgage pricing in 2018 and 2019 (Zhang and Willen, 2021).

REFERENCES

Addo, F.R., Houle, J.N. and Simon, D. (2016). Young, Black, and (Still) in the Red: Parental Wealth, Race, and Student Loan Debt. *Race and Social Problems*, *8*(1), 64–76.

Agenjo-Calderón, A. and Gálvez-Muñoz, L. (2019). Feminist Economics: Theoretical and Political Dimensions. *American Journal of Economics and Sociology*, *78*(1), 137–166.

Albelda, R., Bell-Pasht, A. and Konstantinidis, C. (2020). Gender and Precarious Work in the United States: Evidence from the Contingent Work Supplement 1995–2017. *Review of Radical Political Economics*, *52*(3), 542–563.

American Association of University Women. (2017). *Deeper in Debt: Women and Student Loans*. AAUW, Washington, D.C.

Banks, N. (2020). Black Women in the United States and Unpaid Collective Work: Theorizing the Community as a Site of Production. *The Review of Black Political Economy*, *47*(4), 343–362. https://doi.org/10.1177/0034644620962811.

Bartscher, A.K., Kuhn, M., Schularick, M. and Wachtel, P. (2022). Monetary Policy and Racial Inequality. *Federal Reserve Bank of New York Staff Reports* no. 959 (March).

Becker, G. (1957). *The Economics of Discrimination*. University of Chicago Press, Chicago.

Benería, L. (1999). The Enduring Debate Over Unpaid Labour. *International Labour Review*, *138*(3), 287–309.

Bhutta, N., Chang, A.C., Dettling, L.J. and Hsu, J.W. (2020). Disparities in Wealth by Race and Ethnicity in the 2019 Survey of Consumer Finances. *FEDS Notes*, September 28. Board of Governors of the Federal Reserve System, Washington, D.C.

Blecker, R.A. and Seguino, S. (2002). Macroeconomic Effects of Reducing Gender Wage Inequality in an Export-Oriented, Semi-Industrialized Economy. *Review of Development Economics*, *6*(1), 103–119.

Bohren, J.A., Hull, P. and Imas, A. (2022). Systemic Discrimination: Theory and Measurement. *NBER Working Paper* 29820.

Braunstein, E. and Heintz, J. (2008). Gender Bias and Central Bank Policy: Employment and Inflation Reduction. *International Review of Applied Economics*, *22*(2), 173–186.

Braunstein, E., Bouhia, R. and Seguino, S. (2020). Social Reproduction, Gender Equality and Economic Growth. *Cambridge Journal of Economics*, *44*(1), 129–156.

Braunstein, E., Seguino, S. and Altringer, L. (2021). Estimating the Role of Social Reproduction in Economic Growth. *International Journal of Political Economy*, *50*(2), 143–164.

Braunstein, E., van Staveren, I. and Tavani, D. (2011). Embedding Care and Unpaid Work in Macroeconomic Modeling: A Structuralist Approach. *Feminist Economics*, *17*(4), 5–31.

Carpenter, S.B. and Rodgers, W.M. III. (2004). The Disparate Labor Market Impacts of Monetary Policy. *Journal of Policy Analysis and Management*, *23*(4), 813–830.

Carter, M. (1989). Financial Innovation and Financial Fragility. *Journal of Economic Issues*, *23*(3), 779–793.

Chelwa, G., Hamilton, D. and Stewart, J.B. (2022). Stratification Economics: Core Constructs and Policy Implications. *Journal of Economic Literature*, *60*(2), 377–399.

Chiteji, N.S. and Hamilton, D. (2002). Family Connections and the Black–White Wealth Gap among Middle-Class Families. *The Review of Black Political Economy*, *30*(1) (Summer), 9–28.

Danby, C. (2012). Gender. In King, J.E. (Ed.). *The Elgar Companion to Post Keynesian Economics* (pp. 250–255). Edward Elgar Publishing, Cheltenham, UK and Northampton, MA, USA.

Darity Jr, W., Hamilton, D., Paul, M., Aja, A., Price, A., Moore, A. and Chiopris, C. (2018). What We Get Wrong About Closing the Racial Wealth Gap. *Samuel DuBois Cook Center on Social Equity and Insight Center for Community Economic Development*, *1*(1), 1–67.

Darity Jr, W., Hamilton, D. and Stewart, J.B. (2015). A Tour de Force in Understanding Intergroup Inequality: An Introduction to Stratification Economics. *The Review of Black Political Economy*, *42*(1–2), 1–6.

Davidson, P. (1991). Is Probability Theory Relevant for Uncertainty? A Post-Keynesian Perspective. *Journal of Economic Perspectives*, *5*(1), 129–143.

Domínguez, S. and Watkins, C. (2003). Creating Networks for Survival and Mobility: Social Capital Among African-American and Latin-American Low-Income Mothers. *Social Problems*, *50*(1), 111–135. https://doi.org/10.1525/sp.2003.50.1.111.

Dymski, G.A. (2009). Racial Exclusion and the Political Economy of the Subprime Crisis. *Historical Materialism*, *17*(2009), 149–179.

Dymski, G.A. and Aldana, C.B. (2014). The Racial U-Curve in US Residential Credit Markets in the 1990s: Empirical Evidence from a Post Keynesian World. In Holt, R.P.F. and Pressman, S. (Eds). *Empirical Post Keynesian Economics* (pp. 70–109). Routledge, London.

Dymski, G.A. and Kaltenbrunner, A. (2021). Space in Post Keynesian Monetary Economics: An Exploration of the Literature. In Bonizzi, B., Kaltenbrunner, A. and Ramos, R.A. (Eds). *Emerging Economies and the Global Financial System* (pp. 84–98). Routledge, London.

Dymski, G.A., Hernandez, J. and Mohanty, L. (2013). Race, Gender, Power, and the US Subprime Mortgage and Foreclosure Crisis: A Meso Analysis. *Feminist Economics*, *19*(3), 124–151.

Ederer, S., Mayerhofer, M. and Rehm, M. (2021). Rich and Ever Richer? Differential Returns across Socioeconomic Groups. *Journal of Post Keynesian Economics*, *44*(2), 283–301.

Elson, D. and Cagatay, N. (2000). The Social Content of Macroeconomic Policies. *World Development*, *28*(7), 1347–1364.

Federal Deposit Insurance Corporation (FDIC). (2020). *How America Banks: Household Use of Banking and Financial Services – 2019 FDIC Survey.* FDIC, Washington, D.C.

Figart, D.M. (1997). Gender as More than a Dummy Variable: Feminist Approaches to Discrimination. *Review of Social Economy*, *55*(1), 1–32.

Fishback, P., Rose, J., Snowden, K.A. and Storrs, T. (Forthcoming). New Evidence on Redlining by Federal Housing Programs in the 1930s. *Journal of Urban Economics*.

Fishbein, A.J. and Woodall, P. (2006). *Women Are Prime Targets for Subprime Lending: Women Are Disproportionately Represented in High-Cost Mortgage Market.* Consumer Federation of America, Washington, D.C.

Fitzpatrick, K. (2015). Does 'Banking the Unbanked' Help Families to Save? Evidence from the United Kingdom. *Journal of Consumer Affairs*, *49*(1), 223–249.

Folbre, N. (2006). Measuring Care: Gender, Empowerment, and the Care Economy. *Journal of Human Development*, *7*(2), 183–199.

Folbre, N. (2021). *The Rise and Decline of Patriarchal Systems: An Intersectional Political Economy.* Verso Books, London.

Gelatt, J., Capps, R. and Fix, M. (2021). Nearly 3 Million U.S. Citizens and Legal Immigrants Initially Excluded under the CARES Act Are Covered under the December 2020 COVID-19 Stimulus. *Migration Policy Institute.* Last updated January 2021.

Grinstein-Weiss, M., Chun, Y. and Jabbari, J. (2022). Do Racial and Ethnic Disparities in Savings and Job Loss during COVID-19 Explain Disparities in Housing Hardships? A Moderated Mediation Analysis. *The Annals of the American Academy of Political and Social Science*, *698*(1), 68–87.

Grown, C., Elson, D. and Cagatay, N. (2000). Introduction. *World Development*, *28*(7), 1145–1156.

Hamilton, D. and Darity Jr, W. (2010). Can 'Baby Bonds' Eliminate the Racial Wealth Gap in Putative Post-Racial America? *Review of Black Political Economy*, *37*, 207–216.

Hamilton, L., Roll, S., Despard, M., Maag, E. and Chun, Y. (2021). *Employment, Financial and Well-Being Effects of the 2021 Expanded Child Tax Credit.* Social Policy Institute, Washington University, St. Louis.

Hein, E. (2017). Post-Keynesian Macroeconomics since the Mid 1990s: Main Developments. *European Journal of Economics and Economic Policies: Intervention*, *14*(2), 131–172.

Heintz, J., Staab, S. and Turquet, L. (2021). Don't Let Another Crisis Go To Waste: The COVID-19 Pandemic and the Imperative for a Paradigm Shift. *Feminist Economics*, *27*(1–2), 470–485.

Holtzblatt, J. and Karpmann, M. (2020). *Who Did Not Get the Economic Impact Payments by Mid-to-Late May, and Why? Findings from the May 14–27 Coronavirus Tracking Survey.* Urban Institute, Washington, D.C.

International Labour Office [ILO]. (2018). *Care Work and Care Jobs for the Future of Decent Work.* ILO, Geneva.

Kalecki, M. (1937). The Principle of Increasing Risk. *Economica, 4*(16), 440–447.

Kappes, S.A. (2023). Monetary Policy and Personal Income Distribution: A Survey of the Empirical Literature. *Review of Political Economy, 35*(1), 211–230.

Kartashova, K. and Zhou, X. (2021). Wealth Inequality and Return Heterogeneity during the COVID-19 Pandemic. *FRB of Dallas Working Paper* 2114.

Keynes, J.M. (1936). *The General Theory of Employment, Interest, and Money.* Macmillan, London.

King, J.E. (2015). *Advanced Introduction to Post Keynesian Economics.* Edward Elgar Publishing, Cheltenham, UK and Northampton, MA, USA.

Klawitter, M. and Fletschner, D. (2011). Who Is Banked in Low Income Families? The Effects of Gender and Bargaining Power. *Social Science Research, 40*(1), 50–62.

Lavoie, M. (1996). Horizontalism, Structuralism, Liquidity Preference and the Principle of Increasing Risk. *Scottish Journal of Political Economy, 43*(3), 275–300.

Long, M.G. (2018). Pushed into the Red? Female-Headed Households and the Pre-Crisis Credit Expansion. *Forum for Social Economics, 47*(2), 224–236.

Long, M.G. (2020). Informal Borrowers and Financial Exclusion: The Invisible Unbanked at the Intersections of Race and Gender. *The Review of Black Political Economy, 47*(4), 363–403.

Macciò, D.D. (2016). The Apostles' Justice: Cambridge Reflections on Economic Inequality from Moore's Principia Ethica to Keynes's General Theory (1903–36). *Cambridge Journal of Economics, 40*(3), 701–726.

Minsky, H.P. (1982). *Can 'It' Happen Again?: Essays on Instability and Finance.* Routledge, Abingdon, U.K.

Mitchell, W. and Juniper, J. (2007). Towards a Spatial Keynesian Economics. In Arestis, P. and Gennaro, Z. (Eds). *Advances in Monetary Policy and Macroeconomics* (pp. 192–211). Palgrave Macmillan, London.

Morduch, J. and Schneider, R. (2017). *The Financial Diaries: How American Families Cope in a World of Uncertainty.* Princeton University Press, Princeton, NJ.

National Center for Education Statistics [NCES]. (2022). Loans for Undergraduate Students. *NCES Condition of Education.* U.S. Department of Education, Institute of Education Sciences. Last updated May 2022.

Onaran, Ö, Stockhammer, E. and Grafl, L. (2011). Financialisation, Income Distribution and Aggregate Demand in the USA. *Cambridge Journal of Economics, 35*(4), 637–661. https://doi.org/10.1093/cje/beq045.

Park, J. (2021). Who Is Hardest Hit by a Pandemic? Racial Disparities in COVID-19 Hardship in the U.S. *International Journal of Urban Sciences, 25*(2), 149–177.

Petach, L. (2021). Spatial Keynesian Policy and the Decline of Regional Income Convergence in the USA. *Cambridge Journal of Economics, 45*(3), 487–510.

Petach, L. and Tavani, D. (2021). Differential Rates of Return and Racial Wealth Inequality. *Journal of Economics, Race, and Policy, 4*(3), 115–165.

Piketty, T. (2014). *Capital in the Twenty-First Century.* Harvard University Press, Cambridge, M.A.

Pressman, S. and Haywood Scott III, R. (Forthcoming). A Refundable Tax Credit for Children: Its Impact on Poverty, Inequality, and Household Debt. *Journal of Post Keynesian Economics* (Forthcoming).

Rhine, S.L.W., Greene, W.H. and Toussaint-Comeau, M. (2006). The Importance of Check-Cashing Business to the Unbanked: Racial/Ethnic Differences. *The Review of Economics and Statistics, 88*(1), 146–157.

Seguino, S. (2019). Feminist and Stratification Theories' Lessons from the Crisis and Their Relevance for Post-Keynesian Theory. *European Journal of Economics and Economic Policies: Intervention, 16*(2), 193–207.

Seguino, S. and Braunstein, E. (2019). The Costs of Exclusion: Gender Job Segregation, Structural Change and the Labour Share of Income. *Development and Change, 50*(4), 976–1008.

Seguino, S. and Heintz, J. (2012). Monetary Tightening and the Dynamics of US Race and Gender Stratification. *American Journal of Economics and Sociology, 71*(3), 603–638.

Stockhammer, E. and Wildauer, R. (2016). Debt-Driven Growth? Wealth, Distribution, and Demand in OECD Countries. *Cambridge Journal of Economics, 40*(6), 1609–1634.

Takhtamanova, Y. and Sierminska, E. (2009). Gender, Monetary Policy, and Employment: The Case of Nine OECD Countries. *Feminist Economics, 15*(3), 323–353.

Thorbecke, W. (2001). Estimating the Effects of Disinflationary Monetary Policy on Minorities. *Journal of Policy Modeling, 23*(2001), 51–66.

van Staveren, I. (2010). Post-Keynesianism Meets Feminist Economics. *Cambridge Journal of Economics, 34*(6), 1123–1144.

Weller, C.E. and Hanks, A. (2018). The Widening Racial Wealth Gap in the United States After the Great Recession. *Forum for Social Economics, 47*(2), 237–252.

Weller, C.E. and Karakilic, E. (2022). Wealth Inequality, Household Debt, and Macroeconomic Instability. In Whalen, C.J. (Ed.). *A Modern Guide to Post-Keynesian Institutional Economics* (pp. 121–143). Edward Elgar Publishing, Cheltenham, UK and Northampton, MA, USA.

Weller, C.E. and Tolson, M.E. (2017). Too Little or Too Much? Women's Economic Risk Exposure. *The Journal of Retirement, 4*(4), 69–83.

Wyly, E. and Ponder, C.S. (2011). Gender, Age, and Race in Subprime America. *Housing Policy Debate, 21*(4), 529–564.

Zavodny, M. and Zha, T. (2000). Monetary Policy and Racial Unemployment Rates. *Economic Review-Federal Reserve Bank of Atlanta, 85*(4), 1–59.

Zhang, D.H. and Willen, P.S. (2021). Do Lenders Still Discriminate? A Robust Approach for Assessing Differences in Menus. *NBER Working Paper* 29142.

7. The Green New Deal in a Kaleckian model of growth and distribution

Neil Perry

INTRODUCTION

In a post Keynesian model of the economy, policy proposals such as the Green New Deal (GND), which aims to boost employment and growth while transitioning to a low carbon economy, may increase or decrease carbon emissions depending on a few key parameters. While it is important to address the narrative that reducing carbon emissions will undermine the economy, proponents of the GND must also address the fact that economic growth causes carbon emissions and other environmental damages. The throughput of materials and energy in the economy must be reduced, which can only occur when the GND increases the environmental efficiency of technology faster than the growth in the economy itself. Ecological economists refer to this issue as relative versus absolute decoupling (Ward et al., 2016). Relative decoupling occurs when environmental efficiency improves but total environmental impact increases due to increases in production. As such, many ecological economists call for zero growth or a degrowth economy (Kallis, 2011) to achieve absolute decoupling of the economy from material and energy throughput. They argue that degrowth is the only way to achieve many of the objectives of the GND. In this chapter, I explore the impact of the GND on emissions and the economy using a Kaleckian model of growth and distribution.

The GND is a comprehensive policy suite which suggests that transformation to a low carbon economy can be achieved with economic growth and stable employment. It is an important rhetorical tool because the environmental movement has seen a number of potential policy solutions for climate change fail due to the rhetoric of "jobs versus the environment". Examples include the Waxman–Markey Bill (US Congress, 2009) in the United States in 2009 where coal dependent communities, conservative lobbyists and Republican politicians argued that US jobs will be lost to China and India (see for example the analysis by the Heritage Foundation (Kreutzer et al., 2009)). The Bill was eventually defeated in the Senate after passing a Democrat dominated

Congress by the barest of margins. As someone who was lobbying Congress at the time for a non-profit environmental organisation, the predominant attitude for even Democratic representatives of Congress and the Senate was that they could not possibly vote in favour of the Bill and expect to remain in office in the next election cycle. To the Congress representatives, the "jobs will go overseas" argument had won despite the absence of any evidence or logic. The rhetoric was simply too strong amongst their constituents.

In Australia, a similar argument was heard as a carbon pricing mechanism was proposed in 2008. While a policy was eventually enacted in 2011, it was a watered-down policy that provided great concessions to industry (Perry, 2012) and it was eventually repealed as a new government swept to power on the back of a jobs-versus-environment rhetoric. While Europe has been more successful, policies initially granted great concessions to industry which led to windfall profits for the biggest polluters and set real climate action back for years (Martinez and Neuhoff, 2005).

The GND addresses this narrative, but its fundamental purpose is articulated as reducing carbon emissions. Mastini et al. (2021) describe the history of the GND, tracking its increasingly antigrowth, anticapitalist ideas from the GND 1.0 to the GND 2.0. Noting its mainstream origin in a *New York Times* op-ed by Thomas Friedman (2007) and proposed recovery from the Global Financial Crisis, the GND 1.0 is associated with ecological modernisation, which focusses on technical rather than social and political solutions to the climate crisis. Ecological modernisation is associated with orthodox economics approaches to environmental policy such as changing relative prices and it is criticised on the basis that it produces relative versus absolute decoupling (Feindt and Cowell, 2010, pp. 194–5). Sensing that GND 1.0 would not be enough, more radical proposals have since become prominent. Chief among these in a US context is the proposed US Congress (2019) House Resolution 109 proposed by Congress representative Alexandria Ocasio-Cortez in the House and Senator Ed Markey in 2019. This is a nonbinding resolution to create a GND and while it failed to gain congressional approval it provides some detail about the nature of a GND 2.0. Bernie Sanders (2019) also proposed a GND for his failed campaign to win the Democratic nomination. While Joe Biden (n.d.) has also proposed the Clean Energy Revolution and Environmental Justice policies during the presidential elections, which have also become known as a GND, it is the more radical proposals from Ocasio-Cortez and Sanders that we focus on in this chapter.

While all details of the proposals cannot be explained here, the main elements are as follows. The US Congress (2019) House Resolution 109 stated that it is the "duty of the Federal government to create a Green New Deal" that achieves net zero emissions through a just transition, create millions of jobs, invest in infrastructure, secure a clean environment for people, and provide justice and equity for people. A 10-year mobilisation was proposed to build resilience to climate change-related disasters, repair and upgrade infrastructure in the process of eliminating greenhouse gases and pollution, and meet a goal of 100% "clean, renewable, and zero-emission energy sources". There is a strong emphasis on justice and equity in the resolution with the mobilisation also aimed at helping farmers transition, ensuring all buildings achieve minimum energy efficiency requirements, supporting green manufacturing, overhauling transport systems to public transport and fast rail, mitigating health effects from climate change and protecting other species and ecosystems. The resolution has a rhetoric of public ownership and community ownership of resources and public investments to transform. It addresses wage justice by "ensuring that the Green New Deal mobilization creates high-quality union jobs that pay prevailing wages, hires local workers, offers training and advancement opportunities, and guarantees wage and benefit parity for workers affected by the transition". There is also a stated job guarantee embedded into the resolution, which has strong resonance with post Keynesian economics. With regard to the business environment, the resolution states that the Green New Deal will ensure "a commercial environment where every businessperson is free from unfair competition and domination by domestic or international monopolies", which has implications for Kalecki's markup equation.

Bernie Sanders' (2019) proposal is likewise post Keynesian by nature. It provides a timeline for achieving 100% renewable energy and transport by 2030, ending unemployment and creating 20 million union jobs that transform the economy, $16.3 trillion in public investment, a just transition and investing in public lands, amongst other proposals. Sanders states that these investments will pay for themselves, which brings in the critical issue of budget deficits, government debt and government financing. The principal financing mechanisms to pay for the needed public investment are varied but include new taxes on polluters, reducing subsidies for polluters and shifting government funding from defence spending. The latter recognises that spending to halt climate change is a form of pre-emptive defence spending, given the expectation that the climate crisis will itself create wars and mass migrations that threaten national security. Both proposals have been associated with increasing taxes on the rich and corporations. Sanders also proposes that revenue from the sale of electricity from publicly owned energy generation companies can help to keep the policy revenue neutral.

It is challenging to interpret all these proposals in one model of the economy. In what follows I interpret them using a Kaleckian model of growth and distribution with particular emphasis on the impact of the proposals on green productivity and the markup or the distribution of income. However, the following section sets the scene for the model by drawing from the ecological economics literature on decoupling, degrowth and the IPAT equation.

ECOLOGICAL ECONOMICS AND THE GND – CRITICAL ISSUES

While policy to transform the economy is needed, the issue of absolute versus relative decoupling must also be addressed; that is, whether the transformation of the economy actually reduces material and energy throughput. It is possible to increase environmental efficiency and still increase total (absolute) carbon emissions if the consumption per person or the population increases. This draws on the famous IPAT equation in ecological economics (see Chertow, 2000 for a history of the IPAT equation).

The IPAT equation is an identity where total environmental impact (I) (whether this is measured in terms of pollution or carbon emissions or some other measure) equals the size of the population (P) multiplied by consumption per person (Affluence (A)) multiplied by environmental efficiency or environmental impact per unit of consumption (Technology (T)). Environmental efficiency is the target for many advocates of the GND or "green growth" more generally (United Nations Conference on Sustainable Development, 2012). It is argued that technical change and substitutions in production create the conditions for an absolute decoupling while GDP growth continues to increase (Hickel and Kallis, 2020). In contrast, advocates of degrowth such as Kallis (2011) argue that technology can improve environmental efficiency, but further radical changes to the economy are required because population and affluence will continue to grow. Thus, the degrowth advocates argue for reductions in consumption per person, decreased inequality and curbs on population growth, along with forced and incentivised improvements in environmental efficiency.

For post Keynesian economics, these issues are critical to understand because of the traditional focus on employment and growth (Perry, 2013). In the context of the GND's impact on the economy and carbon emissions, there is a tension between the rhetoric of maintaining or increasing employment and growth and the overriding need to reduce carbon emissions. The IPAT equation appropriately demonstrates this tension.

The issue also relates to the debate regarding the appropriate concept of sustainability as a policy objective – that future generations have the same opportunities as the current generation (World Commission on Environment and Development, 1987). Orthodox economists, following Hartwick (1977), suggest that human-made and natural capital are substitutable which leads to "weak sustainability". Weak sustainability suggests that as long as the total capital stock is maintained through time, consumption possibilities are also maintained and well-being is non-declining (Costanza et al., 1997, pp. 85–6, 100–102). Ecological economists have argued that the concept of strong sustainability is appropriate, where substitutions between human-made and natural capital have only limited potential. The issue comes down to non-linearities or thresholds in nature, where many elements of nature cannot be degraded beyond certain limits if the future generations are to be as well off as the current generation.

The technical solution of the GND 1.0 and perhaps 2.0 can be associated with weak sustainability. The GND proposes a substitution between different types of capital from nonrenewable to renewable resources. Strong sustainability implies that more is needed. While capital substitutions and complementarities may not have a lot of resonance for a post Keynesian model of the economy, strong sustainability requires that we analyse the feedback mechanism of new environmental efficiency on growth and the other elements of the IPAT equation. In the following sections, I adjust existing Kaleckian models of growth and distribution to accommodate the concept of environmental efficiency so that the economic and sustainability or decoupling implications of the GND 2.0 can be analysed.

THE KALECKIAN MODEL WITH ENVIRONMENTAL EFFICIENCY

To investigate the impact of the GND 2.0 on the economy, I draw on a Kaleckian model of distribution and accumulation, which is a long-run model consistent with Kalecki's short-run model of the economy (Lavoie, 1992). Following Lavoie (1992), Guarini (2020) and Hein (2012), who draw from Kalecki, the model centres around three elements. The first is the demand regime and the equilibrium established by aggregate savings being equal to aggregate investment and the budget deficit. The second element is the productivity regime which affects investment and is itself affected by capacity utilisation. These two elements come together to determine equilibrium outcomes for the rate of profit, accumulation and capacity utilisation in the long run. The third element relates to the Kaleckian distribution equations.

In particular, to draw conclusions for the impact of the GND on the economy and sustainability, I follow Guarini's (2020) innovation of defining productivity in terms of environmental efficiency. However, Guarini (2020) investigated the Porter Hypothesis – that environmental regulations can force innovation and growth (Porter and Van der Linde, 1995). Guarini (2020) did not consider the GND, which has different implications for the demand and productivity regimes when compared to the Porter Hypothesis. In particular, Guarini did not consider the feedback from environmental productivity to growth or the impact of the policy on the distribution equations, which work through the markup on prime costs, a key feature of Kalecki's model. The markup affects the rate of profit and profit share and the demand and productivity regimes.

Thus, I add to the general literature on Kalecki's model and its application to a post Keynesian Environmental Economics (Perry, 2013).

Specifically, I focus on the impact of the GND on green productivity and technological change, the markup, depreciation and the government budget deficit. Each of these potential effects of the GND work through the demand and productivity regimes to determine the impact on relative versus absolute decoupling and sustainability more generally. For example, an increase in environmental efficiency is represented as a productivity improvement but it also impacts investment and the demand regime and therefore accumulation or growth. This increases capacity utilisation and material and energy throughput in the economy. As such, the overall impact will be dependent on parameters and the GND could conceivably increase carbon emissions rather than reduce them, and it could therefore be seen as a kind of governmental "greenwashing". Greenwashing is usually associated with private companies, who cover up their detrimental environmental practices with tokenistic environmental actions (de Freitas Netto et al., 2020). In this case, the term refers to a nation or government of a nation covering their detrimental environmental impacts with tokenistic national policy to appease others in international environmental agreements.

With regard to the demand regime, the equilibrium condition for a closed economy and including a public sector is, using Lavoie's (1992) notation:

$$g^s = g^i + (b - t) \tag{7.1}$$

where g^s is the rate of savings, or aggregate savings divided by the nominal capital stock (S/K), g^i is the rate of investment (I/K), b is government expenditure as a function of nominal capital, and t is government tax revenue expressed as a function of nominal capital.

As noted earlier, the impact of the GND on the budget deficit is uncertain. Sanders's proposal claims that the impact can be revenue neutral as other areas of government spending will be reduced (such as defence expenditure) and revenues will increase due to prosperity. However, in other estimates there is likely to be a short-term deficit which could become structural. To allow for this, government spending is divided into $b = b_g + b_n$ where b_g refers to the spending associated with the GND and b_n refers to spending under business-as-usual conditions.

The saving function is given in simple terms as:

$$g^s = S_p r \tag{7.2}$$

where S_p is the marginal propensity to save and r is the rate of profit, equal to profits divided by nominal capital (π/K). As modelled in Hein (2012), the savings function can include terms related to retained profits and distributed profits. However, it is assumed that the GND has no implications for the ratio between retained and distributed profits. Similarly, company taxes are ignored. However, it is noted that the rate of profit is dependent on the profit share (h) and the rate of capacity utilisation (u). That is, $r = \frac{\pi}{K} = \frac{\pi}{q} \cdot \frac{q}{K} = hu$, where q is nominal output. In turn, the profit share is determined by the degree of monopoly (m) such that $\partial h / \partial m > 0$ (Hein, 2012, p. 479).

The Kaleckian investment function varies with the issue being investigated but its general form is adjusted from Lavoie (1992, p. 308), Guarini (2020) and Hein (2012) as:

$$g^i = \gamma + g_u u + g_h h + g_z z \tag{7.3}$$

where γ reflects the "animal spirits" of the capitalist class (Hein, 2012, p. 481) and g_u and g_h are parameters for the impact of capacity utilisation and the profit share on investment. Technical progress can be an additional argument in the investment function, which is typically represented by labour productivity as in Lavoie (1992, p. 318) and Hein (2012, p. 480). However, in analysing the Porter Hypothesis, Guarini (2020) introduces the idea that technical progress can be represented by green productivity, which can be defined as $z = q/E$, or the output per unit of environmental impact (E), such as carbon emissions. Guarini (2020, p. 34) justifies this position by noting that green innovations that increase green productivity are more radical than standard labour-saving technologies and that green technical progress is still assumed to be labour-saving and capital embodied. I follow Guarini's approach to analyse the impact of the GND. As such, z is included in the investment function along with the productivity parameter g_z.

Guarini (2020, p. 34) also notes that productivity and the model does not affect the distribution of income by invoking Hein (2014, p. 314), who states that the distribution of income is dependent upon "institutional factors and the relative powers of capital and labour". However, green productivity could affect the Kaleckian price equation through its impact on unit costs related to raw materials including energy, which would affect short-run equilibrium. The GND may also change the institutional factors and relative power of capital and labour due to some of the more radical elements of the proposals, such as government ownership of energy generation and distribution, and the focus on equity and justice. This more direct impact on the degree of monopoly is discussed later in the chapter. Initially, I assume that the Kalecki pricing equation or degree of monopoly is unaffected by the GND.

Equilibrium in the goods market is determined by combining (1), (2) and (3), as well as the identity that $r = hu$ and definition of $b = b_g + b_n$. Equilibrium capacity utilisation, rate of profit and growth (or capital accumulation $= {}^1\!/_K$) are given by:

$$u^* = \frac{\gamma + g_h h + g_z z + (b_g + b_n - t)}{(S_p h - g_n)} \tag{7.4}$$

$$r^* = \frac{h(\gamma + g_h h + g_z z + (b_g + b_n - t))}{(S_p h - g_n)} \tag{7.5}$$

$$g^* = \frac{S_p h(\gamma + g_h h + g_z z) + g_n(b_g + b_n - t)}{(S_p h - g_n)} \tag{7.6}$$

The analysis that follows concerns the relationship between the variables g and z and the impact of the GND on these variables. Following Lavoie's (1992, p. 317) discussion of the impact of technical progress on employment and Guarini's (2020, p. 36) discussion of the equivalent for green technical progress, the overall impact of the GND on absolute decoupling of the economy from carbon emissions depends on:

$$g_E = g^* - z \tag{7.7}$$

As pointed out by Guarini (2020, p. 36), equation (7.7) is the IPAT equation discussed earlier, holding the size of the population constant. In particular, if population is constant, and green productivity increases faster than the rate of accumulation in the economy, total environmental impact decreases. If accumulation is faster than the rate of green productivity growth, the economy experiences relative but not absolute decoupling. This relationship can be represented on a two-dimensional diagram of g^* and z with an expression for z, the green productivity function:

$$z = \varepsilon_0 + \varepsilon_1 g^* + \varepsilon_2 e + \varepsilon_3 b_g \tag{7.8}$$

First, Guarini (2020, p. 35) specifies that, as with labour productivity, green productivity is positively related to accumulation (g^*). This reflects Verdoon's Law and cumulative causation (Lavoie, 1992, p. 322; Hein, 2012, p. 484). Green economies of scale are represented by the parameter $\varepsilon_1 > 0$ (Guarini, 2020, p. 35). Second, Guarini (2020, p. 35) adds the variable e, which represents regulatory policy consisting of "public efforts to promote and sustain ecological conversion of the economic system." It is here that the Porter Hypothesis is invoked as $\varepsilon_2 > 0$ represents a situation where green regulations have a forcing effect on green productivity despite the fact that it may include taxes on traditional industries such as fossil fuels and thereby hurt the economy. The GND includes stricter environmental regulations and reductions in fossil fuel subsidies, which is related to the Porter Hypothesis. However, the GND also involves direct government investment in green technologies such as renewable energy and I add the variable b_g to the function for green productivity and its corresponding parameter ε_3 where $\varepsilon_3 > 0$ by definition.

To visualise the analysis, Figure 7.1 is derived from equation (7.8), the productivity regime (PR), and an algebraic manipulation of equation (7.6), the demand regime (DR):

$$z = \frac{-S_p h (r + g_s h) - g_u (b_g + b_n - t) + (S_p h - g_u) g'}{S_p h g_z} \tag{7.9}$$

Figure 7.1 illustrates a position where the economy is unsustainable in the sense that carbon emissions are increasing through time. Any point below the bisector is a position where $g^{**} > z^*$ and emissions are rising. This is assumed to be the current situation before the GND is applied to the economy. For Figure 7.1, there is a stability condition with the slope of the demand function (7.9) needing to be greater than the slope of the productivity regime (7.8). That is,

$$\frac{(S_p h - g_u)}{S_p h g_z} > \varepsilon_1 \ or \ \left(S_p h - g_u \right) > \varepsilon_1 S_p h g_z \tag{7.10}$$

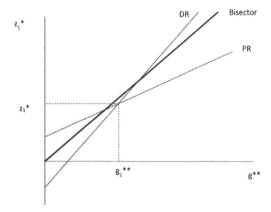

Figure 7.1   *Equilibrium green productivity and accumulation*

By equating equations (7.8) and (7.9), equilibrium green productivity (z^*) and accumulation (g^{**}) are given by:

$$g^{**} = \frac{\left(\epsilon_0 + \epsilon_2 e + \epsilon_3 b_g\right)S_p h g_z + S_p h\left(\gamma + g_n h\right) + g_n\left(b_g + b_n - t\right)}{\left(S_p h - g_n\right) - \epsilon_1 S_p h g_z} \qquad (7.11)$$

$$z^* = \frac{\left(\epsilon_0 + \epsilon_2 e + \epsilon_3 b_g\right)\left(S_p h - g_n\right) + \epsilon_1\left(S_p h\left(\gamma + g_n h\right) + g_n\left(b_g + b_n - t\right)\right)}{\left(S_p h - g_n\right) - \epsilon_1 S_p h g_z} \qquad (7.12)$$

noting that the expressions for equilibrium values have the same stability conditions as above.

ANALYSIS

Given the basic Kaleckian model above, the impact of the GND on the economy and emissions can be discussed. The initial effect to consider is the increase in green productivity that arises from the direct expenditure of the GND. The effect can be analysed using comparative statics[1] and diagrammatically. Diagrammatically, the GND is represented by a shift of the PR curve upwards, which changes the equilibrium values of z^* and g^{**}. The extent to which the new equilibrium position lies above or below the bisector depends on the size of the shift in the PR curve and the parameters related to a change in the variables e and b_g. As illustrated in Figure 7.2, the economy may become sustainable, with $z_2^* > g_2^{**}$. That is, absolute decoupling is occurring.

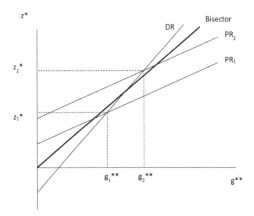

Figure 7.2   The impact of the GND on the PR curve and sustainability

However, the comparative statics reveal that the DR curve will also shift. The GND affects two variables in the equations. The first is the variable e, which was the focus of analysis in Guarini (2020), although Guarini did not discuss the potential implications of this for the DR curve. As mentioned, the variable e relates to environmental regulations such as carbon pricing and the removal of subsidies for fossil fuels. The GND requires the creation of environmental pricing which can have a forcing effect on productivity in the economy as determined by the parameter ε_2. The second variable is b_g, which is the more direct impact of government spending on green productivity. This variable relates to plans under the GND to invest in renewable energy, and it has the effect of shifting the PR curve upwards. The impact of these variables on the DR curve is indirect. Increases in green productivity affect investment, as seen through equation (7.3). The DR curve will increase or shift to the right as the economy grows from the increase in demand due to the variables b_g and e as seen in equation (7.9). This is illustrated in Figure 7.3.

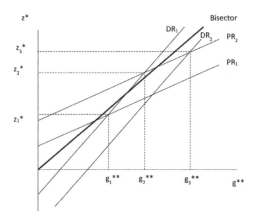

Figure 7.3   *The impact of the GND on the PR and DR curves and sustainability*

As illustrated, the resulting equilibrium position may be $z_3^* < g_3^{**}$, as the indirect and direct effect of spending under the GND and the increased green productivity result in a larger rate of growth. Effectively, the demand effect of the GND is circumventing the increase in green productivity and the economy is only achieving relative decoupling. The GND in this case is a national greenwashing exercise. In particular, the total effect of the GND depends on the size of the change in the variables e and b_g, and the comparative statics of changes in these variables:

$$dg^{**} = de \cdot \frac{\partial g^{**}}{\partial e} + db_g \cdot \frac{\partial g^{**}}{\partial b_g} \tag{7.13}$$

$$\frac{\partial g^{**}}{\partial e} = \frac{\varepsilon_2\left(\left(S_p h g_z\right)\right)}{\left(S_p h - g_u\right) - \varepsilon_1 S_p h g_z} = +ve \tag{7.14}$$

$$\frac{\partial g^{**}}{\partial b_g} = \frac{\varepsilon_3\left(S_p h g_z\right) + g_u}{\left(S_p h - g_u\right) - \varepsilon_1 S_p h g_z} = +ve \tag{7.15}$$

$$dz^{*} = de \cdot \frac{\partial z^{*}}{\partial e} + db_g \cdot \frac{\partial z^{*}}{\partial b_g} \tag{7.16}$$

$$\frac{\partial z^{*}}{\partial e} = \frac{\varepsilon_2\left(S_p h - g_u\right)}{\left(S_p h - g_u\right) - \varepsilon_1 S_p h g_z} = +ve \tag{7.17}$$

$$\frac{\partial z^{*}}{\partial b_g} = \frac{g_u \varepsilon_1 + \varepsilon_3\left(S_p h - g_u\right)}{\left(S_p h - g_u\right) - \varepsilon_1 S_p h g_z} = +ve \tag{7.18}$$

For absolute decoupling to occur:

$$dg^{**} < dz^{*}$$

which implies that

$$de \cdot \left[\varepsilon_2\left(S_p h g_z - \left(S_p h - g_u\right)\right)\right] < db_g \cdot \left[\varepsilon_3\left(S_p h - g_u\right) + g_u \varepsilon_1 - \left(\varepsilon_3 S_p h g_z + g_u\right)\right] \tag{7.19}$$

Clearly, the sustainability of the economy under a GND depends on the size of the shifts in the variables e and b_g and the parameters related to the green productivity equation, the marginal propensity to save, the profit share and the parameters of the investment function.

Two other effects of the GND are the impact on the degree of monopoly and depreciation. Both the Ocasio-Cortez and Sanders proposals have implications for justice and equity in the economy and explicitly for job guarantees, a reduction in monopoly power and increased corporate taxes and taxes on the wealthy. There is also a rhetoric of government ownership which decreases the bargaining power of capitalists. All these effects can be read as a reduction in the degree of monopoly and this will impact the DR curve given in equation (7.9). The degree of monopoly is positively related to the share of profits. When the degree of monopoly decreases, the DR curve will shift to the right. Workers receive a larger share of national income and spend a larger proportion of their income, which increases growth. Specifically, in the Kalecki model, it is assumed that workers spend all that they earn, which relates to

Kalecki's statement that "capitalists earn what they spend, whilst workers spend what they earn" (Sawyer, 1985, p. 73; Lavoie, 1992, p. 313).

There will be a similar effect on the DR curve from the increase in depreciation, which is not included in the model for the sake of simplicity. The GND implies that there is a fast transition to renewable energy and green technology, which will make existing capital obsolete and increase depreciation compared to a business-as-usual transition. The increase in the rate of depreciation can be embedded in the model by noting that depreciation is a cost that reduces the rate of profit and the profit share (Lavoie, 1992, p. 311). Both the reduction in the degree of monopoly and increase in the rate of depreciation will reduce h and increase growth, which is related to the paradox of costs (Lavoie, 1992, p. 313).

ACHIEVING NET ZERO EMISSIONS

It is clear that the GND may increase carbon emissions under very plausible assumptions. This is simply a matter of the GND increasing effective demand and the growth in the economy outstripping the growth in green productivity. In ecological economics, this is referred to as a situation where the economy is relatively decoupling from material and energy throughput but not absolutely decoupling and the above analysis has also assumed a constant population throughout. An increase in the population will further exacerbate carbon emissions.

Proponents of the GND may need to take the call for degrowth (Kallis, 2011) seriously. It is convenient to go to an electorate and argue that we can have our cake and eat it too – that we can have increased prosperity and reduce emissions. But clearly the truth in this political statement depends on the parameters in the economy. In addition, if equation (7.19) is satisfied and the economy is positioned above the bisector in Figure 7.3, absolute decoupling may not occur fast enough to meet the timelines of the GND. It may take many more years than 2050 to reach net zero carbon emissions.

The issue of "net" zero carbon emissions raises the question of how carbon offsets affect the post Keynesian model. The target of reaching net zero by 2050 and the analysis above suggests that carbon offsets will be needed. The controversial aspect of environmental offsets concerns the extent to which they actually reduce CO_2 emissions in the atmosphere, which relates to whether they are additional to what would otherwise have occurred and permanent (Thamo and Pannell, 2016; Lohmann et al., 2006). For example, some international offsets, such as those established under the Clean Development Mechanism of the Kyoto Protocol, have been criticised because the environmental improvement would have occurred without the Clean Development Mechanism incentives (Böhm and Dabhi, 2009). Securing an existing forest that would never have been clear-felled is similarly argued to be not additional to the status quo. Monitoring and enforcement is often difficult and there are questions concerning the neocolonial aspects of international offsets. For example, livelihoods in the global south are often negatively affected due to the production and consumption practices in the global north (Lyons and Westoby, 2014). These issues are important for a discussion on national greenwashing, but for the purposes of analysing offsets in the Kaleckian model it can be assumed that offsets are legitimately additional and permanent.

Offsets can be modelled in a number of ways and are often discussed as voluntary improvements to a public good to offset a negative consumption or production externality or public bad (Kotchen, 2009; Yoshida et al., 2022). In the context of the GND and achieving a target of net zero emissions by 2050, the voluntary nature of offsets is replaced by an imperative and therefore mandatory offsets by either the nation or individual producers. The simplest way to model mandatory offsets is as a form of tax on producers based on their current level of carbon emissions with the tax revenue returned to the economy through government purchases of carbon sequestration, such as reforestation.

As such, offsets can be analysed using post Keyensian tax incidence theory (Kalecki, [1937] 1971; Asimakopulos and Burbidge, 1974; Asimakopulos, 1979; Laramie, 1991; Laramie and Mair, 1993). While it is not possible to fully develop the theory of offsets in the space available in this chapter, an intuitive description should suffice to lay out the basic features and results of the model. The theory of tax incidence revolves around the Kaleckian price equation, the markup and the share of profits, wages and taxes in the economy. The markup pricing rule is given for each firm i as the following:

$$p_i = k_i u_i \tag{7.20}$$

where p_i is price, k_i is the markup on unit prime costs, and u_i is unit prime costs (equal to wage costs (W_i) divided by output (Q_i) in the most basic case). The markup for each firm in the industry is determined by the following (Kalecki, [1971] 1971, p. 160):

$$k_i = 1 + f_i\left(\tfrac{p}{p_i}\right) \tag{7.21}$$

where p is the weighted average price in the industry (weighted by the output of firms), and f_i is an increasing function. That is, a higher average price compared to the firm's price increases the markup. The "degree of monopoly" determines the function f_i, which reflects the process of concentration in the sector, sales promotion, the power of trade unions and the level of overheads (Sawyer, 1985, pp. 24–7).

Note that if all prime costs in the sector increase by a factor, *a*, then all prices (including the average price) increase by this factor with given functions *f*. Note also that prime costs differ amongst firms and a rise in one firm's prime costs by a factor, *a*, will not lead to a rise in its price equal to that factor. In equation (7.2), the ratio of average price to firm price falls for that firm and its markup falls. An environmental tax to fund offsets affects prices in a similar way.

The environmental tax is a tax on emissions, such as a dollar amount per ton of CO_2 released. This new tax is passed on fully to consumers and, at the aggregate level, the profit share remains unchanged, the wage share falls and the tax share increases. However, it is assumed that the government returns the revenue from the tax completely to the economy by purchasing carbon sequestration. In the macroeconomy, this compensates for the reduction in the wage share and revenue neutrality ensures that the economy is no worse off than before the tax. Growth is unaffected.

However, there will be long-run changes in the industrial composition of output. Within each sector of the economy, there will be relatively dirty and relatively clean producers where a dirty firm is defined as one with a higher-than-average ratio of environmental impact (carbon emissions) to wage costs, the other main prime cost. When an environmental tax is imposed, dirty firms experience a larger increase in prime costs than green firms. The relative change in costs for green and dirty firms has implications for profit margins, financing opportunities, firm growth and industrial composition, and this has further implications for the distribution of income and tax revenue.

Recognise that the differential cost change has implications for firm markups, even when the average markup remains unchanged. Dirty firms who want to maintain their market share will need to reduce their markup. This can be seen in equation (7.21) because the markup is dependent on the ratio of average industry price to firm price. This ratio will fall for dirty firms because, due to the tax, their price is increasing faster than the average price in the industry. Thus, the markup for dirty firms falls. The opposite occurs for green firms. Thus, profit margins will necessarily fall for dirty firms and increase for green firms in each industry. This has implications for firm growth in post Keynesian analysis.

Kalecki's principle of increasing risk is the starting point. This principle describes a constraint on the amount of financing available for firm expansion due to the risk associated with continued expansion. The size of a firm is limited by the amount of "entrepreneurial capital" – the capital owned by the firm – because this determines the amount of "rentier capital" – external financing – available to the firm (Kalecki, [1937] 1971, p. 105). The principle of increasing risk ensures this. Thus, "the expansion of the firm depends on its accumulation of capital out of current profits" (ibid., p. 106). As Asimakopulos

(1975, p. 320) states: "A firm's ability to grow thus depends on the profits it can generate to finance its investment plans both directly (retained earnings) and indirectly through borrowing related to its internal funds".

Steindl makes an important contribution to this area. As Bloch (2000, p. 94) points out, "Steindl develops his theorising about industry concentration from an analysis of the process of firm growth". Bloch (2000) establishes three key aspects to Steindl's theory of firm growth and industry concentration of which two are important here (the third aspect is the theory of random influence on firm growth). Initially, Kalecki's principle of increasing risk is important and investment by firms and the growth of firms is tied to their internal accumulation of capital. The size of the firm matters with large firms having an advantage (Bloch, 2000, p. 95). The second aspect is the role of technology. Here, Steindl distinguishes between progressive and marginal firms. The progressive firms are innovators and as a result have lower unit production costs and greater profit margins than marginal firms (ibid., p. 95; see also, Bloch, 2006). As a result, they have the "greatest access to finance to undertake research and development activities with uncertain payoffs" (Bloch, 2006, p. 299). Thus, "investment by firms is tied to their internal accumulation. Higher profits earned by progressive firms therefore lead to expansion of their productive capacity relative to marginal firms. Eventually, the progressive firms become the largest firms in the industry" (Bloch, 2000, p. 96). In Steindl's (1952, p. 41) own terms:

> If there are firms which owing to large scale economies, or, more generally speaking, owing to the adoption of any cost-reducing technical innovations, have greater gross profit margins, and greater net profit margins, than the marginal firms, they will often have a natural tendency to expand relatively to other firms. The reason is that firms with greater profit margins – if we may assume that this also implies a greater profit rate – will accumulate internal funds, and will accumulate them at a rate which is the greater, the greater is their differential advantage.

In general, differential cost advantages and access to financing determine firm growth and industrial concentration.[2] This has obvious implications for the impact of environmental taxes on firm growth and industrial composition. The environmental tax changes the relative costs and the profit margins of firms and therefore their financing opportunities. Over time, holding other impacts constant, green firms will tend to grow and dirty firms shrink as their internal accumulation slows. Green firms will occupy a larger share of the market and gain greater power.

Given the change in industrial composition, the environmental tax will increase green productivity, which can be modelled through the variable e and parameter ε_2 in equation (7.8). The actual spending on the offsets shifts the green productivity curve upwards through the variable b_g, which now incorporates the spending from the environmental tax, and parameter ε_3. In this way, the economy can come closer to the net zero emissions target by 2050. Of course, the allowance to use offsets may have a detrimental effect on the incentive to create new green technologies, which reduces the parameter ε_2 and negates the Porter Hypothesis. However, with offsets assumed to be effective, the economy can continue to grow with zero net emissions.

This analysis has assumed that domestic offsets are employed; that is, the government increases carbon sequestration within the country's borders, for example, by increasing woody vegetation across the country. In contrast, international offsets – which may involve protecting forests in the global south – are often part of proposals for national attempts to achieve carbon neutrality. For example, the US Environmental Protection Agency (2009) estimated that abatement costs associated with the 2009 Waxman–Markey climate bill would be 20% lower with international offsets (Hahn and Richards, 2013). However, in a Kaleckian model of the economy, international offsets will reduce growth as the reduction in the wage share is not compensated by the increase in government spending in the domestic economy. This result arises due to the emphasis in post Keynesian theory on the spending of the working class and distribution amongst the classes more generally.

CONCLUSION

In this chapter I have analysed the impact of the GND in a post Keynesian, and specifically a Kaleckian, model of growth and distribution. By adjusting the green productivity function given in Guarini (2020), it is clear that the GND will not necessarily reduce carbon emissions unless carbon offsets are employed. The positive growth implications of green productivity improvements and government spending on renewable energy increase carbon emissions even as they are falling per unit of output due to the green productivity improvements. In addition, the GND implies a reduction in the markup and an increase in depreciation, which both have the effect of increasing growth. With reference to ecological economics, while relative decoupling of the economy from carbon emissions will occur, absolute decoupling may not. The model has also abstracted from population growth, which would also increase carbon emissions. Even if absolute decoupling does occur, it may not occur fast enough to achieve the timeline of the GND's target to reduce emissions to net zero by 2050, which suggests the need for carbon offsets.

While carbon offsets are rightly viewed sceptically, I have provided an intuitive description of the impact of a carbon offsetting policy on the distribution of income, growth and emissions when the government taxes emissions and returns the tax revenue by purchasing carbon sequestration in the domestic economy. The tax on emissions will not have any growth implications but it will change the structure of industrial composition as dirty firms reduce their markup following Kalecki's markup equation. This impact on the markup of dirty firms relative to green firms (whose markup increases) changes the financing opportunities of dirty firms relative to green firms and green firms tend to dominate each industry and sector of the economy. The change in industrial composition increases green productivity and, even though the potential for offsets may reduce the need to innovate, the net zero target can be reached with a growing economy. This suggests that the argument for the GND is only strong in a Kaleckian model of the economy when carbon offsets are understood to be effective in reducing emissions, which suggests the need to clarify this point in GND literature and proposals. Otherwise, the GND appears to be a national greenwashing exercise and the arguments for degrowth need to be taken seriously.

NOTES

1. While comparative statics can be criticised for invoking notional time, Lavoie (1992, pp. 282–3) argues that it was standard amongst the great post Keynesians of the past and is readily justifiable as a method of analysis.
2. Lavoie (1997, pp. 37–40, 50–51) provides a textbook version of this theory of firm growth.

REFERENCES

Asimakopulos, A. (1979). Tax incidence. In Eichner, A.S. (Ed.), chapter 10. *A Guide to Post-Keynesian Economics*. Macmillan, London.

Asimakopulos, A. (1975). A Kaleckian Theory of Income Distribution. *The Canadian Journal of Economics*, *8*(3), 313-33.

Asimakopulos, A. and Burbidge, J.B. (1974). The short-period incidence of taxation. *Economic Journal*, *84*, 267–88.

Biden, J. (n.d.). *The Biden Plan for a Clean Energy Revolution and Environmental Justice*. Available at: https://joebiden.com/climate-plan/# (accessed 14/04/23).

Bloch, H. (2000). Steindl's contribution to the theory of industry concentration. *Australian Economic Papers*, *39*(1), 92–107.

Bloch, H. (2006). Steindl on imperfect competition: The role of technical change. *Metroeconomica*, *57*(3), 286–302.

Böhm, S. and Dabhi, S. (Eds) (2009). *Upsetting the Offset: The Political Economy of Carbon Markets*. MayFly Books, London.

Chertow, M.R. (2000). The IPAT equation and its variants. *Journal of Industrial Ecology*, *4*(4), 13–29.

Costanza, R., Cumberland, J., Daly, H., Goodland, R. and Norgaard, R. (1997). *An Introduction to Ecological Economics*. St. Lucie Press, Boca Raton, Florida.

de Freitas Netto, S.V., Sobral, M.F.F., Ribeiro, A.R.B. and Soares, G.R.D.L. (2020). Concepts and forms of greenwashing: A systematic review. *Environmental Sciences Europe*, *32*(1), 1–12.

Environmental Protection Agency (EPA). (2009). Analysis of the American Clean Energy and Security Act of 2009 H.R. 2454 in the 111th Congress. Available at: https://www.epa.gov/sites/default/files/2021-06/documents/epa_hr_2454_analysis _appendix_6-23-09.pdf (accessed 19/03/23).

Feindt, P.H. and Cowell, R. (2010). The recession, environmental policy and ecological modernization – what's new about the Green New Deal? *International Planning Studies*, *15*(3), 191–211.

Friedman, T. (2007). A Warning from the Garden. *The New York Times*. pp. A17. Available at: https://www.nytimes.com/2007/01/19/opinion/19friedman.html (accessed on 23/02/23).

Guarini, G. (2020). The macroeconomic impact of the Porter Hypothesis: Sustainability and environmental policies in a post-Keynesian model. *Review of Political Economy*, *32*(1), 30–48.

Hahn, R. and Richards, K. (2013). Understanding the effectiveness of environmental offset policies. *Journal of Regulatory Economics*, *44*(1), 103–19.

Hartwick, J.M. (1977). Intergenerational equity and the investment of rents from exhaustible resources. *American Economic Review*, *67*(5), 972–74.

Hein, E. (2012). 'Financialization', distribution, capital accumulation, and productivity growth in a post-Kaleckian model. *Journal of Post Keynesian Economics*, *34*(3), 475–96.

Hein, E., 2014. *Distribution and growth after Keynes: A Post-Keynesian guide*. Elgar Publishing, Cheltenham, UK and Northampton, MA, USA.

Hickel, J. and Kallis, G. (2020). Is green growth possible? *New Political Economy*, *25*(4), 469–86.

Kalecki, M. [1937] (1971). A theory of commodity, income and capital taxation. Reprinted in *Selected Essays on the Dynamics of the Capitalist Economy: 1933–1970*. Cambridge University Press, Cambridge.

Kalecki, M. [1971] (1971). Class struggle and distribution of national income. Reprinted in *Selected Essays on the Dynamics of the Capitalist Economy: 1933–1970*. Cambridge University Press, Cambridge.

Kallis, G. (2011). In defence of degrowth. *Ecological Economics*, *70*(5), 873–80.

Kotchen, M.J. (2009). Voluntary provision of public goods for bads: A theory of environmental offsets. *Economic Journal*, *119*(537), 883–99.

Kreutzer, D., Loris, N., Lieberman, B., Campbell, K. and Beach, W. (2009). *The Economic Consequences of Waxman–Markey: An Analysis of the American Clean Energy and Security Act of 2009*. The Heritage Foundation. Available at: https:// www.heritage.org/environment/report/the-economic-consequences-waxman-markey -analysis-the-american-clean-energy-and (accessed 14/04/23).

Laramie, A.J. (1991). Taxation and Kalecki's distribution factors. *Journal of Post Keynesian Economics*, *13*(4), 583–94.

Laramie, A.J. and Mair, D. (1993). The incidence of business rates: A post-Keynesian approach. *Review of Political Economy*, *5*(1), 55–72.

Lavoie, M. (1992). *Foundations of Post-Keynesian Economic Analysis*. Edward Elgar Publishing, Aldershot, UK and Brookfield, VT, USA.

Lavoie, M. (1997). *Introduction to Post-Keynesian Economics*. Palgrave Macmillan, New York.

Lohmann, L., Hällström, N., Österbergh, R. and Nordberg, O. (2006). *Carbon Trading: A Critical Conversation on Climate Change, Privatisation and Power*. Dag Hammarskjöld Centre, Uppsala.

Lyons, K. and Westoby, P. (2014). Carbon colonialism and the new land grab: Plantation forestry in Uganda and its livelihood impacts. *Journal of Rural Studies*, *36*, 13–21.

Martinez, K.K. and Neuhoff, K. (2005). Allocation of carbon emission certificates in the power sector: How generators profit from grandfathered rights. *Climate Policy*, *5*(1), 61–78.

Mastini, R., Kallis, G. and Hickel, J. (2021). A Green New Deal without growth? *Ecological Economics*, *179*, 106832.

Perry, N. (2012). A post-Keynesian perspective on industry assistance and Australia's carbon pricing policy. *Economic and Labour Relations Review*, *23*(1), 47–66.

Perry, N. (2013). Environmental economics and policy. In Harcourt, G.C. and Kriesler, P. (Eds). *The Oxford Handbook of Post-Keynesian Economics. Volume 2: Critiques and Methodology* (pp. 391–411). Oxford University Press, New York.

Porter, M.E. and Van der Linde, C. (1995). Toward a new conception of the environment–competitiveness relationship. *Journal of Economic Perspectives*, *9*(4), 97–118.

Sanders, B. (2019). *The Green New Deal*. Available at: https://berniesanders.com/en/issues/green-newdeal/ (accessed 28/03/23).

Sawyer, M.C. (1985). *The Economics of Michal Kalecki*. Macmillan, London.

Steindl, J. (1952). *Maturity and Stagnation in American Capitalism*. Monthly Review Press, New York and London.

Thamo, T. and Pannell, D.J. (2016). Challenges in developing effective policy for soil carbon sequestration: Perspectives on additionality, leakage, and permanence. *Climate Policy*, *16*(8), 973–92.

United Nations Conference on Sustainable Development. (2012). *The Future We Want*. United Nations. Available at: https://sustainabledevelopment.un.org/content/documents/733FutureWeWant.pdf (accessed 25/05/23).

US Congress. (2009). *H.R.2454 – American Clean Energy and Security Act of 2009*. Congress. Gov. Available at: https://www.congress.gov/bill/111th-congress/house-bill/2454 (accessed 14/04/20).

US Congress. (2019). *House Resolution 109*. Congress. Gov. Available at: https://www.congress.gov/116/bills/hres109/BILLS-116hres109ih.pdf (accessed 23/02/23).

Ward, J.D., Sutton, P.C., Werner, A.D., Costanza, R., Mohr, S.H. and Simmons, C.T. (2016). Is decoupling GDP growth from environmental impact possible? *PLoS ONE*, *11*(10), e0164733.

World Commission on Environment and Development. (1987). *Our Common Future*. Oxford University Press, Oxford.

Yoshida, M., Turnbull, S.J. and Ota, M. (2022). Environmental offsets and production externalities under monopolistic competition. *International Tax and Public Finance*, *30*, 305–25.

8. The Green New Deal: economic analysis and practical policy

Jonathan M. Harris

INTRODUCTION

The essential concepts of what is referred to as a "Green New Deal" (GND) have been discussed by ecological and Post Keynesian economists for some time. A GND proposal was formally introduced as a resolution in the 116th U.S. Congress in 2019 and reintroduced in the 117th Congress in 2021. The concept thus gained some political traction and has since led to legislation in both the United States and Europe incorporating some of its proposals. The exact content and policy feasibility of various GND proposals has been subject to much debate. In this discussion, there remains a tension between concepts of "green growth" and limits to growth or "degrowth". Theorists proposing a GND have attempted to resolve this tension.

Major stated goals of a GND include:

1. Transformation to a low-carbon economy including renewable energy sources and energy efficiency;
2. Protection and restoration of forests and wetlands;
3. Sustainable farming and soil restoration;
4. Expanding employment in renewable energy, energy efficiency, infrastructure investment, ecological resilience, and water management, among other areas.

There is a theoretical basis for this program. A "green Keynesian" approach combines a radical Keynesian analysis with ecological priorities such as drastic carbon emissions reduction (Harris, 2013). This approach delinks traditional economic growth, largely based on fossil energy and resource input-intensive techniques, from employment creation and expanding well-being. In part this is a technological issue of employing "green", renewable, and resilient technological options, and in part it represents a shift in consumption patterns from energy-intensive to energy-conserving and service-oriented forms of consumption.

This combination of changes on the supply and demand sides of the economy enables, for example, large-scale reduction in carbon emissions through "lowering the ceiling" of total energy consumption while "raising the floor" of renewable energy supply. This provides an alternative to assertions both by growth proponents who favor expanded traditional economic production, and by proponents of "degrowth" who argue that only radical reductions in consumption and economic growth can achieve ecological balance.

Despite this potential, many popular presentations of the GND have suffered from excessively broad aspirational rhetoric, making it difficult to discern which of the stated goals are feasible. The Congressional resolution (which never passed) was not legislation but a general statement of principles. It proposed a ten-year time frame—clearly insufficient to achieve many of its more ambitious goals. In addition to climate and environmental goals, it included broader issues such as universal health care and guaranteed employment and was vague on the question of costs as well as budget and deficit implications.

In practice, significant aspects of the GND approach were adopted in two major acts that passed the U.S. Congress and were signed into law: the Infrastructure Investment and Jobs Act (IIJA) of 2021 and the Inflation Reduction Act (IRA) of 2022. Despite the title of the latter, its main purpose was not inflation reduction but energy and climate policy, along with health care provisions. The IRA included a substantial part of the Biden administration's original Build Back Better program but was trimmed down to achieve Congressional passage.

The IIJA, passed on a bipartisan basis, included a significant number of "green" investment provisions including public transit, passenger and freight rail, zero- and low-emissions buses and ferries, electric vehicle chargers, and upgrades to the electric grid and water infrastructure. The IRA, adopted through the "reconciliation" process with Democratic votes alone, featured $369 billion in spending on investments related to renewable energy and climate policy "to accelerate the transition to a clean energy economy". It also funded $19.5 billion in Agriculture Department programs to promote regenerative and climate-friendly agricultural techniques (Qiu, 2022).

To justify its "inflation reduction" moniker, the IRA also included $737 billion in new revenues through increased corporate and stock buyback taxes, and more effective tax enforcement, especially targeting high-income tax evasion. The bill thus has the effect of reducing the Federal deficit, with at least a slight anti-inflationary effect (U.S. EPA, 2023; Penn Wharton, 2022; Congressional Budget Office, 2022). During the same period that GND initiatives were being considered, and partially adopted, in the United States, the European Commission adopted a package of policy initiatives known as the European Green Deal. The stated goal of this plan was to make the European Union climate-neutral by 2050. It included a series of initiatives aimed at rapidly reducing greenhouse gas emissions and boosting energy efficiency, as well as promoting biodiversity and sustainable agriculture. The aim was to mobilize over $100 billion euros per year over the next decade for sustainable development by "increasing the resources devoted to climate action under the EU budget, and leveraging additional public and private financing" (European Parliament, 2020).

Thus, important elements of a "GND" are already in place in the United States and Europe. Critics from differing perspectives have argued both that these initiatives are too ambitious and expensive, and that they do not go far enough to address climate and ecological crises. An application of green Keynesian analysis can offer some insights into how GND measures may be able to achieve both economic and ecological goals, subject to both physical/ecological and economic constraints.

KEYNESIAN ECONOMICS, THE ORIGINAL NEW DEAL, AND THE POST KEYNESIAN REVIVAL

The original New Deal under Franklin Roosevelt was not a direct application of Keynesian theory. Its origins were more as a pragmatic response to high unemployment, but its fundamental principles were consistent with the then-revolutionary theories by which Keynes justified the need for government intervention in a depressed economy. Important aspects of the theory included the direct effect of government employment and government spending, as well as the indirect, or multiplier, effects leading to additional economic activity and employment creation. Interestingly, the original New Deal had a significant "green" aspect. Programs such as the Civilian Conservation Corps provided employment in natural resource and conservation areas including erosion and flood control, forest protection and planting, and streambed protection, while agricultural extension programs sought to promote crop rotation and soil restoration (Merrill, 1981).

The basic insight of Keynesian economics was that a social investment function was required in a market system. As Keynes emphasized in the "Concluding Notes" to *The General Theory of Employment, Interest, and Money*, "the outstanding faults of the society in which we live are its failure to provide for full employment and its arbitrary and inequitable distribution of wealth and incomes" (Keynes, 1964 [1936], p. 372). Environmental issues were not central to Keynes's original theory but are an obvious example of the shortcomings of an unregulated market system. Thus, it was quite logical, as the architects of the New Deal looked for opportunities to promote employment through social investment, for natural resource conservation to be one of the areas of focus.

Keynesian approaches fell out of favor with many economists during the period of "great moderation" from the 1980s to 2007, during which economic volatility seemed to recede. Even though the more stable economic situation during these years arose in large part from the long-term "automatic stabilizing" effect of institutionalized government spending on programs such as Social Security and Medicare, many economists felt that macroeconomic problems had been largely solved, so that Keynesian interventionist policies were no longer needed. Robert Lucas of the University of Chicago famously declared that the "central problem of depression-prevention has been solved" in his 2003 presidential address to the American Economic Association (Krugman, 2009). The fiscal crisis of 2007–2008, leading to what has been termed the "Great Recession of 2007–2009", shattered this mainstream consensus and motivated renewed attention to Keynesian theory and policy.

In particular, the Obama stimulus program of 2009–2010 followed a well-established Keynesian pattern. It also had a significant environmental component. In part the stimulus package was directed towards traditional types of spending such as highway maintenance, but a significant portion (about $71 billion) was specifically oriented towards "green" investments, together with another $20 billion in "green" tax incentives (Jacobs and McNish, 2009).[1]

An analysis by economists Alan Blinder and Mark Zandi in 2010 found that the Obama stimulus "probably averted what could have been called Great Depression 2.0… [W]ithout the government's response, GDP in 2010 would [have been] about 11.5 percent lower [and] payroll employment would be less by some 8½ million jobs" (Blinder and Zandi, 2010).

Just as the Great Depression forced the economics profession to abandon strict classical principles, the Great Recession and the subsequent Covid recession of 2020 required a reorientation of theory and policy. Post Keynesians have presented an alternative perspective that is in some respects simply a restatement of fundamental Keynesian principles: the macroeconomy does not necessarily tend to full employment, and government intervention may be required to maintain adequate effective demand. This, of course, is exactly what was demonstrated in both the Great Recession and the Covid recession.

In addition, Post Keynesians emphasize the role of economic inequity and the inherent instability of the financial system, following theories derived from Kalecki (class inequality) and Minsky (financial instability). These theoretical elements also have obvious current relevance. Post Keynesian economists' skepticism about the efficiency of markets and price mechanisms also predispose them towards environmentally oriented macroeconomic policy including government-led "green" investment (King, 2015).

The history of economic theory and policy thus shows a significant overlap between Keynesian and Post Keynesian economics and environmental concerns. This offers a substantial basis for current GND proposals (Harris, 2013).

Because environmental issues today, especially but not only climate change, are much more pressing than in the past, a modern version of the New Deal needs to find its theoretical foundation not only in updated Keynesian analysis, but also in broader Post Keynesian and ecological economics perspectives.

ECOLOGICAL ECONOMICS AND THE GND

Ecological economics, as distinct from mainstream environmental economics, is based on a specific and powerful insight: the economy, as a subsystem of the planetary ecological system, is fundamentally limited by the physical realities of that planetary system. This has always been true, but it was possible to neglect the implications of this basic truth so long as human economic activity was at a relatively low level relative to planetary capacity—allowing economic theorists to take what Herman Daly has referred to as an "empty world" rather than a "full world" perspective (Daly, 1999). In Keynes's time, this was basically still true. Although there was significant evidence of environmental degradation, giving rise to the resource and conservation concerns mentioned in connection with the New Deal, the overall pressures of global population and economic activity were far less than today.

Since about 1950, there have been staggering increases in global population, energy use, and carbon emission more than threefold for global population and more than sixfold for energy use and carbon emissions (Harris and Roach, 2022). While the most obvious and widely known result of this is the current climate crisis, parallel crises have emerged in terms of other resources, including water resources, forests and wetlands, agricultural soils, ocean pollution, fisheries decline, and biodiversity loss. Even assuming optimistic forecasts of population stabilization, these consumption-generated pressures on the global ecosystem can be reliably forecast to increase further during the twenty-first century.

This broader perspective implies that a more drastic change will be required in the nature of economic production than was envisioned in the original Keynesian perspective. Keynes assumed that the goal of government policy was to promote full employment and economic growth. While he speculated about an eventual end to standard economic growth in his essay on "Economic Possibilities for Our Grandchildren" (Keynes, 2009 [1930]), this was not an immediate concern in an era of mass unemployment, nor was it a concern for the policymakers who applied Keynesian economics on a broad scale following World War II. The ecological economics perspective, in contrast, implies that an extraordinary reorientation will be required as the period of steady economic growth, characteristic of the past 200 years and especially of the last 75 years, necessarily comes up against firm ecological limits.

Does this mean an end to economic growth? The issue is a bit more complicated:

There is an extensive debate on the possibility of achieving "absolute decoupling"—reducing overall resource inputs, specifically carbon-based fuels, while "growing" the economy. Advocates of "degrowth" argue that absolute decoupling is unlikely to be possible, meaning that consumption must be reduced if carbon reduction targets are to be achieved. But regardless of whether we anticipate only "relative decoupling"—reducing the carbon intensity of the economy—or absolute decoupling, some form of green Keynesian policies will be essential to redirect economic activity away from a carbon-intensive path. (Harris, 2019, p. 4)

A GND, then, has to envision an economic transition at least as sweeping as that of the original Keynesian revolution, and likely more so. This transition necessarily involves drastic changes both in the structure of production and consumption. It is notable that the full impact of Keynesian policies was only felt with the onset of World War II—a massive transformation of national and global economies—and the permanently altered pattern of government economic involvement in the postwar period. If we take into account the full implications of the ecological economic perspective, the next stage of economic development will necessarily reflect an even greater realignment of economic production—but in a quite different direction.

FUNDAMENTAL GOALS OF A GND

The first goal of GND proposals is an energy transformation to a low-carbon economy. One version of the GND by Data for Progress calls for 100% renewable electricity by 2035, and zero net emissions for energy by 2050. Related goals include 100% net zero building energy standards by 2030, dramatic increases in efficiency standards for appliances, lighting, and equipment, 100% zero-emission passenger vehicles by 2030, 100% fossil fuel free transportation by 2050, and reducing methane leakage 50% by 2030 (Carlock and Mangan, 2018).

An important, and neglected, element of climate policy is the management of forests, wetlands, and soils. GND goals cited by Data for Progress include the preservation of existing forests and reforestation of 400 million acres of public and private land by 2035. Wetland preservation and restoration is another critical component. Wetlands are extremely efficient at carbon storage, and wetland loss is a significant cause of increased carbon emissions (Moomaw et al., 2019; Finlayson et al., 2019). Agriculture is a major contributor to carbon and methane emissions, as well as to pesticide and fertilizer pollution degrading waterways and oceans, but sustainable agricultural practices promoting healthy soils have the potential to turn the agricultural sector into a major net carbon sink (Codur and Watson, 2018).

A third major focus for the GND is infrastructure investment. In addition to infrastructure investment related to the low-carbon energy transition, major investment is urgently needed in water, sewage, transportation, and waste management. A single example gives a sense of the scope of the issue. New Jersey's largest lake, Lake Hopatcong, has recently been closed to recreational uses due to a major bloom of toxic blue-green algae—a problem that affects many inland and coastal waters. The causes include climate change, leading to more intense rainfall, and "older sewer and stormwater systems that have been overwhelmed by fast-moving storms… the Environmental Protection Agency has put the cost of upgrading New Jersey's stormwater system at $16 billion" (Barnard, 2019, p. 1). A price tag of $16 billion, for one major problem in one state, strongly suggests many hundreds of billions in needed infrastructure investment nationwide.

Policies to achieve GND goals can be roughly divided into three areas:

1. Redirection of existing economic activity and investment. These policies could include carbon taxes, elimination of "perverse" subsides for carbon emissions and resource extraction, subsidies for renewable energy or sustainable agricultural and forestry practices, establishing strong fuel and building efficiency standards, renewable energy portfolio standards, and stronger environmental regulation;
2. New public investment in renewable energy, energy efficiency, water and sewer infrastructure, public transit, research and development of new renewable technologies and battery storage, electrical grid integration and modernization, public trust funds for community resilience, and land protection programs;
3. Employment creation programs, overlapping with (2) but also including human resource areas such as health, education, and community services.

Green policies adopted in the United States and Europe include all of these, with substantial public investment accompanied by environmental subsidies and stronger efficiency standards. Carbon taxes have generally not been adopted, although the European Union has an existing carbon trading program that will be ramped up to achieve a more ambitious goal of a 55% reduction in carbon emissions by 2035 (European Environment Agency, 2021).

BUDGET IMPLICATIONS OF A GND

The goals of the GND are extremely ambitious, but do not necessarily involve high economic costs. Many environmental problems arise from the exploitation of "free" or low-priced natural resources. Putting a proper price on these resources can be consistent with both good economic theory and sound ecological principles, and generally implies a shift in economic techniques and activities rather than an absolute cost. In some cases, greater efficiency in resource use can save money as well as reduce ecosystem impact.

While proper pricing of resources can generate significant revenue streams, carbon taxes and other resource taxes are generally regressive. A portion of the revenue stream associated with them therefore needs to be channeled into individual per capita rebates (which have the effect of changing the net tax impact from regressive to progressive or at least proportional), or into social investment that primarily befits lower-income individuals and families, such as health care and education. Another approach, implemented in the U.S. IRA, is to raise corporate taxes or close tax loopholes to provide funding for the green transition.

To the extent that necessary infrastructure investment is not covered by carbon tax, cap-and-trade, or corporate tax revenues, it will need to be funded out of general government budgets. According to standard Keynesian theory, at times of severe recession government deficits are acceptable and indeed necessary to counter a deficiency of private investment. But at times of relatively high employment, budget deficits should be reduced or eliminated. In the United States, this implies at a minimum reversing most of the 2017 tax cuts, especially those for upper-income individuals, and closing loopholes. Another option is a financial transaction or "Tobin" tax, set at a very low rate but with significant revenue potential due to the high volume of financial transactions.

Opponents of a GND argue that its implementation will be enormously costly and require government takeover of major economic functions (Ip, 2019). Some formulations of the GND, including expansive goals and "add-ons" such as the concept of guaranteed jobs, have lent credibility to these critics. But, in fact, implementation of a GND can be flexible and does not necessarily involve high costs.

GND investment policies can both promote employment and advance a transition to a more environmentally sustainable economy at relatively low cost in terms of national budgets and GDP. While the total costs of the IIJA and the IRA, at $1.2 trillion and $369 billion respectively sound fairly large, this spending is spread over a ten-year period, and in the case of the IRA is more than offset by $737 billion in new revenues. In the context of an annual Federal budget of over $6 trillion, these are not very large amounts, and the IRA, as noted above, is projected to achieve an actual decrease in the Federal deficit. A "greener" economic view, taking into account ecological benefits including both climate and collateral pollution reduction benefits, implies that the policies required to promote a massive transition to renewables and greater energy efficiency could overall be considered a net benefit, not a net cost.

An important issue in assessing costs is the standard economic principle of increasing marginal cost. This implies that the initial costs are the lowest, and indeed in the case of greenhouse gas abatement costs a major study by McKinsey & Company found that the costs of abating up to about a third of total emissions were *negative*—implying that for these abatement programs, especially increasing energy efficiency, economic advantages outweighed costs even without considering environmental gains. The second third involved relatively low cost, less than $20 per ton of CO_2 equivalent. On a global scale, the total cost of reducing 2030 emissions by 35% compared to 1990 levels, or 70% compared with business-as-usual levels, would be less than 1% of global GDP (McKinsey, 2009 and 2013).

It would thus be a major mistake to reject the GND based on an inflated estimate of its total potential cost. Unfortunately, some of its early advocacy, linking GND to broad goals of guaranteed employment and health care, encouraged just that perception; that it would involve trillions of dollars in immediate new spending. Many GND policies, as noted above, would require minimal spending and deliver net benefits in terms of employment and environmental advances.

In terms of carbon reduction, the higher costs would potentially come later: 35% reduction would be relatively cheap, 100% could be expensive. By trumpeting a 100% goal within the unrealistically short period of ten years, early advocates did the program a disservice. The Biden administration approach, with an emphasis on energy efficiency, incentives for a transition to renewables, and employment generation, will demonstrate employment and environmental benefits from early rounds of investment and incentives, and can be ramped up over time.

Early investments in research and development of areas such as battery storage and low-carbon techniques for steel, cement, aviation, and maritime shipping can lower the costs of reaching more ambitious carbon reduction goals (Davidson, 2022, pp. 119–121). Mark Jacobson suggests that with improved storage capacity, a wind–water–solar electric generation system can ultimately replace 100% of fossil fuel power generation, while electrification of transport can largely eliminate fossil fuel use in that sector (Jacobson, 2023). A green Keynesian analysis suggests that the overall effects will be both economically and environmentally beneficial, even though higher levels of investment spending would be involved to achieve the eventual net zero goal.

JOB-CREATING IMPACTS OF A GND

Several studies of the impact of the IRA confirm its positive impacts on employment, income, and energy efficiency. According to the Energy Futures Initiative (EFI), modeling the impact of the IRA indicated "the unique benefits that well-directed energy investments can have simultaneously on job growth, GDP, real disposable income, inflation reduction, targeted sectoral energy costs, and greenhouse gas emissions reduction" (Foster et al., 2023, p. iii). The EFI model indicates that the IRA will expand employment in the U.S. economy by 1.5 million jobs by 2030, with much of this increase coming in the first 3 years of implementation, representing a permanent gain rather than short-term employment.

Another study by the Political Economy Research Institute (PERI) at the University of Massachusetts Amherst similarly finds a permanent job improvement, measured at just under a million jobs per year over a ten-year period, for a total job creation of 9.1 million job-years over the period (Pollin et al., 2022). The permanence of the job creation is an important feature, since construction of new power facilities often involves a number of short-term jobs in construction, but few long-term employment benefits.

The job-creation effects are a combination of public and private spending. In the PERI study, $40.6 billion in public spending per year is assumed to be matched by $57.8 billion in private spending for a total of $98.4 billion per year. The incentives for private spending include tax credits for electric vehicles and renewable energy investment, as well as loan guarantees and a national Green Bank underwritten by the Federal government. According to the EFI study, the "domino effect of energy investments speaks to the important role that energy plays in the architecture of modern industrial economies. When combined with public policies that support job quality and access, energy investments can also result in greater social equity" (Foster et al., 2023, p. iv).

The projections of these studies are being borne out by the early record of the IRA in job creation. A CNBC article based on a report by the nonprofit Climate Power, finds that more than 100,000 new clean energy jobs were created in the first six months after passage of the IRA:

In the six months since the landmark climate and clean energy investments became law, clean energy companies have announced more than 100,000 new clean energy jobs for electricians, mechanics, construction workers, technicians, support staff, and many others. As of the end of January [2023], companies have announced more than 90 new clean energy projects in small towns and larger cities in the U.S., totaling $89.5 billion in new investments. The wind, solar and EV manufacturing sectors are creating the new positions, which include electricians, mechanics, construction workers and technicians. Plans include 40 new battery manufacturing sites in states like Arizona, Michigan and South Carolina, according to Climate Power. So far, 22 companies have unveiled plans for new or expanded EV manufacturing in Alabama, Oklahoma and Michigan. And an additional 24 companies have released plans to expand wind and solar manufacturing in Colorado, Ohio and Texas. (Newburger and Cortés, 2023, p. 1)

ACHIEVING EMISSIONS REDUCTION AND SOCIAL EQUITY GOALS

The greenhouse gas emissions reduction expected from the full implementation of the IRA is about 37% relative to a 2005 baseline, according to the EFI study. But the authors also note that additional reductions could be achieved from non-energy sources including agriculture, land use, and forest management, as well as direct carbon removal and waste management. "Such initiatives, supplemented by complementary state policy and regulation, could credibly increase emissions reduction to 50% by 2030" (Foster et al., 2023, p. iv). The IRA thus puts in place policies that can achieve a significant portion of GND goals, both in terms of emissions reduction and job creation.

But it is also true that the IRA falls well short of what is needed to respond fully to the climate crisis. According to Robert Pollin, lead author of the PERI study, "[t]he Inflation Reduction Act is the most significant piece of climate legislation ever enacted by the U.S. government. It is also, in itself, not close to sufficient to move the U.S., much less the global economy, onto a viable climate stabilization path" (Polychroniou, 2023, p 1). Pollin estimates that up to four times as much funding is needed to achieve a 50% emissions cut by 2030 and net zero by 2050. In addition, to gain sufficient political support the IRA was crafted to include expansion of oil and gas leasing as well as gas pipeline permitting—clearly not helpful in reducing overall fossil fuel use.

A related issue is support for carbon capture and storage (CCS). While the IRA does not have fully specified mandates for its funding programs, it means that substantial funding could be directed to carbon capture, a controversial and commercially unproven technology that would, in theory, permit continued use of fossil fuels at the expense of funding for renewable energy. Nuclear energy, which does not involve direct carbon emissions but is associated with nuclear waste and safety problems, also receives funding through the IRA. Nuclear has struggled to compete in the marketplace, with the U.S. Energy Information Administration estimating that the "levelized cost", including construction and operating costs, of nuclear power will be about double that of onshore wind and solar in 2027 (U.S. Energy Information Administration, 2022). Some GND advocates see a possible role for CCS and nuclear, but are generally wary of the danger of exploitation of CCS by the fossil fuel and nuclear industries to delay the development of renewable energy (Davidson, 2022, pp. 119–121).

Pollin also points out two other shortcomings of the IRA. It does not provide transitional and reemployment programs for communities currently dependent on the fossil fuel industry, and has no funding for the global clean energy transition, something that has been a prominent issue in the international climate negotiation process, as developing nations have protested the lack of support provided both for climate mitigation and adaptation. Promised funds have so far largely failed to materialize, despite pledges by richer nations, and the IRA does nothing to fill this gap. The IRA does contain over $60 billion in funding dedicated to low-income communities and communities of color, addressing social justice issues within the United States, but international funding is lacking.

In terms of the emissions reduction and social equity goals of the GND, the IRA is thus at best a partial measure. Its significance lies in being the first substantial climate legislation adopted in the United States, and in demonstrating that aggressive climate policy can be a strong net positive from the point of view of employment. Similarly, the European Green Deal represents a major step forward, but has been criticized for institutional and funding weaknesses that raise doubts as to whether it can achieve its goals of a 55% emissions reduction by 2030 and climate neutrality by 2050 (European Union, 2022). Both initiatives have helped to bring the GND into the political mainstream, but much remains to be done to achieve its full potential.

CONCLUSION: REFORMING ECONOMIC THEORY AND POLICY FOR TWENTY-FIRST CENTURY REALITIES

The Keynesian revolution in economics took place in the context of unavoidable, massive economic problems of large-scale unemployment. Under these conditions, it became impossible to maintain a "classical" view of a self-regulating laissez-faire economy. In a sense, we have come full circle. The very success of the institutionalization of Keynesian policies after World War II made it possible for economists to return to a more classically oriented perspective, downgrading the role of government and blaming government policies for problems such as inflation or low productivity growth. With the currently overwhelming importance of climate and ecological crises, it is once again impossible to ignore what Keynes called the "outstanding faults" of an economic system that lacks any effective mechanism to respond to these crises, and that depends on resource-intensive forms of economic growth that steadily worsen them.

Economic policymakers must adapt to a new reality in which government policy plays an active role in reshaping the economy both to avoid ecological catastrophe and to redress growing inequality and social breakdown. If this necessity is recognized, a wide range of economic tools, including standard Keynesian policy and new approaches such as the GND, is available to respond.

It is true, as conservative critics point out, that government actions can be wasteful, ineffective, or counterproductive—if poorly designed. But the option of forgoing an active government response is no longer open. Thus, the answer to the shortcomings of government policies must be to design effective policies, not abandon the effort or rely on an unregulated "free market" that makes the problems worse. The initial policies being implemented in the United States and Europe are promising, as the analyses reviewed above indicate. Strengthening these policies over time, and adapting them to the international arena, will be essential.

Revised macroeconomic goals should include:

1. Rapid reduction of carbon emissions through investment in energy efficiency and renewables, and through increased carbon storage in forest and soils;
2. Adaptation to ecological limits to growth, including carbon limits but also sustainable use limits related to water, land, forests, fisheries, and other ecosystems;
3. Revenue generation through increased taxes on upper incomes and corporations, carbon tax with partial rebate, and financial transactions tax;
4. Using "green" Keynesian policies for infrastructure investment and development of renewable energy technologies.

Economies based on these principles will look different, with more emphasis on human services and less on resource-intensive goods production, significantly lower overall energy use, and a vastly expanded renewable energy infrastructure. But there is no reason that a combination of existing policy tools and newer ecologically oriented policies cannot promote prosperity and increased employment opportunities, as well as stabilization of both economic and ecological systems. This is the promise of the GND and, despite an uneven start, the future is promising—if policymakers learn the right lessons.

NOTE

1. Specific provisions included energy efficiency in government facilities ($8.7 billion); smart-grid infrastructure investment ($11 billion); energy and conservation grants to state and local governments ($6.3 billion); weatherization assistance ($5 billion); energy efficiency and renewable energy research ($2.5 billion); grants for advanced battery manufacturing ($2 billion); loan guarantees for wind and solar projects ($6 billion); public transit and high-speed rail ($17.7 billion); environmental cleanup ($14.6 billion) and environmental research ($6.6 billion).

REFERENCES

Barnard, Anne. (2019). Algae Bloom Fouls N.J.'s Largest Lake. *New York Times*, August 5.

Blinder, Alan, and Mark Zandi. (2010). How the Great Recession Was Brought to an End. https://www.economy.com/mark-zandi/documents/End-of-Great-Recession.pdf.

Carlock, Greg, and Emily Mangan. (2018). A Green New Deal: A Progressive Vision for Environmental Sustainability and Economic Stability. *Data for Progress*. https://www.dataforprogress.org/green-new-deal-report.

Codur, Anne-Marie, and Josephine Watson. (2018). Climate Smart or Regenerative Agriculture? Defining Climate Policies Based on Soil Health. *GDAE Climate Policy Brief #9, April*. Global Development and Environment Institute, Tufts University. https://sites.tufts.edu/gdae/climate-policy-briefs/.

Congressional Budget Office. (2022). *Estimated Budgetary Effects of H.R. 5376, the Inflation Reduction Act of 2022*. Congressional Budget Office, Washington, D.C.

Daly, Herman E. (1999). *Ecological Economics and the Ecology of Economics*. Edward Elgar Publishing, Cheltenham, UK and Northampton, MA, USA.

Davidson, Eric A. (2022). *Science for a Green New Deal: Connecting Climate, Economics, and Social Justice*. Johns Hopkins University Press, Baltimore.

European Environment Agency. (2021). EU Achieves 20-20-20 Climate Targets; 55% Emissions Cut by 2030 Reachable with More Efforts and Policies. https://www.eea.europa.eu/highlights/eu-achieves-20-20-20.

European Parliament. (2020). *European Green Deal Investment Plan*. https://www.europarl.europa.eu/RegData/etudes/BRIE/2020/649371/EPRS_BRI(2020)649371_EN.pdf.

European Union. (2022). *European Green Deal Barometer*. https://think2030.eu/publications/european-green-deal-barometer-2022.

Finlayson, Max et al. (2019). The Second Warning to Humanity—Providing a Context for Wetland Management and Policy. *Wetlands 39* (February), 1–5.

Foster, David, Alex Maranville, and Sam F. Savitz. (2023). Jobs, Emissions, and Economic Growth: What the Inflation Reduction Act Means for Working Families. *Energy Futures Initiative Policy Paper*, January.

Harris, Jonathan M. (2013). Green Keynesianism: Beyond Standard Growth Paradigms. In Richardson, R. (Ed.). *Building a Green Economy: Perspectives from Ecological Economics* (pp. 69–82). MSU Press, East Lansing, MI.

Harris, Jonathan M. (2019). Responding to Economic and Ecological Deficits. *Tufts University Global Development and Environment Institute Working Paper No. 19-01, April*. https://sites.tufts.edu/gdae/working-papers/.

Harris, Jonathan M., and Brian Roach. (2022). *Environmental and Natural Resource Economics: A Contemporary Approach*, 5th ed. Chapter 2, "Resources, Environment, and Economic Development", pp. 21–26. Routledge, New York and Abingdon, UK.

Ip, Greg. (2019). The Unrealistic Economics of the Green New Deal. *Wall Street Journal*, February 13.

Jacobs, Scott, and Rob McNish. (2009). The U.S. Stimulus Program; Investing in Energy Efficiency. *McKinsey Quarterly*, July 1.

Jacobson, Mark Z. (2023). *No Miracles Needed: How Today's Technology Can Save Our Climate and Clean Our Air*. Chapter 2, "WWS Solutions for Efficient

Generation" and Chapter 4, "WWS Solutions for Transportation". Cambridge University Press, Cambridge, UK.

Keynes, John Maynard. (1964) [original publication 1936]. *The General Theory of Employment, Interest, and Money*. Harcourt, San Diego, New York, and London.

Keynes, John Maynard. (2009) [original publication 1930]. "Economic Possibilities for Our Grandchildren". *Essays in Persuasion*. Classic House Books, New York.

King, John E. (2015). *Advanced Introduction to Post Keynesian Economics*. Chapter 2, "The Core of Post Keynesian Economics"; Chapter 7, "Why it all Matters: Economic Policy"; and Chapter 9, "Post Keynesians and Other Schools of Thought". Edward Elgar Publishing, Cheltenham, UK and Northampton, MA, USA.

Krugman, Paul. (2009). How Did Economists get it so Wrong? *New York Times*, September 2.

McKinsey & Company. (2009 and 2013). *Pathways to a Low-Carbon Economy*. https://www.mckinsey.com/business-functions/sustainability/our-insights/pathways -to-a-low-carbon-economy.

Merrill, Perry H. (1981). Roosevelt's Forest Army, a History of the Civilian Conservation Corps. *Forest & Conservation History 25* (4), 232–233.

Moomaw, William, Susan Masino, and Edward Faison. (2019). Intact Forests in the United States; Proforestation Mitigates Climate Change and Serves the Greater Good. *Frontiers in Forests and Global Change*, June. https://www.frontiersin.org/articles/10.3389/ffgc.2019.00027/full.

Newburger, Emma, and Gabriel Cortés. (2023). Inflation Reduction Act has Spurred 100,000 New Green Jobs so far: Here's Where They are. *CNBC*, February 7. https://www-cnbc-com.cdn.ampproject.org/c/s/www.cnbc.com/amp/2023/02/07/inflation -reduction-act-which-states-have-most-new-green-jobs-so-far.html.

Penn Wharton. (2022). Inflation Reduction Act: Estimates of Budgetary and Macroeconomic Effects. University of Pennsylvania, August 2. https://budgetmodel .wharton.upenn.edu/issues/2022/8/12/senate-passed-inflation-reduction-act.

Pollin, Robert, Chirag Lala, and Shouvik Chakraborty. (2022). Job Creation Estimates through Proposed Inflation Reduction Act. University of Massachusetts Amherst Political Economy Research Institute. https://peri.umass.edu/publication/item/1633 -job-creation-estimates-through-proposed-inflation-reduction-act.

Polychroniou, C.J. (2023). Let's Acknowledge Inflation Reduction Act's Significance— and Its Inadequacy. *Truthout*, August. https://truthout.org/articles/lets-acknowledge -inflation-reduction-acts-significance-and-its-inadequacy/.

Qiu, Linda. (2022). Federal Government's $20 Billion Embrace of "Climate Smart" Farming. *New York Times*, September 26.

U.S. Energy Information Administration. (2022). Levelized Cost of New Generation Resources. *Annual Energy Outlook 2022*. https://www.eia.gov/outlooks/aeo/pdf/electricity_generation.pdf.

U.S. Environmental Protection Agency. (2023). The Inflation Reduction Act. https://www.epa.gov/green-power-markets/inflation-reduction-act.

9. Macroeconomic theory and policy in the capitalism of "permanent catastrophe"

Riccardo Bellofiore and Giovanna Vertova

INTRODUCTION

When Keynes wrote *The Economic Consequences of Peace*, not only Europe but the world was at a turning point. We think that in hindsight it was a more significant watershed for us than the Great Crash of 1929 or the Second World War – "for us", we mean us economists; and, more specifically, "us" non-mainstream economists. In this chapter we shall try to argue how this is one of the lessons we must draw after the multiple shocks of the beginning of the third millennium, like the Great Financial Crisis, the Covid pandemic, climate change, and the Ukrainian war. Moreover, we shall argue that this takes us back to what was the true birth of macroeconomics.

According to Keynes, "the War", as it was called then, had revealed a double deception. In pre-1914 capitalism, workers were receiving the smallest share of wealth while capitalists, who were given the largest slice, were induced not to consume much of it. The justification was the need to overcome capital scarcity and the struggle for subsistence. A few years later, in 1928–1930, Keynes predicted that for his grandchildren (who would perhaps be the parents of Millennials, well before Generation Z or Alpha) the era of abundance economy would finally dawn. Not a dream, but a delusion, which is definitively behind us, attacked as we are by a multiple crisis, designated by some as "polycrisis", borrowing Moren and Kern's term (1999). We are rather dealing with a reality which puts into question, at once, so many economic and social ways of being that we took for granted, and on which our reproduction and identity depend. There is the urgency of a change, without, however, our capacity to cope being guaranteed.

Since when has this intersection of challenges taken place? Certainly not since the invasion of Ukraine, when the term polycrisis was resurrected by Adam Tooze (2022). On closer inspection, the origin could perhaps be traced back to 2000–2003, when the neoliberal configuration of "privatised Keynesianism" (Crouch, 2009; Bellofiore and Halevi, 2006, 2012), based on indebted consumption, capital-assets inflation, and monetary policy began to crack down, anticipating the 2007–2008 collapse. We live near Bergamo, where the Covid pandemic first hit Europe violently in February/March 2020, and three years later we write this chapter, in February/March 2023, one year after the beginning of the war in Ukraine. That is why we shall concentrate on these two historical junctures as starting points of a more general discourse. We are convinced that the sequence of crises since 2000 forces us to return to some fundamental and original issues of macroeconomics, which must consider not only the level of employment, but also what employment is for.

The conclusion will be that, nowadays, it is necessary to radicalise the notion of the "socialisation of investment" (that we borrow more from Minsky than Keynes) by renovating it, into that of the "social production economy", because we are convinced that the challenge before us concerns "how", "what", "how much", and "for whom" to produce.

THE COVID CRISIS: INTERPRETATIONS

The economic policy response to the Covid crisis has been discussed from different angles. In the following pages, we shall only refer to the positions offered by Mario Draghi (who compared the Covid emergency to "war times"), Adam Tooze (who situated it on the background of the "political economy of inflation" and named it as "the first crisis of the Anthropocene"), and Jan Kregel (who argued in favour of a "central role for direct social provisioning" as the most appropriate macroeconomic policy). The pandemic was also instrumental in determining a paradigm shift in European economic policy. Even unlikely thinkers found in it the motive to suggest a break with neoliberalism, either in its 1987–2007 glorious incarnation or in its post-2007 zombie variant.

Mario Draghi (2020), in his article in the *Financial Times* published on 25 March of that year, maintained that the emergency to be addressed was not so much a lack of effective demand (as in the 1930s), nor a sudden collapse of the financing system (as in the 2007–2008 crisis). The health crisis was endangering not only people's lives, but also their livelihoods. Employment and income were threatened as a direct consequence of what were the timely and required actions of governments to prevent hospitals and healthcare systems from being overwhelmed and crushed. After the outbreak of the subprime crisis in 2007, triggering the Great Recession, the world economy was again heading for a global crisis, of a deeper nature, if possible. This time it was not detonated by finance, but by an induced supply shock set off by political decisions. The top-down choice of putting the most advanced economies in an artificial coma was judged inevitable to stop the pandemic. This could only spark downsizing and layoffs, rising the risk of bankruptcies.

One cannot fail to appreciate the boldness with which the former president of the European Central Bank (ECB) endorsed unprecedented policy decisions in favour of health and life versus profits, income, and employment. The survival of businesses (in particular, of the small and medium-sized ones, where most of the workforce is employed) was directly in question. The private sector's loss of income was such that all or part of it had to be taken over by public budgets. The needed economic policy response, together with a cancellation of private debt, the former ECB president predicted, would have made the resulting increase in public debt an enduring feature of economies.

Draghi was clear that the exceptional state action against the pandemic was nothing new. Governments always get involved in national emergencies: the most relevant precedent being the two World Wars. The issue is not whether governments should sustain public deficits, he wrote, but how. Income support, unemployment benefits, tax deferrals, liquidity provision, are the policy interventions that Draghi explicitly endorsed as means to maintain the quality of the labour force and the productive capacity. He insisted on an urgent and full mobilisation of the entire financial system. The interest rate on loans was to be temporarily zeroed for companies that wanted to save jobs. Capital had to be supported with state guarantees, regardless of the costs for the government issuing them. If the pandemic lasted and the lockdowns were prolonged, the private debt incurred by companies to maintain jobs would have to be written off. There was no alternative for the economy and for the government other than the destruction of productive capacity, and thus of the very base on which taxes are levied. In fact, the increase in public debt could be easily financed, thanks to the reduced current and future level of interest rates. This, he argued, is the change of mentality needed to deal with pandemic: as if one were in wartime.[1]

Draghi wrote in the first weeks of the pandemic. Adam Tooze a few months later, when the first wave was winding down. In 2018, Tooze had published *Crashed*, likely the best book on the global financial and geopolitical dimensions of the 2007–2008 crisis. Before the Covid outbreak he planned to write a book on the political economy of energy and climate change. Two good reasons why Tooze was ideally placed to deal with the health crisis, which is the subject of his following book *Shutdown* (Tooze, 2021).

Tooze, like Draghi, is full of admiration for the discretionary lockdowns decided during the first wave: shutting down the economies to preserve human life was indeed spectacular and extraordinary, and we agree with the positive judgement. However, while Draghi insisted that there is nothing new in the Covid crisis, for Tooze we have not seen anything yet: the relation between past experience and the present is fundamentally problematic. The key role of public debt was already evident in 2008–2009, in spite of that, after 2010, austerity had reasserted itself as the only game in town. The economic policy response to the Great Recession confirmed that there was no "technical" difficulty in funding governments in need, but the message was soon forgotten. Covid provided a gigantic opportunity to reiterate the lesson about the fiscal spending capacity of states, and of how a genuinely monetary economy works. In fact, the quantitative amount of monetary and fiscal interventions in 2020 was much larger than in previous crises. It came swiftly and as something quite shocking in the European case. The qualitative break was even more fundamental.

To better understand the nature of the Covid crisis, Tooze's considerations on the formation of the consensus that had been built in the 1970s, and its obsolescence after its undisputed success, are central. As part of the fight against inflation, on the one hand, a campaign for central bank independence was mounted, while, on the other hand, aggressive capital markets supposedly came to the rescue of wealth holders. The reason goes back to what Tooze calls the political economy of class antagonism. In the late 1960s and early 1970s, workers were questioning the way production was organised and how income was distributed. The change in central bank policy was instrumental in crushing the conditions that supported class warfare on the side of labour. By no longer buying treasuries, central banks enhanced the power of the bond market to intimidate progressive politics. Today, as Warren Buffett famously declared, class war has not disappeared, it just has been won by the capitalist class. What was a self-inflicted financial and monetary constraint on political activism can now be removed if necessary. The need to remove it became urgent in 2007–2008 when the Great Financial Crisis broke out: but people panicked because they were not intellectually ready for such a radical change in economic policy.

The Covid pandemic was a sort of "cunning of reason". The long transition from the shock of the class war of the late 1960s (prolonged into the 1970s) to the shock of the global financial collapse (due to the collapse of the North Atlantic banks) was not enough. Another earthquake had to win the last defences. What Tooze tells us is that Covid, this huge trauma experienced in a few years after the great financial crash, has its original roots in the same decades, the 1970s and 1980s, when (after the oil shocks) emerging or re-emerging infectious diseases took over and climate change warnings kicked in. Thanks in part to the spatial compression of globalisation, the Covid health crisis condensed the effects of accelerating economic growth that brought poor food, poor sanitation, and overcrowded housing to some parts of its value chain. Covid was by no means the first in a series of emerging infectious diseases and, like other viruses before it, is linked to the incorporation of animal life into the human food chain. Since the causes are anthropogenic, Tooze calls it the first crisis of the Anthropocene. As others do, we will argue that the imprinting of the capitalist social form is so obvious that it seems more sensible to use the term Capitalocene.[2]

The acceleration of the consequences of the pandemic was exponential, on both the epidemiological and economic fronts. To counter the health risks the measures had to be strong and immediate, but also the responses to economic disruption had to be massive: and, as a matter of fact, they were. Covid made clear how dramatic would have been the cost of inaction and highlighted that only central banks and governments had the size and firepower to ensure economic survival.

Draghi conceptualises the health crisis through a comparison with the mobilisation effort during a war economy, beginning with the First World War. Tooze sees in the policies against the pandemic a radicalisation of the caesura with the political economy of inflation (and class struggle in the 1970s) in place in reaction to the Great Financial Crisis. Kregel's (2020) position is different.[3] This author calls for a return to some aspects of the 1930s New Deal which have been overlooked. Even if Draghi and Tooze made clear that the 1970s stagflation, the Great Recession since 2007, and the health crisis since 2020 cannot be framed through traditional Keynesian lenses, much of the economic policy instrumentation they refer to is still of that kind. In Kregel's argument, although Keynes is certainly most important for the understanding of the nature of the crisis, his policy outlook is far from an endorsement of stimulus programmes.

The economic policy focus was initially to bring about a slowdown in production, but quickly it shifted on preoccupation about the resultant demand slump. Governments and central banks' concerns were to provide financial assistance and huge deficit spending with zero interest. Kregel was crystal clear that these were the wrong responses, descending from a misunderstanding of the crisis. What occurred during the Covid pandemic was a situation in which agents were overwhelmed by "true" uncertainty. The natural way to deal with it, following Keynes's views on probability, would have been to assume the similarity of the new contagion with past virus experiences at the outset, and to prevent panic. When transmission and mortality rates proved to be higher than expected, the unknowability of the key parameters had to be recognised. At that point, the rational response could have been only to inhibit transmission through large-scale lockdowns.

Recession, or more properly depression, was exactly the outcome to be expected from active policy decisions of this kind. That is why the suggestion to proceed with expansionary stimulus – in markets that had been voluntarily shut down, and with production frozen from above – was entirely inappropriate. Job guarantee programmes are not suitable when the target is to close down economic activities. Basic income subsidies are incongruous, if the point is to guarantee provision in kind. Loans to support employment are meaning-less, if workers must stay at home. Kregel thought a different policy had to be found by looking at a different page of the New Deal's response to the Great Depression. The need was for social provision directly ensured by the state as a central organisation. The rise in government deficit spending should have been limited to provide interventions like food distribution for subsistence. Fixed costs for payments should have been deferred. A suspension of finan-cial transactions, rather than their financing, was in order. This would have prevented an escalation in debt levels. The message is clear. Since markets no longer work in lockdowns, the appropriate policy following Keynes is to put in place central controls on what is produced and distributed. The point is to organise the appropriate "direction" of production with a fair sharing of the burden. A policy like this not only affects the level but also the composition of output. If you fight a war, this is what you had to do in the past, Kregel concluded.

It is plain that if Draghi and Kregel disagreed on what was to be done during the pandemic, both think that the Covid pandemic was a short-run shock. A robust and aggressive policy intervention was required, but the emergency was temporary. Tooze, on the contrary, lucidly understands the need for a longer-term transformative policy to deal with the immanent and imminent crisis in the Anthropocene. A paradox is apparent here. The policy that Kregel recommends embodies some characteristics essential to configure economic policy (and politics altogether) to orient the structure of the economy to address this longer-run challenge. In the parallel with a "war economy" – particularly relevant for mass events like the First and Second World War – reminded by Draghi, as well as in the comparison to the New Deal called to mind by Kregel, elements of a "command economy" are brought up. Through direct measures and through government funding, the production system was targeted on two pressing objectives: on the one hand, the war effort, and sending citizens to the front; on the other, meeting the basic needs of the civilian population.

In the meantime, while this discussion went on, the Covid pandemic had done in months, indeed in weeks, what years and decades of prolonged low growth (if not stagnation) had failed to achieve. The Stability and Growth Pact was suspended, making clear that what will happen in future on that front depends not on technical constraints but on political choices. No true limits were set on government bond purchases by the ECB, which acted de facto as the lender of last resort. The speed with which such turnaround took place was astonishing compared to the previous crisis, that of 2007–2008. A significant reversal in European economic policy came to pass. Eurobond financing was seriously discussed, as was the possibility of the management of a European public debt, with a European safe asset. The construction of a true European budget remained a mirage, but a medium-term programme

(NextGenerationEU) was approved, followed by the definition of national recovery plans. Government expenditure in deficit came back as a protagonist.

Coherent with the parallel between the Covid crisis and World Wars, it might have been sensible to consider a partial or total forgiveness of past debts. The form might have been not an open cancellation, but rather a conversion into securities with a very long-term maturity, at a minimum interest rate. This could have been a powerful sign of a collective political investment but was never the subject of debate.

PERMANENT CRISIS AND THE RETURN OF THE STATE

Though it may not appear obvious, we are directed to a similar conclusion to what we argued about the pandemic – namely, the urgency of a structural intervention including elements of a command economy – by the turmoil following, but also immediately preceding, Putin's invasion of Ukraine. Already before the beginning of the Ukrainian war, sharp rises in energy as well as in commodity prices had materialised, both for demand- and supply-side reasons. Inflation had surged everywhere. In the US, in the more classical type of a general inflation affecting all sectors. In Europe, in a more structural instantiation, where changes in relative prices drastically alter the allocation of resources and the distribution of income. In this latter case, it may be hoped to be temporary. However, in the meantime, debtors and creditors are affected differently. The same happens for industries, countries, agents with different balance sheets, social classes. The growing gap between the macroeconomic and structural conditions of the US and of the rest of the world generated fears that the announced abandonment of the low interest rate policy by the central banks, beginning with the Fed, could disarticulate the various areas and ignite uncontrollable fires. The fear became more concrete by virtue also, but certainly not only, of the Russian invasion of Ukraine.

If we dissect also other contradictions that condensed in the last two decades, we recognise a unifying thread. The Great Financial Crisis since 2007, climate change exposing the pathological social relation of human beings with nature, the Covid pandemic as an endogenous shock within the Capitalocene, are all events which laid bare that the challenge in front of us is the monetary and political command over what, where, how, how much, and for whom to produce. What the invasion of Ukraine has accelerated is just to highlight how impossible it is in the advanced countries to address the contradictions on the distribution and employment side without an intervention that is not only macroeconomic, but also financial and structural.

The gap between the two sides of the Atlantic is widening. Europe at risk of recession, the US once again in a kind of full employment, though of pre-

carious labour. The European Union's inability to respond to the crisis with
a leap forward in the federal unification process, its substantial immobility, is
somewhat surprising in comparison to the capacity to react demonstrated in
the pandemic. It would have been conceivable that, albeit on the bad side of
history, the Russian invasion itself could have been an inducement to assume
a leading role in a conflict on its doorstep. On the contrary, Europe, like the
protagonist of a Woody Allen film, is constantly "out of focus", in danger
of falling apart. If there is a designated loser as a backlash to the Ukrainian
crisis, in the first instance, it is her. Meanwhile, in the tearing of international
relations, the advanced areas of the world are suffering, to varying degrees,
from restrictive monetary interventions. But higher energy bills, the return of
inflation, and financial shocks are hard blows that the advanced world could
withstand, and against which it would not be unimaginable to set up safety
nets. Emerging countries, on the other hand, may drown from the tsunami generated in a fragmented and weakened centre. Their marginality renders them
voiceless, predestined to exclusion, deprived of that weapon which would be,
at least, the fear that their difficulties will seriously infect the advanced world.

In the usual progressive agenda, with greater or lesser radicality, the refrain
has long been to counter the mainstream economic policies of monetary
restriction and austerity with an alternative recipe of high public deficit spending and low interest rates. One could be divided on the attitude towards growth,
favoured mostly by economists, while ecologists waved the banner of zero or
negative growth. On this last point, the invasion of Ukraine intervened to
block, or rather, worse, to roll back the timid steps that had been taken towards
a "greening" of economic development and to bring military spending back
into vogue. As we have recalled, the economic policy framework had changed
since 2020, with the unexpected return of deficit spending. The possibility that
all this, in Europe and elsewhere, would mean regaining democratic political
governance of the economic stimulus, however, lasted the space of a few
months. The Russian invasion of the past year has accelerated, but again not
caused, a trend that was already underway towards a different configuration
of economic policy in capitalism than the neoliberal era as we had known it.

Before saying anything about what shape the new capitalist stage looming as
our future is taking, it is worth insisting on the challenge that the very last few
years, even before the Russian invasion, meant for the economic thinking that
precisely pursues the alternative economic policy design we have mentioned.
Jo Michell[4] makes this very clear:

> The current situation of high inflation, driven by energy shortages, war and climate
> change, serves as a sharp reminder that there is something missing in analysis which
> sees higher growth as an entirely free lunch. Almost all economic activity depletes
> scarce physical resources and generates carbon emissions. Higher employment

usually comes at the cost of higher emissions. Furthermore, it is possible that we are now also reaching the end of the historic period in which physical resources were usually immediately available – so that economic activity could quickly rise in response to higher overall spending. The era of the Keynesian free lunch may be ending, replaced by a regime characterised by recurring inflationary episodes. This puts progressive economists, like myself, who believe that the economies of rich countries are predominantly demand driven – meaning that higher overall spending means more jobs and higher incomes – in an uncomfortable position. (Michell, 2022)

Michell is right that the answer to this challenge requires calibrating a macro-economic demand policy with a supply-side sectoral intervention: i.e. transposed into the argument we are articulating necessitates a "socialisation" of investment and a top-down intervention on private consumption, making it "communal". It is hard to escape the conclusion that words that we are accustomed to consider as right wing, such as structural reforms and austerity, should instead be assumed and transformed by the left. A horizon where structural reforms direct a project of higher qualitative development alternative to traditional growth policies, but far from no-growth perspectives, and where a stagnation of GDP as value production may mean no stagnation at all from the point of view of wealth. Austerity, together with highly progressive taxation, may not only rationalise consumption but change its nature, and be an instrument to a different management of social time and a different kind of production.

It can be debated whether nature really has a *horror vacui*, a fear of empty spaces, as Aristotle and Descartes thought. Certainly, it seems so if one looks at the recurrence of "long" capitalist cycles. When a capitalist configuration dissolves, both impersonal forces and political dynamics are set in motion to lay the foundations for a new phase of profit-driven growth that banishes the spectre of stagnation. Sweezy (1982) recalled that permanent stagnation is an impossibility for capital, but he also warned that the countertendencies winning the stagnation can be destructive.

The long cycle of social struggles that helped to close the parenthesis of post-war Keynesianism, based on full employment driven by high investment–high profits–high public spending – the pivot of which was armament spending and waste in the US, the welfare state in some European countries – and the outcome of which was environmental and social degradation – were followed not by a return to laisser faire, but by the triad: casualisation of work/subaltern inclusion of households in money manager capitalism/privatised Keynesianism with debt-driven consumption governed by monetary policy at its centre. When that model collapsed, at the beginning of the third millennium, the pandemic was seized as an opportunity for a reversal of that "privatised Keynesianism", paving the way for the return to state deficit spending.

Beyond what shines at the surface, however, we are still dealing with a "privatised Keynesianism", but of a different nature. The dominance of fiscal policy under the sign of growing public debt does not change the totalising primacy of capitalist logic which, on the contrary, seems to become increasingly ferocious. The explicit and proclaimed reappearance of activism on the side of public spending is bent to private priorities and criteria, fully maintaining austerity for the working and middle classes. The deconstruction of labour is deepened, with cuts in social spending going in parallel with support for business and finance. The criteria to which public intervention must be subject in order to be deemed as "rational" and "efficient", and thus justified, must incorporate a marked allegedly free-market orientation. As Garbellini (2022)[5] wrote:

> Yet on closer examination, the Draghi government's plans, drawing on the loans and grants offered by the European Union's Next Generation EU (NGEU) fund in the wake of the pandemic, show that public spending is not inherently left-wing. What we are instead seeing, in the guise of mass investment and "recovery", is a massive transfer of resources from the public sector to private enterprise.

For the Keynesians, as Sweezy wrote (1942), the economic system is excised from its social context and accounted as if it were a machine to be sent to the repair shop to be overhauled by an engineer state. The return of state activism has, as its hallmark, a social surveillance of labour within production (Zuboff, 2019) and forms of coercion and authoritarian consent in politics, in new and less new forms. As Industry 4.0 and the Chinese peculiar model of capitalism are evidence of, workers and citizens are conceived as passive cogs of a mechanism that naturally must self-regulate. The working conditions take on attributes proper to a slave society. A caste stratification is again on the way to be established, not only related to income and work, but also to wealth and access to finance. The new active and interventionist state assumes the task of restarting what is thought to be an autopoietic system: in Marxian terms, the real social powers of the fetish-character of capital are preserved, fetishistically presuming these powers are natural and not socially specific.

Though it may appear as counterintuitive, the capitalism of the last half-century is reminiscent not so much of Tooze's (2022) "polycrisis", which may seem devoid of a centre, as of Theodor Wiesengrund Adorno's "permanent catastrophe". It is a condition where recurrent destructions of normality obstruct radical changes. Coherently with a world in permanent catastrophe, "permanent crisis" is the engine of economic growth and not its opposite and cancellation.

THE HEALTH CRISIS IS A CRISIS OF THE CAPITALIST SOCIAL FORM OF PRODUCTION AND CONSUMPTION

To imagine an alternative for a world denying its possibility, we have to go back to the Covid crisis. As we have written above, we consider Draghi's reference to wars to understand what to do against the Covid pandemic entirely appropriate, but only if the parallel is developed in the way Kregel did, i.e. looking at the New Deal. Both for the mobilisation of resources and their direction, what counted was essentially the political "command" not only on the level but also on the composition of production. As in the great "social crisis" that hit the capitalist economies in the late 1960s and early 1970s, and as in the great global financial crisis of the early 2000s, the question of "what", "how", "how much", "for whom" to produce was the main issue.

Before coming back to this theme, which we have already suggested, it is prudent to avoid a misunderstanding. The Covid crisis is very often presented as an exogenous shock: something "external" (nature) upsetting the regularity of the economic sphere. We think, on the contrary, that the health crisis is a catastrophic event bringing to light the pathological content behind the supposed normality of our everyday life. The Covid pandemic is inextricably linked to the capitalist social form: that is, to capital as the organiser of the production and circulation of commodities, to the distribution of wealth and income that it determines, to the mode of consumption and the ways of life that it makes universal.

It is customary for economists to present social realities as natural and inevitable events. This is Marx's "fetishism" we mentioned previously. The hope of being able to return to a normal life and the socialisation we are accustomed to, before the virus, removed the ever more decisive need to shape a different mode of production and an alternative societal way of being. The intimate root of the recent crises (and not only the Covid episode) lies in the systematic robbery and destruction of what is "other" than capital: both external nature and human beings, who are themselves part of nature, in their interaction. The capitalist process selects use-values not because they conform to allegedly independent social needs but only insofar as they are functional to valorisation; and then it defines social needs so that those use-values are felt as human needs. Nature is considered as a cost, and workers only as human living bearers of labour power.

The Covid pandemic should not have come as a shocking surprise. The emergence of new diseases and the reappearance of old ones had already been widely discussed in the specialist literature (O'Connor, 1998; Wallace, 2020; Wallace et al., 2020). The same point needs to be made about the consequences of climate change. There is in fact a relationship between global warming and the mutual malignant strengthening of epidemiological infections. One could counter that the issue is not capitalism, but rather industrial production, whatever its social form. Nevertheless, the primacy – in economic policy, and indeed in politics *tout court* – of a profit-driven production system is responsible for global inequality, malnutrition, intensive agriculture, overcrowding in housing, over-urbanisation, pollution, the environmental impact of transports, transnational value chains, and so on. Virus transmission, which otherwise could have been more easily controlled or slowed down, has been dramatically accelerated by all this. The exponential growth in the spread of viruses is the other side of a boundless hunt for profit. During the first wave of the Covid pandemic, the lockdowns implemented in the first half of 2020 were partial, with many non-essential employees in industry and services still at work. During the second wave, manufacturing and business closures were even less strict and the trade-off between economy and human life was soon redefined to the detriment of the latter. The coveted return to "normality" seems to us a very questionable goal, once it is realised how much the previous mode of social coexistence has increased the likelihood of ever more serious health and ecological crises in the future. This professed "normality" was a rather slippery concept, because the benchmark was progressively altered in such a way as to favour a reboot of the economy. Living in a state of emergency and suspending social conflict are becoming established political and economic patterns, to be incorporated into the public policies for ordinary times.

Although the virus is a natural agent, the pandemic is a product of how human beings interact with each other and with nature. The pandemic is endogenous to the social form. It is not the eventual manifestation of some erratic and unpredictable "Black Swan" (if anything, as Tooze puts it, it was a quite predictable "Grey Rhino", or even more like a "White Swan"). The pandemic was heralded by previous epidemics, such as avian flu, SARS, swine fever, MERS. We are not dealing with natural phenomena that do not essentially result from the interaction between human activity and the environment, and which could not have been avoided by timely and targeted interventions in the metabolism (or "organic material exchange") between humans and nature. Contributing factors include anthropogenic erosion, forms of agricultural production, intensive animal farming, loss of biodiversity, population concentration, and (last, but not least) the degradation of workplaces. Similarly, the demolishing of national health systems, with the corresponding privatisation of healthcare and universalisation of market criteria, and more, in general, the cuts in public spending, have all played destructively. The underestimation of risk has been both cause and effect of the Covid pandemic.

MACROECONOMICS BEFORE AND BEYOND MACROECONOMICS

Contrary to the standard accounts, both in mainstream and nonmainstream views, the very birth of macroeconomics is associated to the power of money as capital to control the allocation of resources. This is a theme that goes back to Schumpeter's definition of the concept of "capital" in his *Theory of Economic Development*; and, also, to his conception of money as a social system of accounting and compensation found in *Das Wesen des Geldes.*

In a letter to Dennis Holmes Robertson dated 13 December 1936, just after the publication of *The General Theory*, Keynes dated his emancipation from traditional theory from the discussions between them, that preceded Robertson's *Banking Policy and the Price Level* (1926), and which were contemporary with his early drafts of *The Treatise on Money*. In a later letter to Gottfried Haberler dated 3 March 1938, Keynes identifies the moment of truth that led many economists to break away from "(Neo-)Classical" economics in the (Great) "War".

The First World War, because of its mass character, could not be financed by new taxes or a forced reduction in nominal wages without raising "political complications" or "psychological objections". It was, therefore, financed by the inflow of new liquidity, leading in rebound to the necessary reduction of workers' present consumption through price inflation that was higher than the increase in nominal wages. These were times when it was obligatory to divert productive resources from one use and turn them to something else (in that case war purposes) to a considerable extent, without the possibility of relying on the spontaneous operation of the price system.

Those exceptional conditions disclosed the working of the capitalist mechanism in a true monetary economy. Before the "War", Keynes wrote in the aforementioned letter to Haberler, we were all "Classical" economists, and we were forced to ask what happens when a government gains a command of purchasing power by an inflation of volume of money. The answer was that the consequent "forced saving" may release resources for the government and finance the war. During the following years, Keynes (as well as Robertson) realised that the government gained only in the sense in which every borrower gains. The entrepreneurs were actually those who got a net increment of assets over liability equal to what was lost by the consumers. The war was a special case of the normal operation of a capitalist economy, where bank financing makes entrepreneurs' choices as to the level and composition of output autonomous, while workers' real consumption is dependent on those choices. The immense diversion of resources from the production of "liquid" consumer goods to war production produced precisely the same effect as did – in ordinary times, and in a capitalist and genuinely monetary economy – the increased investment in fixed capital.

Here, the authentic origin of macroeconomics should be recognised. It is from here that we can understand the monetary theories of production and cycle by Robertson in 1926, Kalecki in the early 1930s, and the same in Keynes in between, in his *Treatise on Money*. In this book, savings and investments are independent: consumers decide how to allocate their money income between consumption demand and monetary savings, while entrepreneurs fix the composition of production in the form of consumer goods or capital goods according to their own criteria.

The New Deal logically follows from this new theoretical landscape. It was a strategy of direct job creation by the government that immediately steered output composition, and in this sense it did something irreducible to "Keynesian" economics. Income maintenance came via the provision of work. As Minsky commented, the state had a responsibility to manage markets and create institutions favouring decent wage jobs: what are needed are innovative production and employment schemes that exist outside the market and private enterprise setting. It is a framework that, today, can be adapted to an economy in transition to ecological-friendly production and to progressively more qualified jobs. Minsky called it a "by right program of public employment in useful projects" (Minsky, 1981, p. 58). Once again, the issue of the level of production goes hand in hand with that of its composition.

Our third reference is, maybe, even more unusual. At the end of the 1960s and in the early 1970s the workers' struggle, especially in the Italian case, imposed on politics an unparalleled season of reforms, exactly because of their disregard of short-term capitalist compatibilities. Just to make three examples: on workers' health, on women's bodies, on retirement age. The political command of the composition of production is a normal and permanent feature of capitalism in the 20th century and beyond. It can certainly take on quite different configurations. The armaments economy in the decades of bastard Keynesianism or debt consumption in the decades of privatised financial Keynesianism are two possible examples. Quite divergent, particularly strong configurations are the exceptional conditions during the two world wars, the New Deal of the 1930s, the class warfare of the late 1960s and 1970s, and later the Covid pandemic.

Our position is not too far from the one by Minsky in his 1975 book on John Maynard Keynes, where he declared that he wanted to return to the questions of 1933: "for whom should the game be set, what kind of production should be promoted" (Minsky, [1975] 2008, p. 164). Perhaps these questions are renewed at every historical juncture, when one phase of capitalism is dying and the next is still uncertain in its character. The contradiction opening up between the production of (authentically) social use-values and production for profit is clearly too great to be ignored. What is certain is that our times are not "Keynesian", and that they ask for a revolution coming from a conscious socially oriented transformation of supply.

We know that a proposition like this must be qualified. First, one must distinguish Keynes from "Keynesianism". It is well known the anecdote told by Joan Robinson according to which, in 1946, after having dined in Washington with some of his admirers, Keynes said to Austin Robinson that he was the only non-Keynesian at that dinner. Second, it cannot be forgotten that Keynes's propositions have always been context-sensitive, as the apocryphal phrase so often attributed to him makes plain: when the facts change, I change my mind. Third, it is impossible to pin down Keynes's theory to some particular economic policy. Our point is that the contention, so often reiterated by alternative economists, that in a major crisis, like the ones we are currently experiencing, a lack of effective demand is an important factor, proves too much. Just like Marx's reference to the limited consumption of the masses as the ultimate cause of the crises, such an argument ends up being always true, but precisely because of this it cannot satisfactorily account for any given historical conjuncture. We are convinced that the succession of crises of the last 15–20 years can be deciphered through a Keynesian angle, but only if it is strengthened by embedding it in a structural theoretical construction grounded on Marxian/Schumpeterian foundation.

In December 1971, Joan Robinson claimed that economic theory was experiencing a "second crisis". The "first" was that of the 1930s and had as its rationale the inability of the neoclassical mainstream of the time to account for "involuntary" mass unemployment as an equilibrium position for a free-market economy. The "second" crisis of the 1960s and 1970s, had to do with the failure of the new bastard Keynesian mainstream to answer the other question: what is employment for? The great global financial crisis that erupted in 2007–2008 could have been seen as the occasion of a "third" crisis. At its centre was still a flawed understanding of the endogenous association of money and financing with the level and composition of production.

The first crisis was the background not only to the Keynesian Revolution but also to the Rooseveltian New Deal, which we have seen to be at the base of Kregel's train of thought. The bastard Keynesians degraded the intellectual and political legacy of the years of high theory and forgot Keynes's conservative vision of the socialisation of investment, of which Hyman P. Minsky suggested a radicalisation a few years after Joan Robinson's Lecture. The second crisis had to do exactly with the kind of composition of production that materialised in the so-called golden age of capitalism, which she interpreted (in tune with Kalecki) as a form of military Keynesianism driven by arms spending and (in tune with Baran and Sweezy's *Monopoly Capital*) social and economic waste. Likewise, a similar condemnation of the 1945–1975

Keynesian era is explicit in the last two chapters of Minsky's (1975) *John Maynard Keynes*, partially written in Cambridge (UK) in the early 1970s. The high-profit–high-investment economy of *Les Trente Glorieuses* is, quite literally, accused by Minsky of leading to perpetual deterioration of both the natural and social environment. Nothing like the image of Keynesianism that too often we read in the writings of heterodox, and even radical, economists as it was a kind of *la vie en rose*.

The second crisis also coincides with the class war about which Adam Tooze speaks of, and the acceleration of growth underlying the Anthropocene crisis is from the same period. It is an essential part of our argument that there is an internal connection between the social crisis of the 1960s and 1970s and the ecological crisis we are now finally becoming aware of. The heart of the 1960s and 1970s struggles was not (only) wages, but (above all) the conditions of work effort in the capitalist labour process. The transformation of labour power into living labour passes through the "consumption" of workers as living human bearers of labour capacity. Workers refused to accept to be "used up" by capital and could intervene on the modalities of the extraction of labour much more than in the past. The motto was: "health is not for sale". Struggles went far beyond the factory gates, and social demands extended far beyond their pay: from how to work and for whom, to what kind of production and where to locate it, to how much should be produced and sold on the market.

In fact, we are convinced that one key reason for the crisis of Keynesianism was precisely this social conflict (and sometimes antagonism) that was global in nature, albeit with different characteristics and radicalisations. There was an economist who understood this very well: Michał Kalecki. Not, however, the Kalecki who wrote with Kowalik at the end of the 1960s. Kalecki and Kowalik were convinced that a "crucial reform" of capitalism was underway that would tolerate higher wages and include Western workers as a subordinate subject of the capitalist social order (revolutionary subjects were to be sought in the Third World or in the Western student movement). Very different was Kalecki's 1943 paper "*Political Aspects of Full Employment*". In that article, the Polish economist limpidly grasped that the refusal of the capitalist class to accept permanent full employment policies was not only because, in general, the business class does not like public intervention in employment. Two other specific reasons are more relevant. First, they do not want to lose control of the "direction" of expenditure that drives production: hence, they dislike public investment or support for workers' consumption. Second, captains of industry and company executives know very well that their social and economic power is based on maintaining "discipline" in the workplace. Discretionary economic policies are only accepted if they do not endanger the direct and indirect control of both the level and composition of production by the ruling classes.

This control was at risk in the "class warfare" of the 1960s and 1970s recalled by Tooze.

The myth of central bank independence and the emergence of money manager capitalism as a new stage of capitalism served the purpose of eroding workers' power in production and subjugating households to finance, even before cutting wages or changing distribution. This cannot be mistaken for a return to laisser faire policies, as the label "neoliberalism" may (erroneously) lead one to suspect. We have already mentioned privatised Keynesianism, in its dimension of a very active political management of effective demand, and thus as a way of determining both the level and composition of production. The great global financial crisis indicated the final internal collapse of the mode of regulation and the mechanism that governed the accumulation of capital, as they had been constituted in the 1970s and 1980s. Immediately after, the Covid crisis was a particularly dramatic instance of a loss of control of the organic material exchange between external nature and human intervention.

These two recent crises – the global financial and the health ones – are not imputable to a market once again emancipated from political power. A serious inquiry about the plural forms of the Anglo-Saxon neoclassical mainstream would show that "natural" equilibrium is not so natural, after all, even in theory. It is rather more and more imagined as a biopolitical construction, of the kind Mirowski (2013) has described. Moreover, ordoliberalism supports a top-down planning from strong states in order to win capitalist competition, as Bonefeld (2019) has forcefully argued. In fact, we doubt that "free market" capitalism ever existed. What is for sure is that political command over capitalist dynamics, including state intervention in the innovation process, has never disappeared (Mazzucato, 2013). It has only changed form.

CONCLUSION

In 1973 Suzanne de Brunhoff, Michel Beaud, and Claude Servolin intervened in *Le Monde* in the debate opened by Joan Robinson on the "second" crisis of economic theory. Their contention was that, instead of a crisis of economic theory, one should rather speak of a political crisis of economists. At the time they intended to emphasise that an increasing number of economists were refusing to constrain their reasoning within the compatibilities dictated by the given social order, without questioning the more fundamental nature of the capital order.

Today, we witness an opposite "political crisis" of the economists: the inability to see how the health emergencies and climate change, on the one hand, and the economic and social crisis, on the other, are so inextricably entangled to become inseparable. They cannot be tackled without eradicating capitalist despotism in the labour process (there is no health for all, if it does not include the working conditions) and without opposing capitalist command over the composition of production (there is no health for all, without a different quality of production aimed at satisfying basic social needs). As long as economists imagine that their function is to be "economist-courtiers" providing guidance to save capitalism, this political crisis has no end in sight: their failure will remain without possible redemption, because the very nature of this crisis, whose origin is rooted in capitalist social relationships, is ignored.

What is needed – not just as a temporary response, but as an intrinsic structural property of a truly sustainable new normal – is a radical reorientation of *both* production *and* consumption. The paradox, however, is that the Covid pandemic has revealed that the challenge facing society is more demanding than the paradigm of the socialisation of investments acknowledges. One crisis after the other makes increasingly clear, for us, that the failure of the capitalist mode of production and distribution to provide health and wealth equitably has to be remedied, and it cannot be just proposing a correction to the system. We do not know the recipes for the kitchen of the future, of course, but unless we openly acknowledge that the failure of the capitalist and market economy is the horizon of our action, we will never be able to cope with it. That is why we think that the notion of a socialisation of investment must be radicalised into the idea of an "economy of social production".

Economy of social production is a limit-concept, which insists that the economy should be oriented to the production of immediately socialised use-values by immediately socialised workers. It is not a state but a process that must span an entire historical phase. The concrete ways in which social provisioning is provided – and by which the health emergency and climate change itself are addressed – are the first fundamental steps: "reforms" if you like. A non-exhaustive list includes: a large-scale propulsion of public investment in social "goods", such as health and education; conversion to sustainable ecological production; the establishment of "decent" wages; quality full employment, driven by public spending; an economy more attentive to the "care" of external and human nature, beginning with an uncompromising safeguarding of health within labour processes of any kind; a substantial reduction in working hours, including a lowering of the retirement age.

An epochal transition such as the one just mentioned requires as a stringent condition to be accompanied, in parallel, by the construction of a social protagonism of the working-class movement and of potentially anticapitalist subjectivities. A social "revolution" of this magnitude – which, on the one hand, leads to an economy that interrupts the degradation of nature and improves the health of populations, and which, on the other hand, realises full employment of quality-jobs – can only be gradual. But the "reforms" consistent with such a radical transformation must be energetic and rapid and cannot be separated from progressive social conflicts and deliberative processes that go back from post-democracy to democracy.

It is important that the stress on (even radical) reforms (like these) does not drive us into reformist illusions. Such a "proactive" framework would only be temporarily compatible with capitalism. The same was true for full employment according to the Kalecki of 1943. But it would create a new field of tension in which to intervene more vigorously.

In our time, the critique of political economy must turn into a critique of economic policy. Calling for an economy of social production driven by a social and democratic conflict from below is, of course, strictly speaking, utopian. It is, in fact, a matter of setting oneself a social and political project. Without the definition of a project, no practical intervention, no reform, no economic policy can be subject to a sensible appraisal. One would not know whether one is getting closer to or further away from one's own goal. Of course, stating the terms of a problem is not solving it, nor there can be any illusion of an easy, abrupt, revolutionary way out: but the repeated failures of piecemeal reformism are before our eyes. Against an approach imprisoned within a "sense of realism", it is important to recall the power of the "sense of possibility":

> if there is a sense of reality, and no one will doubt that it has its justification for existing, then there must also be something we can call a sense of possibility. Whoever has it does not say, for instance: Here this or that has happened, will happen, must happen; but he invents: Here this or that might, could, or ought to happen. If he is told that something is the way it is, he will think: Well, it could probably just as well be otherwise. So the sense of possibility could be defined outright as the ability to conceive of everything there might be just as well, and to attach no more importance to what is than to what is not. [...] Such fools are also called idealists by those who wish to praise them. But all this clearly applies only to their weak subspecies, those who cannot comprehend reality or who, in their melancholic condition, avoid it. These are people in whom the lack of a sense of reality is a real deficiency. But the possible includes not only the fantasies of people with weak nerves but also the as yet unawakened intentions of God. A possible experience or truth is not the same as an actual experience or truth minus its "reality value" but has – according to its partisans, at least – something quite divine about it, a fire, a soaring, a readiness to build and a conscious utopianism that does not shrink from reality but sees it as a project, something yet to be invented. After all, the earth is not that old, and was apparently never so ready as now to give birth to its full potential. (Robert Musil, *The Man without Qualities*)[6]

NOTES

1. Subsequently Draghi became the Italian prime minister and, in this role, was, to say the least, disappointing. His appointment was a prime example of what Colin Crouch calls "post-democracy". As if he had forgotten the parallel with wars, he presided over the transition to much-weakened forms of lockdown and early

reopening of business. Meanwhile, for a while, the death toll in Italy rose faster than in other European countries.

2.   A reference to Marx's reflection on nature (starting with Alfred Schmidt's seminal contribution in the 1960s) as well as to the current of Marxian ecological materialism is not possible here. See, at least, Foster (2016) and Cassegärd (2021).

3.   Its content had been anticipated in some videos, such as the IDEAS online streaming in May of that year, *Why Stimulus Cannot Solve the Pandemic Depression*, available on YouTube: https://www.youtube.com/live/rneE9ui9F1c ?feature=share.

4.   Michell J. (2022), *Global Justice – Shifting the Scale of Consumption*. Brave New Europe, 3 August [downloadable here: https:// braveneweurope .com/ jo -michell-global-justice-shifting-the-scale-of-consumption].

5.   Garbellini N. (2022), *Italy's Recovery Plan Shows Why Public Spending Isn't Always "Left-Wing"*. Jacobine, 25 January [downloadable here: https://jacobin .com/2022/01/italys-recovery-plan-shows-why-public-spending-isnt-always-left -wing].

6.   https:// creativecitieseu .files .wordpress .com/ 2015/ 04/ 20040206 -musil -the -man -without-qualities.pdf.

REFERENCES

Bellofiore R. and Halevi J. (2012). Deconstructing Labor: A Marxian–Kaleckian Perspective on What is "New" in Contemporary Capitalism and Economic Policies. In C. Gnos, L.-P. Rochon, D. Tropeano (Eds). *Employment, Growth and Development: A Post-Keynesian Approach* (pp. 11–27). Edward Elgar Publishing, Cheltenham, UK and Northampton, MA, USA.

Bellofiore R. and Halevi J. (2006). Tendenze del capitalism contemporaneo, destrutturazione del lavoro e limiti del "keynesismo". Per una critica della politica economica. In S. Cesaratto and R. Realfonzo (Eds). *Rive Gauche. La critica della politica economica e le coalizioni progressiste in Italia* (pp. 53–80). Manifestolibri, Roma.

Bonefeld W. (2019). Ordoliberalism, European Monetary Union and State Power. *Critical Sociology*, 45 (7), 995–1010.

Cassegärd C. (2021). *Toward a Critical Theory of Nature: Capital, Ecology, and Dialectics*. Bloomsbury, London.

Crouch C. (2009). Privatised Keynesianism: An Unacknowledged Policy Regime. *British Journal of Politics and International Relations*, 11 (3), 382–399.

Draghi M. (2020). Draghi: We Face a War against Coronavirus and Must Mobilise Accordingly. *Financial Times*, 25 March.

Foster B. (2016). Marxism in the Anthropocene: Dialectical Rifts on the Left. *International Critical Thought*, 6 (3), 393–421.

Garbellini N. (2022). *Italy's Recovery Plan Shows Why Public Spending Isn't Always "Left-Wing"*. Jacobine, 25 January [downloadable here: https://jacobin.com/2022/ 01/italys-recovery-plan-shows-why-public-spending-isnt-always-left-wing].

Kregel J. (2020). *Alternative Macro Policy Response for a Pandemic Recession*. Policy Note n. 6, Levy Economics Institute.

Mazzucato M. (2013). *The Entrepreneurial State: Debunking Public versus Private Sector Myths*. Anthem Press, London.

Michell J. (2022). *Global Justice – Shifting the Scale of Consumption*. Brave New Europe, 3 August [downloadable here: https://braveneweurope.com/jo-michell-global-justice-shifting-the-scale-of-consumption].

Minsky H.P. (1981). The Breakdown of the 1960s Policy Synthesis. *Hyman P. Minsky Archive*, Paper 166 [downloadable here: https://digitalcommons.bard.edu/hm_archive/166].

Minsky H.P. ([1975] 2008). *John Maynard Keynes*. McGraw Hill, New York.

Mirowski P. (2013). *Never Let a Serious Crisis Go to Waste*. Verso, London.

Moren E. and Kern A.B. (1999). *Homeland Earth: A Manifesto for the New Millenium. Advances in Systems Theory, Complexity, and the Human Sciences*. Hampton Press, Cresskill.

O'Connor J. (1998). *Natural Causes: Essays in Ecological Marxism*. Guilford, New York.

Sweezy P. (1982). Why Stagnation? *Monthly Review*, 34 (2), 1–10.

Sweezy P. (1942). *The Theory of Capitalist Development: Principles of Marxian Political Economy*. Dennis Dobson Limited, London.

Tooze A. (2022). Welcome to the World of the Polycrisis. *Financial Times*, 22 October.

Tooze A. (2021). *Shutdown: How Covid Shook the World's Economy*. Penguin Random House, London and New York.

Wallace R. (2020). *Dead Epidemiologists: On the Origins of Covid-19*. Monthly Review Press, New York.

Wallace R., Liebman A., Chaves L.F., Wallace R. (2020). Covid-19 and the Circuits of Capital. *Monthly Review*, 72 (1), 1–15.

Zuboff S. (2019). *The Age of Surveillance Capitalism: The Fight for the Human Future at the New Frontier of Power*. Profile Books, London.

10. Lessons from COVID-19: UK experience

Malcolm Sawyer

INTRODUCTION

The focus of this chapter is on the experiences and policy responses in the UK to the COVID-19 pandemic, covering the period from late January 2020 when the first case of COVID-19 was reported in the UK to the end of 2022 by which time the major limitations on everyday life from COVID-19 had been removed.[1]

The policy responses of the UK government, particularly in the first months of the pandemic, were rather slow in implementation and decisions often delayed. Arbuthnott and Calvert (2022) detail the denials of the seriousness of the coronavirus and procrastinations in making decisions, and particularly the role of the Prime Minister Johnson during February and early March 2020. Although the World Health Organization (WHO) declared the coronavirus outbreak a public health emergency of international concern on 30th January 2020, it was only on 2nd March that the first emergency meeting of COBRA[2] chaired by Prime Minister Johnson happened. On 9th March 2020, an action plan was described as having four phases to tackling the virus: Contain, Delay, Research and Mitigate, and "the best thing we can all do is wash our hands for 20 seconds with soap and water" (Johnson, 2020a).

> The government's key advisory committee was given a dire prediction many weeks before the lockdown about the prospect of having to deal with mass casualties as a result of the government's strategy, and yet too little was done. It was a message repeated throughout February, and it became all the louder as deaths started to ramp up elsewhere in Europe in early March and neighbouring countries began taking drastic action. (Arbuthnott and Calvert, 2022, pp. 7–8)

On 12th March, moves to "delay its spread and thereby minimise the suffering" were announced (Johnson, 2020b) with advice to those with coronavirus symptoms to stay at home for at least seven days, seeking to delay the peak of infection by a few weeks. By 16th March (Johnson, 2020c), when cases were doubling every five or six days, the policy became that when anyone in a household had symptoms all of the household should stay at home for 14 days. On 18th March (Johnson, 2020d), it was announced that schools would be closed for most pupils (exceptions for children of key workers and 'vulnerable' children) until further notice. A general lockdown policy was announced on 23rd March, starting three days later, which included the public only being allowed to leave their homes for limited reasons, including food shopping, exercise once per day, medical need and travelling for work when absolutely necessary. All shops selling non-essential goods were told to close, gatherings of more than two people in public banned and events including weddings were cancelled.

From mid-May onward, the lockdown was gradually relaxed. There was then limited reopening of schools in June, and then fully reopening for all in September with the start of the new school year. Throughout the rest of the year, there were frequent changes in regulations and guidance, often operated on a localised basis. A second lockdown started on 5th November, applying to England, with the other nations adopting different timetables and varying in the precise requirements. This lockdown was scheduled to end 2nd December. After relaxations for December, though with some sudden reversals, a third lockdown started in early January 2021. The COVID-19 policy responses were often characterised by delays in taking action, particularly at the beginning, sudden reversals of policy with little notice and degrees of policy differences between the four nations of the UK.[3] The ups and downs with gradual easing of lockdowns and restrictions during 2021 are set out in Arbuthnott and Calvert (2022) chapter 16.

> This slow and gradualist approach was not inadvertent, nor did it reflect bureaucratic delay or disagreement between Ministers and their advisers. It was a deliberate policy – proposed by official scientific advisers and adopted by the Government of all of the nations of the United Kingdom. It is now clear that this was the wrong policy, and that it led to a higher initial death toll than would have resulted from a more emphatic early policy. (Health and Social Care, and Science and Technology Committees, 2021, p. 32)

> As a result, decisions on lockdowns and social distancing during the early weeks of the pandemic – and the advice that led to them – rank as one of the most important public health failures the United Kingdom has ever experienced. This happened despite the UK counting on some of the best expertise available anywhere in the world. (Health and Social Care, and Science and Technology Committees, 2021, pp. 32–3)

The UK should in a number of respects have been in a relatively strong position to confront the pandemic. The UK has a national health system funded by general taxation, generally but not universally free at the point of use, and hospitals that are publicly owned, so that issues of access to treatments and payments do not arise. But the health service had suffered from a decade of austerity and had operated at close to capacity with little room to deal with a large surge of seriously ill people.

The UK government had in place a National Risk Register based on the National Security Risk Assessment. There were other areas of lack of preparedness, for example personal protective equipment. The public accounts select committee concluded in its report in July 2020 that "there were fundamental flaws in the government's central procurement and local distribution of vital goods and equipment … Despite a pandemic being identified as the government's top non-malicious risk, it failed to stock up in advance" (Arbuthnott and Calvert, 2022, p. 107).

One of the early policy decisions (of the Secretary of State for Health and Social Care) which had tragic consequences related to the discharge of elderly patients from hospitals into residential care homes.

> The discharge of elderly people from NHS hospitals into care homes without having been tested at the beginning of the pandemic … had the unintended consequence of contributing to the spread of infection in care homes. The seeding of infections also happened as a result of staff entering care homes, and the failure to recognise this risk early is a symptom of the inadequate initial focus on social care. (Health and Social Care, and Science and Technology Committees, 2021, p. 94)

There were throughout various forces which slowed down responses to COVID-19 in terms of libertarian arguments and COVID-19 denial (often by those who were climate deniers), and arguments to 'protect the economy' based on the reduction in economic activity which comes from lockdowns were influential within government and more widely and often served to slow down policy responses. Rogers (2020, p. 4) argues that when Johnson became prime minister in July 2019, "a swathe of special advisors was put into Downing Street and all key ministries, from the Tufton Street cluster of neoliberal think tanks.[4] The pandemic has been a golden opportunity to accelerate the final stages of the neoliberal transition."

The health effects and the course of the COVID-19 pandemic are briefly summarised in Figure 10.1. The time path of the number of cases reported and the number of deaths attributed to COVID-19 are given. From Office for Health Improvement and Disparities covering England only (part replacement for Public Health England) between 21st March 2022 and 23rd September 2022 registered deaths, 1,255,852 'expected' deaths (based on death rates in previous years), which implies 127,233 'excess deaths' during the COVID-19 pandemic. Another indication of the effects of COVID-19 is that during that period 175,905 death certificates mentioned COVID-19. The waves of COVID-19 are clearly evident with peaks around April 2020 and December

2020. The lower levels during 2021 and 2022 are likely to reflect the success of the vaccination programmes which began in January 2021. The death rate ascribed to COVID-19 for G7 countries places the UK as third highest behind Italy and USA (Table 10.1).

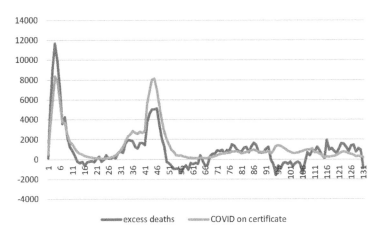

Note: Weekly basis, 27th March 2020 to 23th September 2022.
Source: Calculated from Office for Health Improvement and Disparities.

Figure 10.1   Number of COVID-19 cases in the UK

Table 10.1   Selected international comparisons (G7)

Country	Infection per 100 000	Deaths from COVID-19	Deaths per 100 000
UK	35 250	194 704	287
Canada	11 545	463 89	123
France	55 297	153 688	236
Germany	43 206	154 535	186
Italy	39 640	179 436	301
Japan	18 019	47 139	37
USA	29 146	106 0430	320

Note: Figures to 10th November 2022.
Source: Calculated from Worlddata.info.

The direct impact on economic activity is recorded in the figures for Gross Domestic Product (GDP). There was a sharp decline of 21 per cent in 2020Q2, with recovery of 16.6 per cent in 2020Q3, and thereafter GDP fluctuated, though with a sharp rise of 6.5 per cent in 2021Q2. But by 2022Q4 GDP was nearly 1 per cent lower than in 2019Q4. The UK was the only one of the G7 countries to have GDP lower in 2022Q4 as compared with 2019Q4. Brexit had occurred in February 2020, and much of the decline in GDP may be attributable to Brexit and its impacts on trade.

The employment rate fell from 76.6 per cent in January 2020 down to 74.6 per cent in December 2020, gradually rising thereafter to 75.6 per cent in November 2022. Overall, employment was around a quarter of a million lower at the end of 2022 as compared with the end of 2019. This was largely due to a decline in the workforce through a combination of the effects of Brexit (completed in early 2020), increase in long-term sickness often COVID-19 and 'discouraged worker' effects. Unemployment was just under 4 per cent during 2019 and rose during 2020 to reach over 5 per cent by end of year; during 2021 and 2022 the unemployment rate trended downwards to 3.5 per cent in July and recorded 3.7 per cent at the end of 2020: these were the lowest rates of unemployment since 1974. The effects on unemployment were rather muted, particularly by the furlough scheme.

MACROECONOMIC POLICY RESPONSES

The government budget for the financial year 2020/21, presented to Parliament on 11th March 2020, included some fiscal measures responding to the coronavirus included late on in the budget-making process. Further fiscal measures were announced on 20th March. The budget 2020 contained a fiscal loosening of £18 billion based on pre-COVID-19 assumptions, and then an additional £12 billion. In specific respect of the coronavirus, there was announcement that "whatever extra resources our NHS needs to cope with coronavirus – it will get" (Sunak, 2020), with a £5 billion emergency fund allocated immediately.

The range of fiscal measures made in response to the COVID-19 pandemic and its effects on incomes, economic activity and employment is given in Table 10.2 along with the scale of expenditure. The IMF (2022) estimate that policy measures (announced up to 27th September 2021) would involve for the UK additional spending and foregone revenues relating to health of £102 billion (4.8 per cent of GDP) and other additional spending and foregone revenues of £305 billion (16 per cent of GDP). Contingent liabilities including loans amounted to £352 billion.

The fiscal policy responses were notable for the scale of the resulting budget deficit, amongst the largest in the world. Fiscal policy rules with numerical targets for budget deficit and debt level were quickly placed in abeyance. These fiscal measures included various forms of income support, employment support measures (including the furlough scheme, job retention bonus and job support scheme), loans and grants to firms to support their continual operations and aids to cash flow.

Table 10.2   Fiscal measures related to COVID-19 through to 27 September 2021

	£billions	%GDP
Additional spending	100	
Funding for the National Health Service, including to expand the number of hospital beds, medical staff and equipment		
Forgone revenue	2	
Waiver of VAT and customs duties on critical medical imports		
Additional spending	102	14.4
	271	
Coronavirus Job Retention Scheme to subsidise furloughed employees' wages (initially for 3 months and extended several times until September 2021) and firms' social security contributions (until the 1st August 2020)		
Income support for the self-employed (initially for 3 months, but extended too until September 2021)		
Paid sick leave for self-isolating individuals and compensation for small firms needing to close for over 2 weeks, and support for low-income people in need to self-isolate		
Grant support for sectors impacted by local and national restrictions		
Support for low-income households by temporarily increasing Universal Credit and Working Tax Credit by £20 per week in 2020–21. The increase to Universal Credit was extended by a further 6 months from April 2021 and a one-off payment of £500 was provided to eligible Working Tax Credit claimants in April 2021		
Rent support by increasing the Local Housing Allowance		
International support, with £150 mn made available to the IMF's Catastrophe Containment and Relief Trust and £2.2 bn loan to the IMF Poverty Reduction and Growth Trust to help low-income countries		
Government support for charities		
Cover the cost of 25 hours' work a week at the National Minimum Wage for 6 months for hired unemployed up to 24 years old		
Boost of Active Labour Market Policies, including 250,000 subsidised jobs for young people		
Entitle every diner to a 50% discount of up to £10 in August		

Post Keynesian economics

	£billions	%GDP
Public sector and social housing decarbonisation and Green Homes Grant		
Support for low-income people in need to self-isolate		
Funding of 40,000 traineeships and doubling the number of work coaches to 27,000		
Additional transfers to devolved administrations	305	16
Forgone revenue	34	
Property tax (business rate) holiday for firms in affected sectors		
Temporary cut on stamp duty land tax until June 2021		
VAT reduced at 5% for hospitality, accommodation and attractions until the end of September 2021, at 12.5% until March 2022, after which it will return to normal		
Accelerated spending	5	
Bring forward public infrastructure spending to FY2020/21		
Deferred revenue	7.5	
Deferral of VAT for the second quarter of 2020 until June 2021		
Deferral of income tax (self-assessment) of the self-employed until the end of January 2021		
Extension to reduced VAT rate for hospitality, accommodation and attractions (5% to 30th September 2021 then 12.5% to 31st March 2022)		
Extension of the window for starting deferred payments through the VAT New Payment Scheme by up to 3 months		
Stamp Duty Land Tax: maintain nil-rate band at £500k until 30th June 2021, £250k until 30th September 2021		
Fuel Duty: one year freeze in 2021–22. Alcohol Duty: one year freeze in 2021–22		
Contingent liabilities	12.5	0.6
The government has put in place a £1 bn program to support firms driving innovation and development through grants and loans	1.3	

	£billions	%GDP
The government has provided a £30 mn convertible loan to the steel company, Celsa		
The Coronavirus Business Interruption Loan Scheme (CBILS) launched with the British Business Bank supports SMEs with access to loans of up to £5 mn and for up to 6 years. The government provides lenders with a guarantee of 80% on each loan and covers the first 12 months of interest payments and any lender-levied fees	352	16.7
The Coronavirus Large Business Interruption Loan Scheme (CLBILS) provides a government guarantee of 80% to enable banks to make loans of up to 25% of companies' turnover, or up to £200 mn to firms with an annual turnover above £45 mn		
Under the COVID-19 Corporate Financing Facility (CCFF), the Bank of England will buy short-term debt from larger companies		
The Bounce Back Loan Scheme (BBLS) will help SMEs to borrow between £2K and £50K for up to 6 years, with the government guaranteeing 100% of the loan and SMEs not paying any fees or interest in the first 12 months. The combined cost of the CBILS, CLBILS, CCFF and BBLS was £112 bn as of their expiration in end-March 2021		
In March 2021, a new government-backed loan scheme – the Recovery Loan Scheme (RLS) – was announced. The RLS is to help businesses of any size access loans and other kinds of finance, with up to £10 mn per business. The government guarantees 80% of the financing. The scheme is open until 31st December 2021, subject to review, and is estimated to cost £12 bn		
Trade Credit Insurance for business-to-business transactions will receive up to £10 bn of government guarantees through the Trade Credit Reinsurance scheme. The scheme is for 9 months		

Source: IMF (2022).

Post Keynesian economics

Table 10.3   Sectoral balances % GDP

	Household	Corporate	Public	Rest of world
2020Q1	0.5	1.3	-4.1	2.7
2020Q2	14.9	6.6	-24.8	1.6
2020Q3	5.3	6.3	-13.9	1.7
2020Q4	5.2	0.1	-10.6	4.9
2021Q1	9.3	1.8	-13.4	2.1
2021Q2	3.6	3.0	-9.2	2.4
2021Q3	1.8	1.3	-7.6	4.3
2021Q4	0.1	1.2	-4.3	3.2
2022Q1	-0.2	-0.3	-3.8	4.3
2022Q2	-1.3	1.6	-4.6	4.4
2022Q3	-1.7	1.5	-4.3	4.6
2022Q4	-2.4	1.4	-3.8	4.9

Source: Office for Budget Responsibility: statistics.

Monetary policy was loosened through cuts in the bank rate by the Bank of England, which was lowered from 0.75 per cent to 0.25 per cent, and then to 0.1 per cent on 23rd March 2020 where it remained until December 2021 when it rose to 0.25 per cent, beginning its climb through 2022 to 3.5 per cent by the end of 2022. The Bank of England engaged in further Quantitative Easing (QE) on 19th March, increasing its holdings of UK government bonds and sterling nonfinancial investment-grade corporate bonds by £200 billion to a total of £645 billion, followed by an additional £100 billion in June 2020.

Table 10.3 reports the sectoral balances on a quarterly basis. The public sector recorded a balance of nearly -25 per cent of GDP in 2020Q2, reflecting the sharp increase in expenditure and the loss of tax revenue resulting from lockdown. High borrowing continued through 2020 into early 2021, then returned to more usual levels.

Total government spending expanded from 39.1 per cent (of GDP) during 2019–20 to 51.6 per cent in 2020–21 and then 44.5 per cent in 2021–22. Public sector net debt as ratio of GDP rose from 82.8 per cent at the end of FY 2019–20 to 93.9 per cent at the end of 2020–21, with a further rise to 95.5 per cent at the end of 2021–22.

There was a vigorous fiscal policy response with sharp (and appropriate) rises in budget deficit and there were the usual voices raised against budget deficits. Much concern has been expressed over the higher debt ratio and a push to constrain future fiscal policy to reduce the ratio. However, the high inflation of 2022/23 has done much of that work – if nominal GDP were to be, say 15 per cent higher at the end of 2023 than the beginning of 2022 the debt ratio would be reduced by circa 13 per cent. Monetary policy adopted an historically low policy rate of interest and a substantial increase in QE. The QE policy meant a failure to 'lock in' low borrowing costs as interest (at bank rate) paid on bank reserves which increased as result of QE (at time of writing this means payment to banks of the order of £30 billion a year).

NEOLIBERALISM AND THE PRIVATE/PUBLIC INTERFACE

There were four particular interfaces between the public sector and the private sector which received much attention. One was the development of policies on 'test and trace' as a means to limiting the spread of COVID-19, and the relative roles of public provision and private provision. Another was the acquisition of PPE. The third was contracts and appointments. And the final one was the development and then roll-out of effective vaccines. I now consider these in turn.

Test and Trace

The importance of testing for coronavirus was stressed early on by the World Health Organization. On 20th May 2020, Prime Minister Johnson told the House of Commons that "We will have a test, track & trace operation that will be world-beating, and yes, it will be in place by 1 June," and as was to often happen the outcomes on test and trace were far below the claims. The test-and-trace systems have been a major source of difficulties in counteracting the coronavirus, as Rogers (2020, p. 3), puts it "the immediate crisis is being made far worse by an appallingly incompetent national test-and-trace system that is rapidly coming apart at the seams." Rogers views "the combining of test and trace largely contracted out to private companies with Public Health England which had been starved of funds over the previous decade of austerity as developing this neoliberal agenda." The key difficulties can be identified as arising from "the chaotic and hugely expensive privatisation of the whole process instead of properly funded use of local experts" (Rogers, 2020).

Taylor (2020), Conn and Geoghegan (2020), Calver and Pogrund (2020) and Sikka (2021), amongst others, document cases of inexperienced firms contracted for test and trace, and often the close links of companies with Conservative politicians.

The Department of Health and Social Care (2020) indicate a range of failures of NHS Test and Trace. These include a failure to:

> meet a target to provide results within 24 hours for tests carried out in the community. 93 per cent of results provided within 24 hours in June falling to low of 14 % in

mid-October. It did not plan for a sharp rise in testing demand in early autumn when schools and universities reopened. (p. 10)

There was much further evidence of inefficiencies. For example, "there has been no shortage of central tracers and, at times, parts of the national tracing service have been barely used" (Department of Health and Social Care, 2020, p. 12), and reports that in mid-June there were utilisation rates of Specialist health professionals of 4 per cent and call handlers 1 per cent. Further, the Scientific Advisory Group on Emergencies (SAGE)[5] provided "advice on what a testing and tracing system needs to achieve in order to be effective; to date NHST&T has not achieved these standards" (Department of Health and Social Care, 2020, p. 13). SAGE's advice was that an effective test and trace system needed to reach 80 per cent of close contacts, whereas between 28th May and 4th November 66 per cent of close contacts were reached. "The high reported levels of non-compliance with self-isolation represent a key risk to NHS Test and Trace's success; national and local government have been trying to increase public engagement" (Department of Health and Social Care, 2020, p. 13).

The Public Accounts Committee (2021) note that the NHS Test and Trace is one of the most expensive health programmes with an allocation of £37 billion over two years, equivalent to one-fifth of the 2020–21 NHS England budget. In 2020–21, NHS Test and Trace had paid £3.1 billion for laboratory capacity to process PCR tests and £911 million for contact tracing, though only a minority of the laboratory and contact centre capacity that had been paid for was used. There was criticism of overreliance on consultants, paid an average £1,100 a day.

Personal Protective Equipment

Arbuthnott and Calvert (2022, p. b7) report that hundreds of witnesses including scientists, academics, paramedics, emergency planners and public officials

> told us that, contrary to the official line, Britain was not in a state of readiness for the pandemic. Emergency stockpiles of personal protective equipment (PPE) had severely dwindled and were out of date because they had become a low priority in the years of austerity cuts. The training to prepare key workers for a pandemic had been put on hold for two years while contingency planning was diverted to deal with a possible no-deal Brexit.

Throughout the first months of the coronavirus crisis, there was a great shortage of personal protective equipment (PPE), reflecting the lack of preparedness for a pandemic, and "in the six years before the COVID-19 pandemic, the commitment to austerity, ran down the emergency PPE stockpile by 40%"

(Sikka, 2021). "Many companies with proven track records offered to make or obtain PPE, but most were rejected or ignored by Public Health England (PHE) and the Government. Instead, rules for emergency procurement were used to commission many other companies that had no experience and little or no trading history" (Colegrave, 2020). Colegrave (2020) reports the purchase of faulty antibody tests from China (£129 million), and the ordering of 10 million tests from Roche and Abbott with little evidence of effectiveness (£919 million).[6]

The National Audit Office (2023) found "a lack of adequate governance, oversight and control at UKHSA." "A lack of sufficient, appropriate audit evidence and significant shortcomings in financial control and government meant he [the head of the NAO] was unable to provide an audit opinion on the accounts of the UK Health Security Agency (UKHSA)."

The DHSC (Department of Health and Social Care) estimates that in 2021–22 there was a £6 billion reduction in the value of items procured relating to the pandemic, with a £2.5 billion write-down on items costing £11.2 billion no longer expected to be used or for which the market price is now lower than the price paid, and a write-down of £3.5 billion on PPE, vaccines and medication which the DHSC committed to purchase but no longer expected to use. There had been an £8.9 billion write-down in the 2020–21 accounts. The DHSC estimated "that ongoing storage and disposal costs for its excess and unusable PPE will be £319 million"; and at the end of March 2022 estimated monthly spending on storing PPE was £24 million.

Durrant et al. (2021, p. 16) report that

> the National Audit Office found that business allocated to the "high-priority line" for PPE contracts were 10 times more likely to get a contract than others. Businesses were allocated to this group based on leads from ministers and officials. The NAO found that the reasons for particular awards were often not documented, leaving the government open to charges of cronyism.

Durrant et al. (2021, p. 3) report that of the £17.3 billion spent on such contracts, only 1 per cent was awarded through competitive tendering. Around 38 per cent was awarded through existing framework agreements which are designed to allow governments to procure goods and services quickly when needed. The remaining 61 per cent was awarded directly to contractors without any competition.

Vaccination Roll-Out

The Public Accounts Committee (2022a) described the vaccine programme in England as "highly successful."[7] COVID-19 vaccines became available at the end of 2020, and vaccination became central to the government's pandemic response. UKHSA "estimated that by the end of September 2021, vaccinations may have averted as many as 128,000 deaths and 262,000 hospitalisations by September 2021" (National Audit Office, 2022a).

NHS England and NHS Improvement led on operational delivery of vaccinations, working with Public Health England and its successor body (UKHSA) on vaccine supply, storage and distribution within England. Local healthcare providers including NHS hospitals, GPs and community pharmacies administered vaccines on their own premises and in dedicated vaccination centres. The National Audit Office (2022a, p. 5) report that the general uptake of COVID-19 vaccination had reached 90 per cent of adults (based on two doses by the end of May 2022). But it was much lower in some groups, such as 38 per cent of 12–15 year olds and 55 per cent of 16-and 17-year-olds, and 58 per cent of pregnant women (as of February 2022). And "compared with people of White British origin, people of Black, Black British and Pakistani origins were less than half as likely to have had their boosters" (National Audit Office, 2022a, p. 5).

The Public Accounts Committee (2022a) attributed the success to two factors. "First, the Taskforce secured early access to the vaccines the UK needed, by signing contracts before regulatory approval. Second, NHS England ensured a range of different routes for people to get vaccinated, while clearly prioritising those most at risk" (Public Accounts Committee, 2022a).

Contracts and Appointments

The VIP lane was operated for recommendations by MPs, peers and other politically connected people. Conn and Evans (2023) report that companies referred by the route had a ten times greater success rate for being awarded contracts than those without VIP treatment (based on the National Audit Office Report).

UKHSA (2022) provided (following a Freedom of Information request) a list of suppliers who had been referred by ministers or senior officials to the VIP testing route. The Good Law Project calculated that £5 billion worth of contracts were introduced by six Conservative politicians. Only Conservative Party peers, MPs and donors appear to be named as referrers with no politician from another political party on the list.

"The *New York Times* analysed a large part of expenditure on PPE involving around 1,200 central government contracts that have been made public, together worth nearly $22 billion. Of that, about $11 billion went to companies either run by friends and associates of politicians in the Conservative Party, or with no prior experience or a history of controversy. Meanwhile, smaller firms without political clout got nowhere." They report that about $5 billion went to politically connected companies (former ministers and government advisers on staff, donations to the Conservative Party); around \$6 billion went to companies without prior experience in supplying medical PPE – including fashion designers, pest controllers and jewellers winning contracts. Over \$5 billion went to "companies with histories of controversy, from tax evasion and fraud to corruption and human right abuses" (Bradley et al., 2020).

Conn and Evans (2023) report that Andrew Feldman, former Conservative Party chairman and advisor to the government during the pandemic, helped SG Recruitment to secure PPE contracts worth £50 million after introduction by Tory peer Lord Chadlington. Chadlington had financial interest in SG Recruitment as director and shareholder of its parent company Sumner Group Holdings which is registered in Jersey.

Conn (2023) reported that PPE Medpro, a company closely linked with Conservative peer Michelle Mone, had been accused by the UK government of supplying defective gowns that could have compromised the safety of patients had they been used in the NHS. The DHSC paid PPE Medpro £122 million for 25 million sterile surgical gowns under a contract awarded in June 2020 after Mone approached ministers offering to supply PPE. DHSC alleged the gowns were rejected because they were not sterile, their technical labelling was invalid and improper, and they cannot be used within the NHS for any purpose.

The DHSC awarded contracts worth almost £777 million to Randox Laboratories for COVID-19 testing services and goods. "However, the Department's poor record-keeping means that we cannot be sure that all these contracts were awarded properly. Even allowing for the exceptional circumstances at the start of the pandemic, basic civil service practices to document contract decision making were not followed" (Public Accounts Committee, 2022b, p. 3).

Investigation by the Good Law Project (2023) uncovered profits of £17 million made by Zoe Ley after she brokered a £250 million PPE deal for Worldlink Resources, a firm which landed two contracts via the unlawful 'VIP' lane. Worldlink Resources won their PPE contracts after being referred onto the VIP lane by former Cabinet Minister Lord Agnew. The firm won two contracts: a £178 million deal to supply goggles awarded in June 2020 and a £80 million contract, awarded in May 2020, to supply surgical gowns. Zoe Ley partnered with former Conservative Party MP Brooks Newmark to lobby Matt Hancock (the Secretary of State for Health and Social Care) and other ministers on behalf of Worldlink Resources.

Transparency International (2023) in their report on the Corruption Perception Index (CPI) for 2022 find a decline from 78 in 2021 to 73 in 2022 (on a scale of 0 to 100). Alongside attacks on democratic institutions and a reduction of opportunities for parliamentary scrutiny, there is reference to the fact that:

> Individuals with political connections were appointed to senior public-sector roles during the COVID-19 pandemic. ... A fifth of UK COVID-19 contracts raised red flags warranting further investigation. The systematic bias in the awarding of PPE contracts to those with political connections, government's "VIP lane." This cross-over of vested interests and political power puts money at risk and impairs the government's response to the economic crisis.

IMPLEMENTATION AND EFFECTIVENESS OF POLICIES

There were a number of substantial initiatives to provide support to employment, incomes and business during the COVID-19 pandemic. In this section there is a brief review of their operations.

Furlough

The Coronavirus Job Retention Scheme (CJRS), 'furlough scheme,' paid 80 per cent of wages for those unable to work through COVID-19 limitations, which was undertaken for the first time in the UK, with no limit on the amount of funding available for the scheme, and a willingness to support as many jobs as necessary. The CJRS was initially intended for three months, backdated to 1st March, refecting views of how long the pandemic would last, but then extended at various times to at least the end of March 2021 and variations in the contribution of government to wages of those furloughed. At its peak in early May 2020, the CJRS was supporting 8.9 million jobs, equivalent to over a quarter of the workforce, and overall costs of £96.9 billion (National Audit Office, 2022b).

There have been estimates (subject to considerable degree of uncertainty) that £4.6 billion in JRS payments may have been claimed fraudulently or paid out in error (National Audit Office, 2022b).

The National Audit Office (2022b) concluded that "the employment support schemes achieved their primary objectives of protecting jobs and businesses during the COVID-19 pandemic" (p. 6). There were inevitable flaws in schemes introduced at remarkable speed. Some changes were made to the schemes but more could have been done "in bearing down on deadweight loss and the cost of error and fraud" (p. 11).

"It established that furloughing was a successful response to the COVID-19 crisis, partly because it challenged the traditional UK crisis response of non-state intervention in the labour market. Furloughing prevented higher unemployment and enabled a swifter recovery." It argues "that key lessons from furloughing (including the direct support for job retention) should be used to devise new state policies aimed at promoting a more sustainable and equal economy" (Spencer et al., 2023, p. 81).

Loans

> The taxpayer is expected to lose billions of pounds from the increased risk of fraud and error in the Government's COVID-19 schemes. Government acted quickly to provide vital support to vulnerable businesses and individuals in response to the pandemic but in doing so significantly increased its exposure to fraud and error. This is in part due to the need to work at pace, but also because departments decided to relax or modify controls in place to prevent or detect fraud and error, and to provide support to people and businesses that government did not have a prior relationship with. Launching multiple large-scale support programmes, such as the Bounce Back Loan Scheme, markedly changed the risks BEIS must manage leaving it reliant on banks that it admits lack incentives given it is not their money on the line. BEIS estimates it could lose up to £27 billion through fraud or credit issues on the Bounce Back Loan Scheme. Local authorities are responsible for delivering several government support schemes, but their services are already under pressure and their capability to take on additional counter fraud activities varies considerably. Universal Credit fraud and error rose by £3.8 billion to an all-time high of £5.5 billion between April 2020 and March 2021. (Public Accounts Committee, 2022c, p. 3)

Around £47 billion of COVID-19 'bounce back loans' were handed out to smaller firms to support them during UK lockdowns. The Department of Business, Energy & Industrial Strategy "estimates it could lose £16 billion to £27 billion through fraud or credit risks on loans issued under the Bounce Back Loan Scheme" (Public Accounts Committee, 2022c, p. 10).

Eat Out to Help Out

'Eat Out to Help Out' in participating businesses offered 50 per cent discount Monday to Wednesday, up to £10 per person on food and non-alcoholic drinks consumed on premises, from 3rd to 31st August 2022. It has become apparent that concerns were raised on this scheme: "the publication of former health secretary Matt Hancock's WhatApp messages appears to confirm that there were concerns about the then chancellor's scheme in summer 2020 driving an increase in infections" (Ungoed-Thomas, 2023). Fetzer (2022) found that the scheme "had a significant causal impact on new cases, accelerating the subsequent second COVID-19 wave ... Areas with higher take-up saw both a notable increase in new COVID-19 infection clusters within a week of the scheme starting and a deceleration in infections within two weeks of the program ending" (p. 1200).

THE UNEQUAL IMPACTS OF COVID-19 AND POLICY REACTIONS

The ways in which COVID-19 impacted on different income groups and different ethnic groups generally reflected and exacerbated pre-existing ine-qualities. In this section there is a brief review.

Differential Incidence of COVID-19 and Ill-health

Judged by excess death calculations, males were more prone to die than female. Over the period of 21st March 2020 to 23rd September 2022, excess deaths as a proportion of deaths were 10.1 per cent for men and 8.3 per cent for women.

Education

The shut-down of schools and the use of online and home learning are likely to accentuate the socio-economic divide in educational attainment. It is reported that "pupils at private schools were twice as likely as state-school pupils to get daily online lessons during lockdown. Within the state sector, pupils from better-off homes were more likely to receive active support from schools and to have a better home learning environment" including more space, better access to broadband and computer facilities and availability of parents working from home to provide some assistance. And pupils from poorer areas and households have been more likely to miss days from school (Johnson et al., 2021, p. 3).

Cattan et al. (2021, p. 26) report

> a strong socio-economic gradient in the children who opted to return to school. We find that better-off children – who, on average, enjoyed better resources and spent more time on learning at wave 1 – were far more likely than their poorer classmates to return to school. Even more concerning, amongst children who chose to return, better-off students continued to spend more time on learning than their peers from poorer families.

Eyles et al. (2022, p. 4) calculate that "intergenerational income persistence is set to rise by somewhere between 4.8 percent and 11.9 percent due to the steep socioeconomic gradient in lost learning hours during the pandemic."

Employment and Earnings

Blundell et al. (2020) find that most people in the bottom tenth of the earning distribution (apart from key workers in health and social care) are in sectors that were forced to shut down, and 80 per cent are either in a shut-down sector or are unlikely to be able to do their job from home. This compares with only a quarter of the highest earning tenth. Young people and those of Pakistani, Bangladeshi or black ethnicity are also more affected than others in these respects.

Johnson et al. (2021, p. 3) report that the COVID-19 crisis "exacerbated inequalities between the high- and low-paid and between graduates and non-graduates ... Non-graduates were far more likely than graduates to work in a locked-down sector and far less likely to be able to work from home." In the third quarter of 2020, there had been a 7 per cent reduction in the number of graduates but a 17 per cent reduction in the number of nongraduates doing any hours of paid work in a given week. The authors also find that the COVID-19 crisis particularly hit the self-employed and others in insecure and nontraditional forms of employment. The Self-Employment Income Support Scheme did not cover around 2 million people who had some self-employment income, nor a substantial additional number with incorporated businesses which took income in some combination of salary and dividends. As they remark, this is an illustration of the difficulties which the state has in setting a safety net for those in nontraditional forms of employment.

Inequalities in Illness and Death

There have been significant disparities in illness and death rates. The largest disparity found by age – among those diagnosed with COVID-19 people 80 or older were 70 times more likely to die than those under 40. The death rates have been higher in males than females (Public Health England, 2020). The inequalities between areas of the country based on deprivation are illustrated in Table 10.4. The decile of areas with the highest index of multiple deprivation has death rates (adjusted for age) COVID-19 related of the order of two to two-and-a-half times the death rates of the least deprived area. The degree of inequality revealed for COVID-19 tends to be somewhat greater than death from all causes.

Public Health England (2020) report that the highest diagnoses and death rates are in mostly urban local authories. The death rates in London from COVID-19 being more than three times higher than in the south-west of England (with the lowest rate). The degree of inequality between regions is found to be much greater than the inequalities in all-cause mortality rates in earlier years. It has also been found that there is a particularly high increase

Table 10.4   Death rates by quintile of deprivation

Quintile of deprivation	Deaths	Expected deaths	Excess deaths	COVID-19 on death certificate
IMD1	288 379	257 628	30 751	40 925
IMD2	276 752	251 034	25 718	37 329
IMD3	282 972	257 536	25 436	34 663
IMD4	277 429	253 573	23 856	33 028
IMD5	257 553	236 073	21 480	29 960

Source: Calculated from Office for Health Improvement and Disparities, covers period 21st March 2020 to 23rd September 2022.

Table 10.5   Death rates by ethnic group

	Deaths	Expected deaths	Excess deaths	COVID-19 on death certificate	Excess deaths as proportion of deaths
Asian	50 071	38 860	11 208	11 872	0.224
Black	26 767	20 396	6 361	5 649	0.238
Mixed	6 139	4 796	1 339	931	0.218
Other	5 055	4 320	741	884	0.147
White	1 286 827	1 178 363	108 461	156 321	0.084
All	1 374 859	1 246 735	128 110	175 657	0.093

Source: Calculated from Office for Health Improvement and Disparities.

(over previous years) in all causes of death among those born outside the UK and Ireland, those in a range of caring occupations, those driving passengers in road vehicles, those working as security guards and related occupations, and those in care homes.

Ethnicity

Table 10.5 illustrates differences between ethnic groups. The white population recorded an excess death rate of 8.4 per cent over the period, whereas the black, Asian and mixed-race population recorded a rate of over 21 per cent.

The death rate has been higher in those in Black, Asian and minority ethnic (BAME) groups than in white ethnic groups. "These inequalities largely replicate existing inequalities in mortality rates in previous years, except for BAME groups, as mortality was previously higher in White ethnic groups" (Public Health England, 2020).

> Ethnic minority people experience a much higher risk of COVID-19 related death, a stark inequality that impacts on all ethnic minority groups, including white

minority groups such as Gypsies and Irish Travellers. ... Ethnic inequalities in relation to COVID-19 mirror longstanding ethnic inequalities in health. A large body of evidence has shown that these inequalities are driven by social and economic inequalities, many of which are the result of racial discrimination. (Nazroo and Becares, 2021, p. 1)

Curry et al. (2022) show that black Britons "are more exposed to losses that can be catastrophic in crisis periods" (p. 79).

Blacks are two to three times more likely than whites to have been diagnosed with COVID-19) ... and are over four times more likely to die .... Black Britons accounted for 11% of those hospitalized with COVID-19 but over 36% of those admitted to critical care, after adjustment for age, sex and location ... (Curry et al., 2022, p. 79).

The pandemic widened the gap in unemployment rates: "Black African and Black Caribbean men are 50% more likely than white British men to be found in shut-down sectors (Platt & Warwick, 2020). In November 2020, 11.6 % of Black Britons were unemployed more than double than the unemployment rate of whites" (Curry et al., 2022, p. 80).

CONCLUDING COMMENTS

In something of an understatement, "in the early days of a crisis, scientific advice may be necessarily uncertain: data may be unavailable, knowledge limited and time may be required for analysis to be conducted. In these circumstances it may be appropriate to act quickly, on a precautionary basis, rather than wait for more scientific certainty" (Health and Social Care, and Science and Technology Committees, 2021, p. 127). In the world of fundamental uncertainty, there is always uncertainty, and knowledge is always limited. People's behaviour in response to the experiences of COVID-19 and to policy initiatives addressing the pandemic is further subject to uncertainty. Post Keynesians and many others have long recognised that the world is subject to fundamental uncertainty (rather than risk). Paraphrasing Donald Rumsfeld, there are known knowns, known unknowns and the unknown unknowns. The COVID-19 pandemic had many elements of 'unknown unknowns' and also 'known unknowns.' The delays and false turns on policies could be attributed to the difficulties of decision-making and implementation in conditions of fundamental uncertainty. But a pandemic, rather like a financial crisis, comes in the category of a 'known unknown' – that is a pandemic can be envisaged and a high probability attached to its occurrence at some time for which policy preparations can be envisaged. In a number of areas, British policy preparations were grossly inadequate – a notable example being the lack of stock of PPE.

A strong package of fiscal measures was introduced, which cushioned the effects of lockdown on unemployment. Fiscal policy temporarily disregarded obsessions with reducing deficits and public debt and acted in a socially responsible manner. It was accompanied by a programme of QE and an interest rate close to zero, which has had the eventual effect of higher borrowing costs for government than could have been the case.

The programmes of public expenditure had to be introduced rapidly to address the scale of the pandemic but showed a lack of preparedness often leading to programmes being poorly designed and subject to fraud. The furlough scheme was generally successful and helped to minimise unemployment effects and may serve as the introduction of such policies to the UK which can be drawn on in future crises. Other programmes, notably the 'Eat Out to Help Out,' were failures.

The test-and-trace experiences illustrated the pitfalls of contracting out services which are in their nature public health programmes. The contractual arrangements for the purchase of equipment (particularly PPE) were riddled with inefficiencies and corruption. The vaccination programmes were generally deemed to be successful, which is a tribute to the leading roles of institutions of the National Health Service, and the success of public provision.

The impacts of COVID-19 often illuminated the prevailing inequalities and, in many cases, notably education, significantly worsened those inequalities. There were often considerable differences between ethnic groups in the experiences of COVID-19, generally to the disadvantage of minorities.

NOTES

1. In Sawyer (2021), I focused on the UK experience in the first 12 months (February 2020 to January 2021).
2. COBRA is the acronym Cabinet Office Briefing Room A, a series of rooms located in the Cabinet Office in 70 Whitehall and is the government's emergency situation committee.
3. See, for example, Calvert et al. (2020), McTague (2020), Sinclair and Reed (2020) on delays, missteps, etc. on the UK government's responses to the pandemic.
4. This refers to a number of free market think tanks, including the Institute of Economic Affairs, the Taxpayers' Alliance and the climate denial Global Warming Policy Foundation who share the office address of 55 Tufton Street (and also a reputation for lack of transparency over source of funds). See, for example, https://www.desmog.co.uk/55-tufton-street.
5. SAGE is the key body providing scientific advice to government.
6. Bright (2020) provides further examples of contracts awarded to inexperienced companies, and reports estimates that £190 million worth of PPE contracts were awarded to individuals with links to the Conservatives. Sikka (2020) indicates the extent to which the contracts have been awarded without the use of competitive tendering and to businesses close to the Conservative Party.

7.   The reports discussed here refer only to England. Health is a devolved responsibility, and hence national governments in Northern Ireland, Scotland and Wales have responsibilities for health services in general and dealing with COVID-19 in particular.

REFERENCES

Arbuthnott, G. and Calvert, J. (2022). *Failures of State: The Inside Story of Britain's Battle with Coronavirus.* London: Harper Collins Publishers.

Blundell, R., Costa Dias, M., Joyce, R., and Xu, X. (2020). *COVID-19 and Inequalities.* Institute for Fiscal Studies.

Bradley, J., Gebrekidan, S., and McCann, A. (2020). Waste, negligence and cronyism: inside Britain's pandemic spending. *New York Times*, 17 December 2020.

Bright, S. (2020). Government awards £122 million PPE contract to one-month-old-firm. *Byline Times*, 14 September 2020.

Calver, T. and Pogrund, G. (2020). Rugby stars dodge testing chaos thanks to Randox lab that misses targets for public. *Sunday Times*, 20 September 2020.

Calvert, J., Arbuthnott, G., and Leake, J. (2020). Coronavirus: 38 days when Britain sleepwalked into disaster. *Sunday Times*, 18 April 2020.

Cattan, S., Farquharson, C., Krutikova, S., Phimister, A., Salisbury, A., and Sevilla, A. (2021). *Inequalities in Responses to School Closures over the Course of the First COVID-19 Lockdown.* Institute of Fiscal Studies.

Colegrave, S. (2020). Boris Johnson's great spaffometer. *Byline Times* (https://bylinetimes.com/2020/07/24/boris-johnsons-great-spaffometer/). 24 July 2020.

Conn, D. (2023). PPE Medpro: UK government alleges firm supplied defective gowns to NHS. *Guardian*, 4 January 2023.

Conn, D. and Evans, R. (2023). Conservative peer helped land £50m PPE contract for firm linked to fellow Tory. *Guardian*, 9 January 2023.

Conn, D. and Geoghegan, P. (2020). Revealed: travel agent staff running COVID-19 track and trace. *Open Democracy*, 9 August 2020.

Curry, F., Dymski, G., Lewis, T., and Szymborska, H.K. (2022). Seeing Covid-19 through a subprime crisis lens: how structural and institutional racism have shaped 21st-century crises in the U.K. and the U.S. *The Review of Black Political Economy*, 49(1), 77–92.

Department of Health and Social Care (2020). The government's approach to test and trace in England – interim report: report by the Comptroller and Auditor General.

Durrant, T., Pope, T., Lilly, A., Guerin, B., Shepheard, M., Nickson, S., Hagen Schuller, J-A., Mullens-Burgess, E., and Dalton, G. (2021), *Whitehall Monitor 2021.* Institute for Government.

Eyles, A., Major, L.E., and Machin, S. (2022). *Social Mobility – Past, Present and Future.* The Sutton Trust.

Fetzer, T. (2022). Subsidizing the spread of COVID-19: evidence from the UK's Eat-Out-to-Help-Out scheme. *Economic Journal*, 132(April), 1200–1217.

Good Law Project (2023). REVEALED: Politically connected broker made £17m profit on 'VIP' PPE contracts. 24 January 2023. (goodlawproject.org/revealed-politically-connected-broker-made-17m-profit-on-vip-ppe-contracts/).

Health and Social Care, and Science and Technology Committees (2021). *Coronavirus: lessons learned to date, Sixth Report of the Health and Social Care Committee and Third Report of the Science and Technology Committee of Session 2021–22* HC 92.

IMF (2022). *Fiscal Monitor: Database of Country Fiscal Measures in Response to Pandemic*. Washington: IMF.

Johnson, B. (2020a). Prime minister's statement on coronavirus (COVID-19): 9 March 2020. (www.gov.uk/government/organisations/prime-ministers-office-10-downing -street).

Johnson, B. (2020b). Prime minister's statement on coronavirus (COVID-19): 12 March 2020. (www.gov.uk/government/organisations/prime-ministers-office-10 -downing-street).

Johnson, B. (2020c). Prime minister's statement on coronavirus (COVID-19): 16 March 2020. (www.gov.uk/government/organisations/prime-ministers-office-10 -downing-street).

Johnson, B. (2020d). Prime minister's statement on coronavirus (COVID-19): 18 March 2020. (www.gov.uk/government/organisations/prime-ministers-office-10 -downing-street).

Johnson, P., Joyce, R., and Platt, L. (2021). *The IFS Deaton Review of Inequalities: A New Year's Message*. Institute for Fiscal Studies.

McTague, T. (2020). How the pandemic revealed Britain's national illness. *The Atlantic*, 12 August 2020.

National Audit Office (NAO) (2022a). *The rollout of the COVID-19 vaccination programme in England* HC 1106.

National Audit Office (2022b). *Delivery of employment support schemes in response to the COVID-19 pandemic* HC 656.

National Audit Office (NAO) (2023). *Press Release on Department of Health and Social Care annual report and accounts 2021–22*. 26 January 2023.

Nazroo, J. and Becares, L. (2021). *Ethnic Inequalities in COVID-19 Mortality: A Consequence of Persistent Racism*. Runnymede Trust.

Public Accounts Committee (2021). *Test and Trace in England—progress update* HC 182.

Public Accounts Committee (2022a). *The rollout of the COVID-19 vaccine programme in England* HC 258.

Public Accounts Committee (2022b). *Government's contracts with Randox Laboratories Ltd* HC 28.

Public Accounts Committee (2022c). *Fraud and Error* HC 253.

Public Health England (2020). *Disparities in the risk and outcomes of COVID-19*. https://assets.publishing.service.gov.uk/media/5f328354d3bf7f1b12a7023a/ Disparities_in_the_risk_and_outcomes_of_COVID_August_2020_update.pdf.

Rogers, P. (2020). Is it time to use the F-word about Boris Johnson's disastrous regime. *Open Democracy*, 18 September 2020.

Sawyer, M. (2021). Economic policies and the coronavirus crisis in the UK. *Review of Political Economy*, 33(3), 414–431.

Sikka, P. (2020). The government is using the pandemic to give contracts to cronies. 24 August 2020. (https://leftfootforward.org/authors/prem-sikka/).

Sikka, P. (2021). Tories waste billions of taxpayers' money. *Chartist*, 5 January 2021.

Sinclair, I. and Reed, R. (2020). I Coronavirus crisis. *Byline Times*, 20 April 2020.

Spencer, D.A., Stuart, M., Forde, C., and McLachlan, C.J. (2023). Furloughing and COVID-19: assessing regulatory reform of the state. *Cambridge Journal of Regions, Economy and Society*, 16(1), 81–91.

Sunak, R. (2020). Budget Speech. (https://www.gov.uk/government/speeches/budget -speech-2020), p. 4.

Taylor, D. (2020). Servo wins Covid-19 test-and-trace contract despite £1m fine. *Guardian*, 6 June 2020.

Transparency International (2023). CPI 2022 for Western Europe & EU: undue influence and fragmented anti-corruption measures hurt progress. transparency.org/en/news/cpi-2022-western-europe-eu-corruption-undue-influence-hurt-progress.

UKHSA (2022). Referrers to the Covid testing 'VIP' route. drive.google.com/file/d/1i1DhMGaIvuQlfqn2tTUiBC0TcNy5rYll/view.

Ungoed-Thomas, J. (2023). Matt Hancock leaks lead to cover-up fears over 'eat out to help out' scheme. *Guardian*, 5 March 2023.

11. Inequality after Piketty

John E. King

INTRODUCTION

There are three reasons why many Post Keynesians take a strong interest in the extent of inequality in the distribution of income and wealth. First, and most obvious, it is well known that the propensity to save of the well off is (much) higher than that of the poor, and the propensity to consume is (much) lower. Thus, an increase in inequality raises the possibility that it will result in a deficiency in effective demand, which has been recognised for at least two centuries and underpinned the underconsumption theories of economic crisis that were influential in the nineteenth century and were revived in the wake of the Great Depression of the 1930s. This aspect of the story has become more dynamic in recent years, with the emergence of a theory of wage-led growth, and I shall focus on this question in the first part of the present chapter.

Second, Post Keynesians have always been interested in the ethical issues that are posed by economic inequality, though they have possibly paid these questions less explicit attention than they might have done. I am ashamed to admit that there is no reference to 'inequality' in the index to my own *History of Post Keynesian Economics* (King, 2002), an omission repeated in the extensive indexes to the 1100-page, two-volume *Oxford Handbook of Post-Keynesian Economics* (Harcourt and Kriesler, 2013). However, politically, the great majority of Post Keynesians are left of centre and share a presumption that greater equality in income and wealth is always to be preferred, unless there are strong arguments against it (involving, for example, the need for incentives to work harder and take risks).

Third, perhaps less obvious but arguably even more important, is the substantial increase in inequality that has taken place in all advanced countries since the late 1970s, which is often interpreted (not only by Post Keynesians) as evidence of the emergence of a new stage in capitalist development. The 'crucial reform' of global capitalism that was achieved after 1945 – the phrase originated with the Polish Post Keynesians Michał Kalecki and Taddeusz Kowalik (1971[1990]) – involved a substantial reduction in inequality in income and wealth, along with a firm commitment to full employment, the introduction of free public education and health services and the provision of effective social services for those in need. These big changes ushered in what French thinkers described as the '*trentes glorieuses*' (thirty glorious years) that came to an end with the implementation of neoliberal policies by right-wing politicians such as Margaret Thatcher and Ronald Reagan. This important historical development has cast doubt on the possibility of any permanently effective reform of capitalism and reopened the debate that was so prominent in the 1930s concerning the desirability of a socialist alternative to capitalism, which the Post Keynesians, who strongly supported the crucial reform, had always denied.

In the last decade there has been a new and very important contributor to these discussions: the French economist Thomas Piketty, whose two massive books on the distribution of wealth deal more or less effectively with all these questions. The first of these two volumes, *Capital in the Twenty-First Century*, was first published in French in 2011 and in a very good English translation three years later (Piketty, 2014). It generated a massive critical literature, some of which I surveyed in an article that was written in early 2016 and was published in the following year (King, 2017). Several of the contributors to this literature were Post Keynesians. They included Steven Pressman, the author of the companion chapter in the present volume, who wrote an entire book on Piketty's work (Pressman, 2016). Piketty was criticised for neglecting the ethical issues that are posed by inequality, and also for taking an unduly moderate position on the policy remedies that are required. Neither of these objections applies to his second treatise, *Capital and Ideology* (2020), which has yet to receive the critical attention (by Post Keynesians or others) that it deserves. But I suspect that *Capital and Ideology* will eventually be systematically addressed by Post Keynesians, and hope that the present chapter will encourage such a development.

WAGE-LED GROWTH

There is a substantial literature on wage-led growth, to which Post Keynesians have made a substantial contribution. The underlying macroeconomics is Kaleckian. In the simplest possible model, in a closed economy with no government, the aggregate income of the capitalist class is equal to their total expenditure on consumption and investment, with causation running from expenditure to income: workers spend what they get, but capitalists get what they spend (Kalecki, 1954). Investment expenditure is determined by the expected profitability of new investment projects, which is strongly influenced by working-class consumption spending. Any tendency for the profit share to rise at the expense of wages poses a potentially serious contradiction for the system, since it will reduce consumption and may also reduce investment via the accelerator mechanism that links investment to the rate of change of consumption. Thus, employer pressure to reduce wages may benefit the individual capitalist, viewed in isolation, but be bad news for the profits of the capitalist class as a whole. This contradiction, derived by Kalecki from his reading of the Great Depression, is the fundamental proposition of the twenty-first-century literature on wage-led growth (Hein, 2017; Lavoie and Stockhammer, 2013).

Kalecki himself believed that many capitalists had themselves begun to understand the dangers posed by resistance to rising real wages and had therefore supported the 'crucial reform' of the system after 1945, with governments' commitment to full employment, a comprehensive welfare state and a tightly regulated labour market allowing real wages to rise at least as fast as labour productivity. As I noted in my survey of the relevant literature, 'Kalecki's discovery of the "crucial reform" is a fine example of Hegel's Owl of Minerva, which spreads its wings at dusk: you only find out what is going on when it is about to stop' (King, 2018, p. 309). The re-emergence of free market liberalism in the late 1970s saw increasing resistance by capitalists to all forms of government intervention, and in particular to regulation of the labour market.

The phenomenon of wage theft – systematic and comprehensive underpayment of workers' legal entitlements – became the most obvious and significant economic consequence of these ideological changes, not least in Australia, as I documented a few years ago in my analysis of the obstacles to wage-led growth. As I noted, there are good reasons why non-Australians should pay attention to the Australian experience: 'For most of the 20th century there was a comprehensive system of compulsory arbitration, with state and federal tribunals setting legally-binding wages and conditions of employment' (King, 2018, p. 310), which had only very recently (but also very rapidly) been undermined. If wage theft could happen on a large scale in Australia, it was possible anywhere.

The implications of the waning of the crucial reform were set out very clearly by the German sociologist Wolfgang Streeck, who noted that:

> having no opposition may actually be more of a liability for capitalism than an asset .... Capitalism as we know it has benefitted greatly from the rise of counter-movements against the rule of profit and of the market .... Under Keynesianism and Fordism, capitalism's more or less loyal opposition secured and helped stabilize aggregate demand, especially in recession .... Seen this way, capitalism's defeat of its opposition may actually have been a Pyrrhic victory, freeing it from countervailing powers which, while sometimes inconvenient, had in fact supported it. Could it be that victorious capitalism has become its own worst enemy? (Streeck, 2016, pp. 60–61)

For Streeck this demonstrated that:

> capitalism, if unchecked, [is] a self-destructive social formation. Capitalists, at least some of them, may well recognize this; as capitalists, however, they typically face a fundamental collective action problem that prevents them from acting on their preferences, in particular their longer term, enlightened ones. This is why politics and political power are essential under capitalism, and indeed a politics that supports capitalist markets, not by supporting but by counterbalancing and constraining them, so as to protect them from themselves .... [But the] regulatory institutions restraining the advance of capitalism for its own good have collapsed, and after the final victory of capitalism over its enemies no political agency capable of rebuilding them is in sight. (ibid., pp. 224 and 72)

When I began work on this chapter, in November 2022, I discovered a newly published survey of the recent literature by three political economists at the left-leaning Australia Institute in Canberra, in which Jim Stanford, Fiona Macdonald and Lily Raynes showed how money wage growth in Australia had decelerated in the past decade and was now only half that experienced before 2013. This led to a pronounced and significant decline in real wages, despite the continuing growth of labour productivity – something not experienced before at any point in the country's post-war history. In consequence the share of labour income in GDP also fell sharply, as revealed in the dramatic Table 2 in their report. From a peak of 58% in the early 1950s, the labour share had already declined to just below 50% by 2013. In 2022 it was down to 44%, the lowest level recorded in the official statistics since the current series began in 1959 (Stanford, Macdonald and Raynes, 2022, p. 10).

Stanford and his colleagues argue convincingly that this dramatic development cannot be explained by labour market imbalances, but instead results from institutional and structural changes, above all from the collapse of trade union power and the related decline in the coverage of collective bargaining, which has been more pronounced in Australia than in almost any other advanced capitalist economy. They offer qualified support for the federal Labour government's proposed *Secure Jobs, Better Wages* legislation, which aims to restore the coverage and effectiveness of multiemployer collective bargaining, even if it does not go as far as they would like. They note that this would have important macroeconomic implications, since it would 'partly offset the impact of current rapid inflation on the real purchasing power of working families and support stronger household financial stability' (ibid., p. 35).

There are three underlying issues here that should concern all Post Keynesians. First, and possibly most important, we need always to be aware of the way in which politics affects economics: the increasing penetration of extreme neoliberal free market thinking into all areas of economic life has underpinned the attack on working people and their wages. Second, and closely related to this, is the need to maintain an autonomous macroeconomics that cannot be reduced to its supposed 'microfoundations'. As I noted some years ago, there are at least two compelling reasons for this: the fallacy of composition (the whole is not a simple sum of the parts), and downward causation (the macro affects the micro, no less than the micro influences the macro). King (2013) provides a book-length examination of these issues. Third, there are some very large policy questions that must be addressed. Can neoliberal capitalism still be reformed, quickly and emphatically, or do we need to consider an alternative, noncapitalist mode of production, as Thomas Piketty has recently proposed? The literature that I have discussed thus far has conclusively confirmed a large increase in recent decades in inequality in the distribution of income, but it has had little or nothing to say about the distribution of wealth. This is where Piketty's very impressive contributions have been made.

PIKETTY MARK I

The first and most obvious point to make about *Capital in the Twenty-First Century* (2014) is that it is a very long book: 577 pages of text and a further 76 pages of notes. Even the 'contents in detail' that Piketty provides at the very end of the book, listing the section headings of his introduction, 16 chapters and conclusion, runs to eight pages (pp. 657–64). It is, of course, very scholarly, drawing on a wide range of primary and secondary sources and providing a very great amount of statistical and other empirical evidence on the distribution of income and wealth over several centuries. 'To the extent possible', Piketty writes, 'I will explore the dynamics of the distribution of wealth between and within countries around the world since the eighteenth century' (p. 27). As he concedes, however, the book 'relies primarily on the historical experience of the leading developed countries: the United States, Japan, Germany, France and Great Britain' (p. 28).

After an introductory two-chapter section on 'income, output and growth' (part 1, pp. 37–109), there follows a four-chapter discussion of 'the dynamics of the capital–income ratio' (part 2, pp. 111–234), six chapters on 'the structure of inequality' (part 3, pp. 235–467) and the final four chapters on 'regulating capital in the twenty-first century (part 4, pp. 469–570)'. It is obviously impossible in a brief chapter to discuss the great majority of Piketty's work in any detail, and so my treatment will necessarily be highly selective.

In chapter 1 he sets out what he describes as 'the first fundamental law of capitalism: $a = r \times \beta$'. Here a is the share of profits in national income (P/Y), β is the capital–output ratio (K/Y) and r is the rate of profit (P/K). If $\beta = 6$ and $r = 5\%$, then $a = 30\%$. This, Piketty acknowledges, is 'a pure accounting identity',

but it is nevertheless important, because it 'exposes a simple, transparent relationship among the three most important concepts for analysing the capitalist
system' (p. 55).

More than 100 pages later, he presents 'the second fundamental law of capitalism: $\beta = s/g$', where β is again the capital–output ratio (K/Y), s is the savings
rate (S/Y) and g is the rate of growth (ΔY/Y). If $s = 12\%$ and $g = 2\%$, then β
$= 6$. The formula, Piketty maintains, 'reflects an obvious but important point:
a country that saves a lot and grows slowly will over the long run accumulate
an enormous stock of capital (relative to its income), which can in turn have
a significant effect on the social structure and distribution of wealth' (p. 166).
Unlike the first law, this is 'a long-term law', which is valid *only* in the long
run (p. 168). Piketty suggests that it explains the 'strong comeback of private
capital in the rich countries since 1970, or, to put it another way, the emergence
of a new patrimonial capitalism'. This has been the product of slower growth
in the 1980s and 1990s, a high saving rate, the privatisation of public assets
and the rapid growth of real estate and stock market prices, all 'in a political
context that was on the whole more favourable to private wealth than that
of the immediate postwar decades' (p. 173). These few pages constitute the
theoretical core of the book.

Some of the implications are described in chapter 10, where Piketty analyses
'the mechanism of wealth divergence: r versus g in history'. In traditional
agrarian societies, 'and to a large extent in all societies prior to World War I',
wealth was hyper-concentrated, 'as these were low-growth societies in which
the rate of return on capital was markedly and durably higher than the rate of
growth' (p. 351). After 1914, however, the rate of profit fell, and in the three
decades after 1945 the growth rate was exceptionally high. Between 1945 and
1970, 'for the first time in history, the net return on capital was less than the
growth rate' (p. 356) and inequality fell very sharply.

It has to be said that Piketty's discussion of the implications of these changes
is not entirely clear, a problem compounded by his presentation of statistics for
the rate of profit and the growth for 1950–2012, taken as a single period. This
is not easy to reconcile with his earlier account of the strong comeback of
private capital in the rich countries after 1970. He would probably justify this
in terms of his desire to make very long-term predictions, right down to 2100,
as illustrated in figures 10.9, 10.10 and 10.11 (pp. 354–7).

Piketty's policy proposals occupy much of the four chapters of part 4 of the
book, beginning with the need to re-establish a 'social state' in the 'twenty-first
century', continuing with his thoughts on the future of progressive income
taxation and the case for a global tax on capital, and ending with a substantial
discussion of the economics of the public debt. Here he touches briefly on the
ethics of distribution, suggesting that 'social inequalities are acceptable only if
they are in the interest of all and in particular of the most disadvantaged social

groups'. He finds this principle to have been expressed as early as 1789 in the US 'Declaration of the Rights of Man and the Citizen', and notes that '[t]he "difference principle" introduced by the US philosopher John Rawls is similar in intent' (p. 480). This is the only reference to Rawls in the entire book.

In the following two chapters Piketty argues that a progressive tax on income and wealth (especially inherited wealth) is 'a crucial component of the social state; it played a central role in its development and in the transformation of the structure of inequality in the twentieth century, and it remains important for ensuring the viability of the social state in the future'. He argues that it should be supplemented by a global tax on capital, although he admits that the latter is 'a utopian idea', to implement which 'would require a very high and no doubt unrealistic level of international cooperation' (p. 515). At all events, 'taxation is by far preferable to debt in terms of justice and efficiency' (p. 540), and so Piketty devotes the last numbered chapter of the book to the question of public debt and how it might be significantly reduced.

In the seven-page unnumbered 'conclusion', Piketty reaffirms his belief that $r > g$ is the 'central contradiction of capitalism'. 'The right solution', he maintains, 'is a progressive annual tax on capital. This will make it possible to avoid an endless inegalitarian spiral while preserving competition and incentives' (p. 572). 'The difficulty', he concedes, 'is that this solution, the progressive tax on capital, requires a high level of international cooperation and regional political integration' (p. 573). He continues by restating an important methodological principle that had been set out in the introduction: the case for 'a political and historical economics'. As he had maintained in the introduction, 'I see economics as a subdiscipline of the social sciences, alongside history, sociology, anthropology, and political science'. 'For far too long', he continues, 'economists have sought to define themselves in terms of their supposedly scientific methods ... [and] themselves succumb at times to a certain scientist illusion' (pp. 574–5). The book concludes with a rather strange discussion of 'the interests of the least well-off', which nowhere refers to Rawls, but does strongly criticise the influence of 'Marxist intellectuals' in the advanced capitalist world (pp. 575–7).

A huge critical literature soon emerged, much of which I surveyed in a paper written in early 2016 but only published in the following year (King, 2017). I distinguished nine separate criticisms. The first was the conservative/neoliberal argument that inequality in the distribution of wealth does not matter, since a rising tide lifts all boats. Second, it was claimed that Piketty's prediction of continuously increasing inequality and the return of 'patrimonial capitalism' was unjustified. Third, the quality of the empirical evidence that he cites was questioned, on a number of quite different grounds. Fourth, some critics objected that Piketty's explanation of long-run trends in the distribution of wealth was too general and too theoretical. Fifth, he was criticised for using the correct (neoclassical) theory incorrectly, exaggerating the elasticity of substitution of capital for labour. Against this Post Keynesian critics claimed, sixth, that Piketty was using the wrong theory, and should have drawn on the Kaldor–Pasinetti model of distribution and growth and not the discredited neoclassical analysis. Seventh, he was criticised for ignoring the distribution of wealth in developing countries. Eighth, there was a wide range of objections to his most striking policy proposal, for a progressive global wealth tax, for being both utopian and (some on the left claimed) inadequate. Finally, several critics from outside economics complained that Piketty had neglected a number of noneconomic dimensions of inequality.

He took this critical literature very seriously and began to respond to it almost as soon as the book had appeared (Piketty, 2015a, 2015b). He rejected the first criticism, since it came from the neoliberal authors whose underlying ideas he had always opposed, and was broadly unsympathetic to the second criticism, on similar grounds. He denied the general significance of the third criticism, but did show some sympathy for the fourth. While never explicitly confronting the fifth criticism, Piketty does seem to have taken it seriously, making little or no favourable reference to neoclassical theory in his later writings. While not openly endorsing the sixth criticism, he accepted it in an indirect way by soon abandoning the g, r model. He agreed with the authors of the seventh criticism and attempted to fill this large gap in his later work. Implicit acceptance of the eighth criticism can be inferred from his new policy proposals, which were much more radical than those made in the 2014 book. Finally, he regarded the ninth criticism as very largely unjustified, given his recognition in the book that economics was part (but only part) of a much broader social science.

PIKETTY MARK II

All these questions were addressed, to a greater or lesser extent, in *Capital and Ideology*, which was published in French in 2019 and in English (in another excellent translation) in the following year. It was even longer than *Capital in the Twenty-First Century*, with 1041 pages of text, this time including the notes, which now came at the bottom of the relevant page rather than all together at the end of the book. There was a brief glossary, a list of tables and illustrations, and a 'contents in detail' section that ran to 13 pages, concluding with a 29-page index: 1,093 pages all up.

After a 47-page introduction, part 1 (pp. 49–200) dealt with 'inequality regimes in history' in five chapters, which set out Piketty's interpretation of 'ternary societies' with their three functional groups (clergy, nobility and workers), and the emergence in Western Europe of 'ownership societies' where property was the crucial characteristic. Part 2 (pp. 201–412) was devoted to 'slave and colonial societies'. Here, chapter 6 analysed the extreme inequality found in slave societies, while chapters 7–9 focussed on colonial societies, with particular reference to India. In part 3 (pp. 413–716) Piketty turned to 'The great transformation of the twentieth century', with four chapters dealing in turn with the crisis of ownership society, the greater but still highly incomplete equality that characterised social democratic societies, the nature of Communist and post-Communist societies, and what Piketty now described as the 'hypercapitalism' of the early twenty-first century.

Post Keynesian readers will probably be most interested in the equally lengthy part 4, which is given over to 'rethinking the dimensions of political conflict'. It opens with chapter 14, which has the slightly misleading title 'borders and property: construction of equality'. In fact, it concentrates on the political changes that in recent decades have changed the nature of both the 'electoral left' and the 'electoral right'. By the second decade of the twenty-first century, Piketty maintains, there were four, roughly equal, political groupings: 'egalitarian internationalists', 'inegalitarian internationalists', 'inegalitarian nativists' and 'egalitarian nativists' (see figure 14.19, p. 791). Chapter 15 is devoted to what Piketty now describes as the 'Brahmin left' and its relationship with the 'merchant right', with a particular emphasis on the United States:

> If redistribution between the rich and poor is ruled out ... on the grounds that the laws of economics and globalization strictly prohibit it, then it is all but inevitable that political conflict will focus on the one area in which nation-states are still free to act; namely, defining and controlling their borders. (p. 831)

In chapter 16, 'social nativism: the postcolonial identitarian trap', the analysis is extended to several European countries and to Australia, New Zealand and Canada. Here Piketty discusses the arguments around 'tax competition' between nations and the possibility of sanctions being imposed on tax havens. He regards the 'Swedish decision to abolish the inheritance tax in 2005, at practically the same time as Hong Kong' (p. 925) as a particularly instructive example of left-leaning politicians deciding that the benefits of fiscal competition (lower taxes) outweigh the costs of the endless race to the bottom that is entailed. However, chapter 17, 'elements for a participatory socialism for the twenty-first century', strikes a more optimistic note. Here Piketty argues for the introduction or maintenance of progressive taxes on income and wealth and discusses the ethics of redistribution at some length. I shall have a lot more to say about these proposals very shortly, noting here only that a mere seven pages (pp. 1035–41) was sufficient for Piketty to set out his conclusions to the book as a whole.

It should be evident from this brief summary that *Capital and Ideology* is a very different book from *Capital in the Twenty-First Century*. Piketty acknowledges as much in his introduction. One significant improvement concerns the data sources. The earlier book, he writes, had:

> included a too-exclusive focus on the historical experience of the wealthy countries of the world (that is, Western Europe, North America, and Japan), partly because it was so difficult to access historical data for other countries and regions. The newly available data enabled me to go beyond the largely Western framework of my previous book and delve more deeply into the nature of inequality regimes and their possible trajectories. (p. 14)

At the theoretical level, he accepted that '[o]ne of the most important shortcomings of my previous book … was its tendency to treat political and ideological changes associated with inequality and redistribution as a black box'. He had written on this question in the earlier book, but 'I never really tackled head on the question of how inegalitarian ideologies evolve' (p. 16). Piketty returns to this question in the conclusion, which he begins by citing Marx and Engels on human history as the history of class struggles. 'Their assertion remains pertinent', he concedes, 'but now that this book is done, I am tempted to reformulate it as follows: The history of all hitherto existing societies is the history of the struggle of ideologies and the quest for justice' (p. 1035). While these 'political-ideological transformations' were crucially important, they 'should not be seen as deterministic', since '[m]ultiple trajectories are always possible' (p. 1037).

This was an (implicit) abandonment of the r, g model, which plays no significant part in *Capital and Ideology*. In fact, Piketty concludes the book by repeating his 2014 claim that economics should consider itself as a companion to the other social sciences, but he now draws more radical conclusions. 'I am convinced', he writes,

> that some of today's democratic disarray stems from the fact that, insofar as the civic and political sphere is concerned, economics has cut itself free from the other social sciences … In reality, it is only by combining economic, historical, sociological, cultural, and political approaches that progress in our understanding of socioeconomic phenomena becomes possible. (pp. 1039–40)

I shall have more to say in the concluding section of this chapter on the ethics of distribution, which certainly receives more attention in *Capital and Ideology* than it did in the earlier book. But I want to conclude this section with an appraisal of Piketty's proposal for a new participatory socialism to replace the deregulated capitalism that has taken over the world in the half-century after 1970, since this is a crucial issue that Post Keynesians must consider.

Right at the start of the book he set out:

> the outlines of a new participatory socialism for the twenty-first century. By this
> I mean a new universalistic egalitarian narrative, a new ideology of equality, social
> ownership, education, and knowledge and power sharing. This new narrative pre-
> sents a more optimistic picture of human nature than did its predecessors – and not
> only more optimistic but also more precise and convincing because it is more firmly
> rooted in the lessons of global history. (p. 3)

The predecessors presumably included Piketty himself, who in the earlier
book had been outspokenly antisocialist, proclaiming that 'I have no interest
in denouncing inequality or capitalism per se' (Piketty, 2014, p. 31). But
he remains steadfastly anti-Communist, noting in the new book that the
post-Communist societies of Russia, China and Eastern Europe 'have become
hypercapitalism's staunchest allies ... a direct consequence of the disasters of
Stalinism and Maoism and the consequent rejection of all egalitarian interna-
tionalist ambitions' (p. 8). He expands on these themes in the 70-page chapter
12 on 'Communist and post-Communist societies' (pp. 578–647).

He remains highly critical of European social democracy, as can be inferred
from the title of chapter 11: 'social-democratic societies: incomplete equality'. Their encounter with just taxation was a regrettable missed opportunity,
Piketty maintains: 'The dramatic rise of progressive income and inheritance
taxes in the period 1914–1945 generally came about as an emergency response
and was never fully integrated into party doctrine, either intellectually or
politically', contributing to the fragility of these changes after 1980. Moreover,
'faith in state centralization as the only way to transcend capitalism sometimes
led to neglect of tax-related issues, including what should be taxed and at
what rates as well as issues of power sharing and voting rights within firms'
(p. 547). And the social democratic regimes that held power and did institute
more progressive taxation after 1945 failed to encourage the measures of international cooperation needed to protect it from global tax evasion, and also 'too
often neglected the idea of a progressive wealth tax, despite its importance for
any ambitious attempt to transcend private capitalism' (p. 548).

As a consequence of these defects, the social democrats had been unable to
resist the emergence after 1980 of 'proprietarianism', which Piketty defines
as 'a political ideology based on the absolute defence of private property'.
The increasing inequality in income and (especially) wealth had greatly
strengthened the political influence of the wealthy, ushering in a new stage of
capitalism featuring 'the extension of proprietarianism to the age of large-scale
industry, international finance, and more recently to the digital economy'
(p. 971). There are lessons to be learned, he argued, from those earlier changes
in the legal and social system that had restricted the power of the owners of

property, in particular labour codes that limited the power of shareholders and inheritance taxes which further curtailed their rights.

The underlying principles of Piketty's new socialism were derived directly from these considerations and involved substantial changes to the legal and fiscal systems to 'establish true social ownership of capital by more extensive power sharing within firms' and by making 'ownership of capital temporary by establishing progressive taxes on large fortunes and using the proceeds to finance a universal capital endowment, thus promoting permanent circulation of property' (p. 972). The details of these changes are discussed in great detail in chapter 17, and there is an excellent summary in the second page of the conclusion (p. 1036).

Piketty begins chapter 17 with an analysis of the principles of social justice. A just society, he suggests, 'is one that allows all of its members access to the widest possible range of fundamental goods', which he understands to include 'education, health, the right to vote, and more generally to participate as fully as possible in the various forms of social, cultural, civic, and political life' (pp. 967–8). He notes the affinity of this definition of social justice with that proposed by John Rawls in 1971 (p. 968), and with the 'Germano-Nordic co-management model' that had been influential in the mid-twentieth century (p. 975). If this conflicted with the absolute rights of property owners, so be it. Accumulation was a social process and could never be regarded as a purely individual affair (p. 990).

There are very clear implications for fiscal policy. To prevent excessive wealth concentration, progressive taxes on inheritance and income are essential, but they are not sufficient, and 'need to be complemented by a progressive annual tax on wealth, which I see as the central tool for achieving true circulation of capital' (p. 976). Part of the proceeds should be used to provide a universal capital endowment (pp. 979–81), as had been advocated in 1795 by Tom Paine in his book on *Agrarian Justice* (p. 984), and also a universal basic income, to be set at 60% of average posttax income (pp. 1000–1004). This again, Piketty insisted, is necessary but not sufficient, and must be complemented by the taxation measures previously discussed and by 'an ambitious social state' (p. 1004).

Further elements in Piketty's model of participatory socialism include a progressive carbon tax to fight global warming (pp. 1004–1007) and the construction of 'a norm of educational justice', involving the provision of more resources to less advantaged schools, university admission principles that take students' social origins into account and a progressive tax on university endowments to finance an endowment fund for the poorest universities (pp. 1007–1016). There is an important international dimension to all this, with the need to rethink social federalism on a global scale and to establish social justice on a transnational basis (pp. 1022–30). Thus 'existing trade agreements should be replaced with much more ambitious treaties that seek to promote equitable and sustainable development' (p. 1022), with vital global issues such as tax evasion and carbon emissions regulated by a transnational political assembly (p. 1026).

CONCLUDING REMARKS

What, then, should Post Keynesians make of Piketty's work? I think that they should be very broadly sympathetic to his theoretical and political arguments, especially in *Capital and Ideology*, while recognising the need to add a macroeconomic dimension – the economics of wage-led growth – that is missing from it. Personally, I also find his case for participatory socialism to be convincing, since the political and social changes that have accompanied the huge increase in inequality in the last half-century do cast grave doubt on the prospect of a return to the reformed and much more egalitarian capitalism of the *trentes glorieuses*. I suspect, however, that many Post Keynesians will disagree, and will continue to echo Keynes himself in regarding all this as unnecessary and perhaps also quite dangerous. I hope to see these big issues being debated in Post Keynesian circles before too long.

I would like to end this chapter with some remarks on the ethics of distribution. Although Piketty does pay much more attention to this important question in *Capital and Ideology* than he had done previously, his focus is almost exclusively on the Rawlsian approach, which emphasises the well-being of the least well off. But there are other ways of approaching these important matters, which Post Keynesians do need to consider. The best short treatment that I have ever encountered is the work of my late colleague and friend Michael Schneider, in a fine chapter of his book on *The Distribution of Wealth* (Schneider, 2004, ch. 5), which was repeated, very largely unchanged, in the expanded and co-authored second edition (Schneider, Pottenger and King, 2016, ch. 6).

The four views of society that Schneider deals with are the conservative, the libertarian, the utilitarian and the egalitarian. He takes Edmund Burke and Michael Oakeshott as representatives of the conservative position, which 'is based on the idea that the best societies are those in which there is continuity between the past, the present and the future' (Schneider, 2004, p. 71). There is a strong consequentialist element in Burke's conservatism, since 'his case for a substantially unequal distribution of wealth is […] not merely that what has been inherited from the past should be conserved, but that unless there is unequal distribution the whole institution of private property will be endangered' (ibid., p. 72).

For some utilitarians, beginning with the pioneering marginalist William Stanley Jevons, the case for inequality was reinforced by a refusal to accept the legitimacy of interpersonal comparisons of utility and hence to insist on the need for all important economic policy measures to be (strong or weak) Pareto improvements, a position which is today widely accepted by mainstream welfare economists. 'Thus', Schneider concludes, 'with respect to distribution the current mainstream-economist view of society coincides with the conservative view, supporting the status quo' (ibid., p. 73).

The libertarian view of society, as promoted by Robert Nozick, is very different. Nozick maintains that this approach can be traced back to John Locke. It is based not on end-result principles but rather on an entitlement theory, according to which 'the holdings of a person are just if he is entitled to them by the principles of justice in acquisition and transfer' (ibid., p. 74, citing Nozick, 1974, p. 153). In Nozick's words: 'From each according to what he chooses to do, to each according to what he makes for himself (perhaps with contracted-for aid of others) and what others choose to give him or what they've been given previously (under this maxim) and haven't yet expended or transferred' (Nozick, 1974, p. 160, cited by Schneider, 2004, p. 75).

Accordingly, libertarians endorse all existing inequalities, unless there is strong evidence of historical injustice in the establishment of today's distribution of wealth. However, the logic of utilitarianism implies that 'there may be relatively little happiness in a libertarian society' (Schneider, 2004, p. 76). Schneider associates the origins of the utilitarian view of society with Jeremy Bentham and John Stuart Mill. He emphasises the twentieth-century arguments advanced by John Harsanyi and Jack Smart, both of whom see no difficulty in making interpersonal comparisons of utility or in using them to justify the redistribution of wealth (in the extreme case, from billionaires to homeless people living on the street).

Among the egalitarian critics of utilitarianism, Schneider draws on the contributions of R.H. Tawney, Ronald Dworkin and Amartya Sen. All three agree that there is more to the ethics of distribution than the mere promotion of the greatest happiness of the greatest number. Schneider quotes Tawney as arguing that while people 'differ profoundly as individuals in capacity and character, they are equally entitled as human beings to consideration and respect', and:

> the well-being of a society is likely to be increased if it so plans its organization that whether their powers are great or small, all its members may be equally enabled to make the best of such powers as they possess. (Tawney, 1952[1931], cited by Schneider, 2004, p. 78)

Dworkin and Sen both agreed with Tawney that the individual's self-realisation was an important ethical criterion, and that equality of resources and capabilities matter no less than equality of welfare. Schneider noted that these considerations do not imply support for an entirely equal distribution of wealth, but rather 'the view that wealth should be distributed sufficiently equally for the achievement of equality in capability, or its equivalent' (Schneider, 2004, p. 80). He also recorded the objections of Isaiah Berlin, who feared that the pursuit of equality would come into conflict with 'the desire [...] for colour and variety in a society' (Berlin, 1956, p. 319, cited by Schneider, 2004, p. 80).

Schneider also comments on John Rawls's 'maximin principle', which shares with the egalitarians a deep concern for equality of resources, and on Amartya Sen's closely related 'weak equity axiom' (Schneider, 2004, pp. 80–82). He concludes his account of these alternative views on the ethics of distribution with a very interesting criticism by the Australian economist Wylie Bradford (2000), who argued that Rawls fails to demonstrate that the right to participate in the management of production is any less basic a liberty than the primary goods that he [Rawls] lists. Once again, self-realisation features as a major element in the assessment of distributive outcomes, along with, and possibly no less important than, the allocation of financial claims to goods and services.

These arguments continue, and they do need to be taken into account by Post Keynesians in their thinking about inequality and the different ways in which it might effectively be reduced. Again, I would like to think that Piketty's work will stimulate such discussion.

REFERENCES

Berlin, I. (1956). Equality. *Proceedings of the Aristotelian Society*, *56*, 301–26.
Bradford, W.D. (2000). 'Value and Justice: Property, Economic Theory and Rawls', unpublished PhD thesis, University of Cambridge.
Harcourt, G.C. and Kriesler, P. (2013). *The Oxford Handbook of Post-Keynesian Economics*, two volumes. Oxford University Press, Oxford.
Hein, E. (2017). Post-Keynesian macroeconomics since the mid 1990s: main developments. *European Journal of Economics and Economic Policies: Intervention*, *14*(2), 131–72.
Kalecki, M. (1954). *Theory of Economic Dynamics: An Essay on Cyclical and Long-Run Changes in Capitalist Economy*. Allen & Unwin, London.
Kalecki, M. and Kowalik, T. (1971). Observations on the "crucial reform". *Politica ed Economics 2–3*, 190–196, reprinted in Osiatýnski, J. (Ed.) (1990). *Collected Works of Michał Kalecki. Volume 1. Capitalism, Business Cycles and Full Employment*, pp. 466–76, Clarendon Press, Oxford.
King, J.E. (2002). *A History of Post Keynesian Economics since 1936*. Edward Elgar Publishing, Cheltenham, UK and Northampton, MA, USA.
King, J.E. (2013). *The Microfoundations Delusion: Metaphor and Dogma in the History of Macroeconomics*. Edward Elgar Publishing, Cheltenham, UK and Northampton, MA, USA.
King, J.E. (2017). The literature on Piketty. *Review of Political Economy*, *29*(1), 1–17.
King, J.E. (2018). Some obstacles to wage-led growth. *Review of Keynesian Economics*, *7*(3), Autumn, 308–20.

Lavoie, M. and Stockhammer, E. (Eds) (2013). *Wage-Led Growth: An Equitable Strategy for Economic Recovery*. Palgrave Macmillan and the International Labour Office, Basingstoke, UK.

Nozick, R. (1974). *Anarchy, State and Utopia*. Blackwell, Oxford.

Piketty, T. (2014). *Capital in the Twenty-First Century*. The Belknap Press of Harvard University Press, Cambridge, MA.

Piketty, T. (2015a). About *Capital in the Twenty-First Century*. *American Economic Review*, *105*(5), 48–53.

Piketty, T. (2015b). Putting distribution back at the center of economics: reflections on *Capital in the Twenty-First Century*. *Journal of Economic Perspectives*, *29*(1), 67–88.

Piketty, T. (2020). *Capital and Ideology*. The Belknap Press of Harvard University Press, Cambridge, MA.

Pressman, S. (2016). *Understanding Piketty's Capital in the Twenty-First Century*. Routledge, London and New York.

Schneider, M. (2004). *The Distribution of Wealth*. Edward Elgar Publishing, Cheltenham, UK and Northampton, MA, USA.

Schneider, M., Pottenger, M. and King, J.E. (2016). *The Distribution of Wealth – Growing Inequality?* Edward Elgar Publishing, Cheltenham, UK and Northampton, MA, USA.

Stanford, J.. Macdonald, F. and Raynes, L. (2022). *Collective Bargaining and Wage Growth in Australia*. Centre for Future Work at the Australia Institute, Canberra.

Streeck, W. (2016). *How Will Capitalism End? Essays on a Failing System*. Verso, London.

Tawney, R.H. (1931). *Equality*. Allen & Unwin, London, 1952.

12. Piketty, Post Keynesian economics and income distribution

Steven Pressman

INTRODUCTION

There are many differences between the work of Thomas Piketty and the work done by Post Keynesian economists. Several, in particular, stand out. Piketty was trained as a neoclassical economist (Pressman, 2016, ch. 1), while Post Keynesian economics arose in opposition to neoclassical economics (King, 2002). Piketty is an empirical economist, while Post Keynesians tend to be more theoretical. Piketty is a microeconomist who focuses on the personal distribution of income. Post Keynesian economists, following John Maynard Keynes, are mainly concerned with macroeconomic issues. To the extent that they study income distribution, Post Keynesians tend to look at the functional distribution of income rather than the personal distribution of income. Despite these differences, there are some noteworthy similarities. History features prominently in the work of Piketty and Post Keynesians. Taking account of historical time, rather than assuming an effortless movement to equilibrium, is a characteristic of the Post Keynesian approach (Eichner & Kregel, 1975; Lavoie, 2006, ch. 1). Piketty reports (Pressman, 2016, p. 4f.) that his childhood heroes were left-wing French economic historians, such as Ferdinand Braudel, and his main research concerns the history of income distribution. In addition, his work is full of historical examples illustrating the points made in his extensive empirical analysis. For example, when discussing the primacy of property in *Capital and Ideology* (hereafter *C&I*), Piketty (2020, p. 235) notes that when slavery ended in the US, former slaves did not receive the 40 acres and a mule they were promised; rather, slave owners were compensated by the government for their loss of property.

Neither Piketty nor Post Keynesian economists see economic outcomes as optimal. For Piketty, the problem is considerable income inequality. For Post Keynesians, the business cycle, which leads to high rates of unemployment, is the main problem, although Keynes (1936, p. 372) noted that both unemployment and the unequal distribution of income and wealth were the "two outstanding faults of the economic society in which we live." Also, both Post Keynesian economics and Piketty have a progressive orientation, and Piketty has been moving to the left over time (Pressman, 2023).

Finally, both Piketty and Post Keynesian economics are policy oriented. They look to government policy to solve the problems that arise in market economies and advocate progressive fiscal policies. *Capital in the Twenty-First Century* (Piketty, 2014; hereafter *C21*) famously advocated a wealth tax to reduce inequality, while Keynes (1936, ch. 24) advanced socializing investment in order to stabilize capitalist economies. Piketty and Keynes also hold similar views regarding government deficits and debt, although taking different roads to this end. For Piketty, a balanced government budget is desirable because of its distributional consequences. Keynes saw a balanced government budget over the business cycle as desirable for political reasons more than economic reasons. In bad economic times, high debt left over from the good economic times would increase and would lead governments to push for austerity, worsening the economic situation. Little or no debt would generate more support for greater government spending during times of recession.

Going further, much can be learned from combining the wisdom of Piketty and Post Keynesian economics. This is especially true regarding income distribution. Post Keynesian thought provides theoretical grounding for Piketty's claim about the cause of rising income and wealth inequality. It also provides some insights into the macroeconomic consequences of rising inequality. Similarly, Piketty's work developing and analyzing data provides some empirical lessons for Post Keynesians.

In what follows, I examine Piketty and Post Keynesian economics in terms of the causes of inequality, the consequences of inequality and one key policy issue related to inequality – government debt.

Sections 2 and 3 argue that Piketty and Post Keynesian economics have similar analyses of the causes of inequality, and that the controversial equation in *C21* that is supposed to explain inequality follows straightforwardly from Post Keynesian analysis. Section 4 looks at the consequences of inequality for Piketty and for Post Keynesian economists. As Pressman (2016, ch. 3) points out, *C21* assumes that inequality is bad but doesn't explain why this is so. *C&I* remedies this to some extent by focusing on voting outcomes and the threat to democracy from high and rising inequality. Section 4 also sets forth two Post Keynesian perspectives on the consequences of inequality – one concerning the theory of effective demand and one concerning productivity. Section 5 looks at the issues of government deficits and debt. It makes the case that Piketty and Keynes held similar views on government debt. Section 6 concludes.

PIKETTY ON THE CAUSES OF INEQUALITY

C21 is about inequality. It presents extensive historical data on inequality for many developing nations that go back more than a century. This should be seen as a set of stylized facts about income distribution. Its second important contribution is a unique measure of inequality, which focuses on the changing share of total income going to the rich – the top 1% (really, the top 0.01%) of the income distribution. This measure of inequality has the virtues of being easy to comprehend and focusing our attention on where the action has taken place over time.

Given this data, one question that springs to mind immediately is why the share of total income received by the top 1% has risen over the past several decades and now approaches levels from the Gilded Age. Piketty's answer to this question in *C21* is r>g. In *C&I* Piketty ignores r>g. Instead, he discusses how ideology supports and sustains inequality (Pressman, 2021). While *C&I* is right that ideology is important in maintaining inequality, this doesn't explain the tendency for inequality to rise over time. In the work of Piketty, this job still falls squarely on the shoulders of r>g. The r in this inequality represents the rate of return on wealth; the g represents the average growth rate of incomes (including both the growth of income from wealth and labor incomes).

Piketty (2014, p. 353) takes r>g as an historical fact rather than some theoretical truth or "natural law". It is an empirical regularity. Given how far back his data goes, it is probably not a characteristic of capitalism, as this relationship holds during feudalism as well as capitalism. Perhaps the best way to describe the scope of r>g is that it is an empirical regularity of human societies once they abandoned hunting and gathering and settled down in agricultural societies (see Widerquist & McCall, 2021; Wisman, 2022).

The consequence of r>g is that income grows more for those with wealth than the economy-wide average increase in income (g). Over time it enables the rich to accumulate more, augmenting their wealth. Greater wealth, earning large returns (r), leads to further income and wealth inequality. Compounding, along with r>g, entails that income and wealth inequality will grow with time. And the greater the difference between r and g, the faster inequality will increase. A concrete example helps demonstrate this.

You and a good friend start working at the same time, and you each make $100,000 annually. However, you have an inheritance of $100,000 while your friend does not. You can consume your wage income and all your wealth this year, spend your income and not touch your wealth, or choose some intermediate path. To keep things simple, we assume there is no consumption from wealth or its returns, and that all income from both wages and wealth grows at the rate of 1% every year (i.e., r=g). Consequently, your wealth and your labor income will grow in tandem over time. After 35 years, your assets will be worth $140,000 and you will make $140,000 through your work. Your annual income (from work and from returns on your assets) remains 1% greater than the annual income of your friend, while keeping your wealth intact. Over time, the level of inequality remains the same. You can potentially consume as much as twice your income, or you can consume the returns on your wealth only and increase your standard of living by 1%, or you can keep your wealth growing by not spending more than your income.

Now consider what happens if your wealth grows at a rate of 5% per year instead of 1%. After 35 years, a typical working life, your labor income still increases to $140,000 but your wealth increases to well over half a million dollars. With a 5% return on this money, you can consume more than $25,000 in goods and services in addition to what is possible through your wages. Your standard of living is nearly 20% greater than before and nearly 20% greater than that of your friend. After several generations, or 100 years, this divergence becomes even greater. Your great grandchild (assuming continuous 1% wage growth) would make $268,000 but would have $12.5 million in assets. With a 5% rate of return, his or her income from wealth would exceed $600,000, dwarfing your great grandchild's labor income. Inequality has soared.

It should be noted that rising wealth inequality is not inevitable because r>g. People can consume a good portion of their wealth or save some of their income and add to their wealth. People can retire earlier or work longer. People can be unemployed for a number of years, while others get lucky and remain employed continuously. Returns to wealth, or wealth itself, can be taxed. Wealth also gets diluted when a family divides up their estate among several children, and estate taxes can reduce inequality across generations. Further, some people may earn much more than the average rate of return, while others make investments that lose money over the long haul. Nonetheless, to keep inequality from rising, those without wealth must get lucky, or they must save some money in order to generate wealth and catch up to those who already have substantial wealth, while those with wealth must get unlucky or consume their own wealth.

Returning to the real world, Figure 12.1 contains Piketty's estimates of r and g stretching far back in time. It is the weighted average of r for developed countries. Piketty (2014, fig. 10.7) also provides data for France. This data underpins Piketty's empirical case that r>g.

The value of g for Piketty depends on two things. First, a growing labor force means there will be more workers to produce the national output of goods and services, and more income. Second, productivity growth determines how much, on average, each worker produces. These two factors determine how much output gets produced, and by how much it grows annually. Piketty (2014, table 2.1) finds that g has ranged between 1% and 2% over several

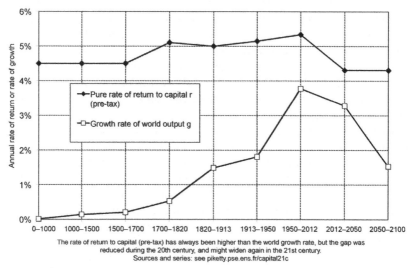

The rate of return to capital (pre-tax) has always been higher than the world growth rate, but the gap was reduced during the 20th century, and might widen again in the 21st century.
Sources and series: see piketty.pse.ens.fr/capital21c

Source: Piketty, 2014.

Figure 12.1   *Rate of return vs growth rate at the world level, from Antiquity until 2100*

centuries but is pessimistic about the future. For the 21st century, he thinks the best we can do is g=1 because of zero or negative population growth and productivity growth at a bit more than 1%. Ever the optimist, Piketty (2014, p. 95) thinks this is not so bad: "a per capita output growth rate on the order of 1 percent is in fact extremely rapid, much more rapid than many people think". It will increase living standards by 40% over a period of 35 years, around one generation. On the other hand, Piketty presents no theory regarding why productivity growth should fall to 1%; Section 4 provides an explanation based on Post Keynesian theory.

However, the big problem is Piketty's assumption of a constant r, or r=5, the main force generating greater inequality. This assumption runs counter to standard economic theory, which holds that when something is more abundant, its return should fall. As wealth grows relative to the size of the economy, returns to wealth should decline. Piketty struggles mightily to circumvent this conclusion and gets himself into a great deal of trouble trying to do so. At one point, Piketty (2014, pp. 215–22) contends that a high elasticity of substitution (greater than 1) between capital and labor maintains the value of r in the face of a growing supply of capital. Unfortunately, this claim runs counter to empirical estimates of this elasticity of substitution (see Semieniuk, 2017). At another point, Piketty (2014, 26f.) regards r as a standard feature of capitalism.

However, as noted earlier, a constant r also characterizes pre-capitalist modes of production according to Piketty's data.

In sum, Piketty's problem is that it is not clear what keeps r constant at 5% or why it should remain at this level as the share of wealth relative to GDP rises. Section 3 provides an answer that comes from basic principles of Post Keynesian economics.

WHY R IS CONSTANT: A POST KEYNESIAN VIEW

Starting with the Cambridge savings equation (Kaldor, 1955–56), we can provide a simple explanation for why r>g. We let S = savings, I = investment, K = capital stock, P = profits, r = rate of return on capital and s = the savings propensity of capitalists. For simplicity we assume there is no government and no foreign trade. We also make the simplifying assumption that workers don't save and don't receive any profits or returns to wealth. This last assumption doesn't matter a great deal because Luigi Pasinetti (1974) has shown that the Cambridge Post Keynesian results hold even if workers save and receive nonwage income.

With no worker savings, total savings equal the propensity to save by capitalists times their capital income or profits

$$S = sP \tag{12.1}$$

As investment and savings must be equal in the absence of a government and foreign sector, it follows that

$$I = sP \tag{12.2}$$

Rearranging slightly, we get

$$P = (1/s)I \tag{12.3}$$

Dividing everything by K, the capital stock, we have

$$P/K = (1/s)(I/K) \tag{12.4}$$

If economic growth (g) requires a constant capital–output ratio, g will equal I/K. In addition, since P/K is the rate of profit or rate of return (r) on capital, it follows that

$$r = (1/s)\, g \tag{12.5}$$

Equation (12.5) resembles Piketty's fundamental inequality, r>g, but tells us a great deal about the relationship between r and g. If and only if capitalists save all their income (or s=1), does r=g. If capitalists spend only a bit of their income, s<1, r will exceed g. Further, the more capitalists spend out of their income, or the smaller the value of s, the greater the distance between r and g, and the faster inequality increases.

We can even add some empirics to equation (12.5). If capitalists save around half their capital income, as some Post Keynesians have estimated (Hein & Vogel, 2008; Stockhammer & Stehrer, 2011), we come close to Piketty's empirical estimates of r and g. Piketty finds (see Figure 12.1 again) that r has averaged between 4.5% and 5.0% over many centuries, and since the 19th century g has averaged a bit over 2%. As a result of this, r should be around half of g, which equation (12.5) tells us should be the case according to Post Keynesian theory.

The macroeconomic approach of Post Keynesian economics elucidates why r>g. Keynes (1936) showed that an increase in savings will lower demand and that the resulting economic slowdown will hurt business profits. Michał Kalecki (1954, 1962, 1971) maintained that with more savings and less consumption by capitalists, effective demand will be lower; this will lower profits, leading r to fall. This led to Nicholas Kaldor's (1955–56, p. 96) pithy conclusion that: "Capitalists earn what they spend". Looking at income distribution, we can revise this aphorism somewhat: "Capitalists gain relative to everyone else based on their spending rate". As such, Post Keynesian ideas underpin Piketty's fundamental inequality. They explain rising inequality based on savings and spending propensities. More important, they do this without relying on neoclassical theory or the circularity in that theory, as made clear in the Cambridge capital controversy (Harcourt, 1972; Cohen & Harcourt, 2003).

Still, it is not clear why r remains constant in the face of rising wealth. I see two possible explanations. One comes from Marx, who thought that r could be maintained by continually increasing the exploitation of workers or squeezing more surplus value out of them. This involves things like speeding up the production process, having workers do more in one day or increasing the number of working days. Marx thought that competition would push down the rate of profit while increased exploitation to reverse this tendency would lead to social unrest, making capitalism unsustainable in the long run. But this has some shortcomings as an explanation for why r>g in the long run, as capitalism has shown remarkable sustainability despite the problems pointed out by Marx. And in the short term, there are limits to the exploitation of workers, or limits to speeding up the assembly line or increasing the workday and the workweek. Also, Marx's prediction of a longer working day and week has not been borne out. Working time has declined throughout the developed world over the past century (Messenger, 2018), although not to the extent predicted and desired by Keynes (1930a).

Post Keynesian economics provides an alternative explanation for the constant r over long periods of time. If r=5 for a long time, it becomes the accepted or accustomed rate of return on wealth. People expect such returns over the long haul, and these expectations (whether they are rational or not) impact behavior.

If returns to wealth begin falling, people can modify their portfolios in order to maintain their accustomed r. Concretely, r is the average return to stocks, bonds, savings accounts, real estate and other assets that people own. Not all wealth, and not everyone's wealth, grows by this amount. In general, riskier assets (such as stocks) receive higher returns than less risky assets (such as corporate bonds and real estate), which in turn earn higher returns than virtually riskless assets (government bonds and insured bank deposits). Likewise, wealth does not grow by r every single year. Rather, r is how much wealth grows each year on average over relatively long periods of time.

For example, suppose stocks yield 10% over long periods of time, bonds yield 6%, housing 4% and cash provides a 1% rate of return. If my portfolio consists of half stocks, 30% bonds and 20% cash, my expected return is the weighted average of these, or 7%. By modifying my asset portfolio, making it slightly more risky, I increase my expected return. Using my cash to buy a home raises my rate of return to 7.6%. Alternatively, putting half my cash into bonds raises my expected return on all assets to 7.5%. Such actions counter any tendency for r to fall. Similarly, within each asset class, I can buy slightly more risky assets that yield higher rates of return. Selling government bonds and buying more corporate bonds raises my return on bond holdings (the average return on all bonds). Holding growth stocks rather than income-generating stocks will increase the average rate of return on stock holdings. Putting my cash into long-term certificates of deposit will (under normal circumstances) increase the return on cash holdings.

"Financial innovation" can also increase the rate of return on asset classes. Junk bonds (and other bonds) can be packaged together and sold as a less risky asset with a higher expected return due to diversification. Going further, these bonds can be cut into several tranches, with some tranches earning higher returns for their owners.

All these actions increase r. They also increase individual risk and increase the financial fragility of the economy, as Hyman Minsky (1977) pointed out. Yet they do keep r constant at 5%, despite a rising stock of wealth that creates pressures for a lower r.

PIKETTY, THE POST KEYNESIANS, AND THE CONSEQUENCES OF INEQUALITY

Both Piketty and Post Keynesian economists believe that high levels of inequality are undesirable. Piketty just assumes this to be the case in *C21*. *C&I* does a bit better. It examines the political consequences of rising inequality.

Pressman (2016, ch. 3) points out many negative microeconomic consequences of inequality, including increased crime, reduced family formation, greater health problems and a failure to work hard because of perceived unfairness. There are also negative macroeconomic consequences of inequality. Two have been of particular concern to Post Keynesian economists. One is well known – inequality leads to lower demand and higher unemployment. The other is not – slower productivity growth and lower living standards result from greater inequality. We begin with how inequality impacts demand.

In the simple Keynesian consumption function, consumption depends on disposable income, or income less income taxes. In addition, Keynes (1936, chs 8–9) identifies six objective and eight subjective factors that impact consumption. His fifth objective factor is income distribution.

Given a certain level of aggregate income, how that income is distributed among the population determines aggregate consumption. This stems from the different spending propensities of households with different income levels. Greater income equality puts a larger share of total income in the hands of people with lower incomes, who have high spending propensities. Redistributing income from the wealthy to others thus increases total consumption. In contrast, as Keynes (1936, p. 262) notes: "the transfer of income from (low income) wage-earners to other factors is likely to diminish the propensity to consume" because the rich have a smaller spending propensity (and a higher marginal propensity to save) than the middle class, the working class and the poor. Piketty's measure of inequality – the fraction of total income going to the top 1% – captures this distributional issue much better than the favorite inequality measure of most economists (the Gini coefficient), as the very top of the income distribution is where high saving propensities predominate.

Saving considerable money out of their income, the rich spend less; and since consumption is by far the largest component of effective demand, rising inequality will tend to have a negative economic impact. To compensate for this and maintain employment levels, greater spending must come from elsewhere. Those who are not rich typically save very little of their income; and they can't cut their savings enough to compensate for the savings done by the rich. Traditional economic analysis focuses on how savings get funneled into investment, which was true historically because banks would lend to businesses but not individuals (Hyman, 2012). However, as Keynes (1936, ch. 8) noted, if firms are not selling goods, they are not likely to increase their productive capacity by investing more.

Keynes wanted government deficit spending to fill the breach, especially investment-like spending. Absent the willingness of governments to do this, we are left with just one possibility – savings by the wealthy must fund borrowing by other individuals for consumption purposes. Economists are just beginning to pay attention to the issue of rising consumer debt.[1]

Greater household debt has its own distributional consequences. Because inequality data, including the data of Piketty, ignore household debt and the expenditures necessary to repay that debt, these measures underestimate inequality in living standards, something at least as important as income inequality (Pressman & Scott, 2009).

Moreover, although greater household debt is a possible short-term solution to demand problems in the face of rising inequality, it is not a viable long-run solution; households can carry only so much debt relative to their income (Scott & Pressman, 2019; Setterfield & Kim, 2022). Once this limit is reached, households will not be able to get additional credit and will be forced to cut their spending. The result will be Minsky-like cycles – but with consumer debt (rather than business borrowing) maintaining sufficient spending until the financial situation of households becomes too risky (Minsky's Ponzi finance), and loans are unlikely to be repaid.

A second macroeconomic consequence of greater inequality, slower productivity growth, has been explored only tangentially by Post Keynesians. Nonetheless, the Post Keynesian approach is very different from the standard economic approach, which sees productivity growth as depending on incentives, flexible wages and prices, and substitution to enhance efficiency. In contrast, for Post Keynesians demand is the key to understanding productivity and productivity growth.

The theory of effective demand is the major idea distinguishing Post Keynesian from neoclassical economics. One way to encapsulate this difference is to note that income effects are more important than substitution effects for Post Keynesians (Davidson, 2005; Pressman, 2011). Instead of looking at the supply side of the economy, or at incentives to produce more efficiently, Post Keynesians focus on spending. Demand determines productivity and productivity growth for Post Keynesians. There are three related reasons for this. Combined, they form a theory of productivity growth that depends on the changing demand for manufactured goods, the changing demand for services and the changing relative demand for goods and services produced by these two sectors.

Adam Smith ([1776] 1937, bk I, ch. I) noted that productivity improves when firms can divide up tasks, have individuals become proficient in narrow duties and enable machinery to assist workers. Smith held that this was possible only if firms sell enough goods to justify investment in machinery and the restructuring of production. Accordingly, the greater "the extent of the market", to use Smith's phrase, the greater firm sales and firm productivity will be. After Smith, this idea remained dormant in economics until the early 20th century when Allyn Young (1928) revived it when he noted that many industries operate under conditions of increasing returns to scale (as opposed to the neoclassical assumption of diminishing returns). Increasing returns mean that productivity grows as output expands; conversely, during times of slow economic growth, productivity grows slowly as output growth slows.

Following Smith and Young, demand determines productivity and productivity growth for Post Keynesians. When unemployment is low and the economy booming, firms must figure out how to use existing labor more efficiently and how to take advantage of economies of scale. During recessions firms focus on maintaining sales and surviving the difficult economic times. They think about cutting costs immediately rather than worker productivity and long-run growth (Sylos-Labini, 1983–84). As a result, productivity suffers in both the short run and the long run.

Productivity growth is also demand driven in service sectors, as William Baumol (2012) has argued. Consider a symphony orchestra. The productivity of the orchestra does not depend on how fast the musicians can play a piece of music (a supply-side concern). Rather, orchestra productivity depends on the amount of money received through ticket sales. When economic growth slows, or when this is feared, people will be reluctant to spend money and they will hesitate to attend the symphony. The productivity of the orchestra languishes. On the other hand, in a booming economy the concert hall will be full and the productivity of the orchestra (the value of its output, or ticket sales divided by the number of players) will be much greater. The orchestra may also produce CDs containing their music, a manufactured good. Here too demand determines the productivity of orchestra members. The value of the output created by the orchestra in this case is determined by how many CDs are sold. When demand is high and sales boom, productivity soars. When people cut back on their purchases of CDs, orchestra member productivity falls.

What is true of the symphony orchestra is true of most service occupations. It is total demand, or the extent of the market, that matters – not the individual. Teachers are more productive when they have more students in their classes. Greater demand for higher education improves the productivity of college teachers. The productivity of real estate agents and the productivity of newspaper reporters likewise depend on the value of firm sales. When home sales fall due to poor macroeconomic conditions, the productivity of realtors drops. When newspaper sales decline and advertising revenue falls because people are not spending money, everyone working at the newspaper becomes less productive.

A final reason demand determines productivity is that aggregate productivity is a weighted average of productivity in different economic sectors, and productivity will change as the sectoral composition of a nation changes. As demand shifts to goods produced by more productive economic sectors, average productivity levels will increase; if demand shifts to goods produced by less productive sectors, productivity growth will stall.

This insight was the basis for the dynamic Tableau of François Quesnay (see Pressman, 1994); but it was then ignored by economists until Nicholas Kaldor (1967, 1996) stressed the composition of demand as a key determinant of productivity growth. Unlike Quesnay, but like Smith, Kaldor saw the manufacturing sector rather than the agricultural sector as the engine for productivity growth. Tony Thirlwall (1983, 1987) has identified several core ideas in Kaldor's theory. First, following Young, due to economies of scale, the growth of the manufacturing sector determines productivity growth in the manufacturing sector. Second, spin-offs from manufacturing mean that the faster the manufacturing sector grows, the greater productivity outside the manufacturing sector increases. Finally, according to Kaldor, manufacturing production depends on overall demand in the economy and by the demand for manufactured goods relative to the demand for other goods and services. Greater demand for manufactured goods therefore boosts productivity in the manufacturing sector (due to increasing returns) and increases productivity for the whole economy (due to spillover effects and the nature of weighted averages).

While *C21* is silent on the question of the costs of inequality, Piketty (2020) devotes the last third of *C&I* to discussing the political consequences of inequality. His focus is on how disillusioned citizens, who have strong feelings of being ignored by the government and by left-of-center political parties, tend to vote. The political consequences of this are fairly well known. Right-wing populism has led to bad policies being enacted throughout the world – Brexit in the UK and austerity policies most everywhere. And right-wing autocrats have either won national elections (Jair Bolsonaro in Brazil, Viktor Orbán in Hungary, Andrzej Duda in Poland, Recep Erodoğan in Turkey and Donald Trump in the US) or have done very well and have come close to winning (Marine Le Pen in France). Even Nordic countries, where people seem willing to pay taxes to support a large welfare state, have not been immune from right-wing populism. The Danish People's Party, which supports immigration restrictions and is highly critical of the European Union, received 21.1% of the vote in the June 2015 general election, making it the second largest party in Denmark (Judis, 2016, p. 132).

C&I documents changes in voting behavior over time in the US, France and the UK. All three countries experienced a marked shift in who supports different political parties. Lower income individuals have gone from supporting left-of-center parties and candidates to supporting parties and candidates that are far to the right of center. Conversely, more educated individuals with higher incomes have come to support left-of-center parties and candidates rather than conservative parties and candidates.

In the 1948 US presidential election, 62% of voters without a high school diploma cast their ballot for Democratic candidate Harry Truman; 50% of voters with a high school degree and no additional education voted for Truman. Yet only 30% of those with a college degree or more voted for Truman. The least educated adults elected Truman president (Piketty, 2020, p. 809). During the 1970s and 1980s, educational differences by party narrowed. Starting in the 1990s, those with more education became more likely to vote for Democrats. By 2016 more educated voters strongly favored Democrat Hillary Clinton; those with little education supported Trump (Piketty, 2020, p. 817).

In France, from the 1950s to the 1970s, the 10% of the population with the most education tended to vote for right-wing candidates; everyone else tended to vote Socialist (Piketty, 2020, p. 724). Over the subsequent two decades, the well educated in France came to vote for candidates on the left to the same extent as candidates on the right. Starting in the mid-1990s, and continuing until today, the better educated were 12 percentage points more likely to vote for the left candidate than the right candidate. In the 2012 election, Socialist François Hollande beat Nicolas Sarkozy, 52% to 48%. Hollande received the support of only 18% of voters with only a primary degree, but 50% of voters with a secondary school (high school) degree and 58% of voters with a college degree (Piketty, 2020, p. 745).

Changes in UK voting propensities were similar to that of the US and France, although the timing was different. It was not until the 2010s that more educated workers were more likely to support Labour and less-educated workers became more likely to support the Conservatives (Piketty, 2020, p. 812, p. 833, p. 846). In the Brexit vote, people with lower levels of education, income and wealth voted by nearly two-to-one to leave the European Union; those in the upper levels voted to remain by more than two-to-one.

Piketty's election survey data demonstrate the seismic shift in voting propensities that have taken place around the world over many decades. Historically, the left has been the party of the worker and those with less education; well-off, better-educated voters supported candidates from right-leaning parties. Today, left-leaning parties attract more affluent and better-educated voters; those with lower incomes and less education support parties on the right of the political spectrum. For Piketty, this stems from rising inequality and belief that left-leaning parties have abandoned their traditional constitutions and have come to support the educated and those who are well off.

PIKETTY AND THE POST KEYNESIANS ON PUBLIC DEBT

Since Post Keynesian economics seeks to expand and develop the ideas of Keynes (King, 2002), we must consider the views of Keynes to be part of the Post Keynesian perspective on government debt. However, it should be noted that an offshoot of Post Keynesian economics, modern monetary theory (Kelton, 2020; Mitchell et al., 2019), takes a different and more radical approach towards government debt, holding that there is no need to worry about government debt under certain circumstances. This is not true of Keynes.

The key policy lesson of *The General Theory* (Keynes, 1936) is that budget deficits were necessary during recessions. Despite losing tax revenues due to the recession, and contrary to the conventional wisdom at the time, Keynes held that fiscal policy had to be expansionary in bad economic times. Government spending had to increase. Balancing the budget by cutting government spending, or engaging in austerity policies, would only worsen economic slumps. The correct policy during a recession was more government spending and greater debt. Keynes wanted that spending to be government investment in things like education, health care and infrastructure. And, many times, Keynes (1980, p. 225, p. 277, p. 352, p. 406) distinguished capital and current government budgets, similar to what business firms do. He thought that the current budget should be balanced all the time and that the capital budget should finance government investment.

There is no doubt that Keynes supported greater government borrowing and government investment during difficult economic times. A little less clear is whether Keynes favored continued budget deficits and rising debt over the long term. It appears not. He seems to have supported running budget deficits during times of recession and then surpluses of equal value during economic expansions, or cyclically balanced government budgets (Kregel, 1983; Seccareccia, 1995; Brown-Collier & Collier, 1995). Another question is whether Keynes thought that the capital budget should be balanced over the business cycle. Here, also, Keynes seemed to favor a balanced capital budget over the business cycle. In a letter to James Meade, Keynes (1980, pp. 319–20) contended that government capital expenditures would pay for themselves, implying a balanced capital budget over time. In addition, Keynes (1980, p. 278) called the accumulation of public debt to finance government expenditures "dead-weight loss", suggesting that he wanted government borrowing during bad economic times and wanted governments to run budget surpluses in good economic times, using the surplus to repay prior government debt.

In chapter 16 of *C21*, Piketty took a somewhat anti-Keynesian position. He seemed to advocate a balanced budget in order to reduce inequality, arguing that the government should tax the rich rather than borrowing money from them when it needed to increase government spending to create jobs. To be clear, Piketty was not opposed to progressive and stimulative fiscal policy to deal with unemployment. Rather, he wanted governments to use progressive taxation to reduce inequality. Piketty argued that rather than borrowing from the wealthy in order to support public expenditures to benefit everyone, a better way to fund these programs, a way that would reduce inequality, would be to tax the rich. More recently, Piketty (2021) seems to have moved away from this view, supporting more Keynesian policies during recessions and even modern monetary theory, although his view on permanent deficits remains unclear (Pressman, 2023).

One way to connect the views of Keynes and Piketty, and to underline the importance of distribution in their fiscal policy proposals, is through the balanced budget multiplier. This notion was formulated by Paul Samuelson (1948) in an attempt to deal with the budget problems facing the US economy after World War II as well as the prediction of Alvin Hansen (1939) and others that developed nations faced the possibility of "secular stagnation" or regular depressions caused by shortfalls in effective demand. If this were to be the case, the Keynesian policy solution would necessitate continual government budget deficits and rising government debt. A cyclically balanced budget was impossible with continued stagnation.

Samuelson figured out a clever way for fiscal policy to circumvent this. His solution depends on the higher marginal propensity to consume as one goes further down the distribution of income. Taxing the rich, who have greater marginal propensities to save, and then spending the tax revenue, or using it to transfer money to middle-income and low-income households, would promote consumer spending and economic growth.

The balanced budget multiplier of Samuelson solves the joint problems of inadequate demand and high government debt levels via Keynes's fifth objective factor – the distribution of income. As Trygve Haavelmo (1945) astutely recognized, this solution works only because it changes income distribution. If the government were to tax people and then return to them the same income that they taxed away, there would be no change in consumption and no fiscal stimulus. Only through taxing the wealthy and providing benefits to everyone, depending on the different propensities to consume, would the economy expand and the government budget deficit remain the same. Households would all spend and save as before. This analysis dovetails nicely with Piketty's analysis that seeks to tax the rich in order to finance government spending. Raising taxes on the wealthy would also provide the revenues for greater spending to support government programs that would improve the lives of all citizens and have positive spillover effects.

There are a few other ways that the tax policies of Piketty and Keynes overlap in their desire to tax the rich and provide additional revenue for government investment expenditures. Piketty (2014, ch. 14, 2021) supports higher corporate income taxes to deal with the problem of globalization, where capital is mobile and labor immobile, giving capital or wealth a huge advantage when it comes to negotiating low taxes with different nations. Keynes (1930b) also supported taxing profits rather than forcing firms to increase wages. It is well known that Piketty (2014, ch. 15) proposed a global net wealth tax each year of around 1% to 2% (depending on the level of wealth) to reduce both income and wealth inequality. As far as I know, Keynes never advocated an annual wealth tax or a global tax. However, he did support a onetime wealth tax or capital levy to support the war effort (Keynes, 1940). Such a tax would overcome a number of objections frequently raised against taxing wealth (Advani et al., 2020). Because it is imposed only once, the tax due could be spread out over several years, mitigating any liquidity problems due to having to pay the tax. And, because it is a "one off", neither capital flight nor large administrative burdens would arise as problems as a result of the tax.

SUMMARY AND CONCLUSION

Piketty got a number of important things right about inequality. He was right that inequality began rising in developed nations in the late 20th century. He was right that this was due to a larger share of income going to those at the very top of the income distribution, something captured by his measure of inequality but not by other inequality measures. Piketty also got many things wrong, including the nature of the Cambridge controversy and the reason that r>g. He also ignored important issues such as the negative consequences of inequality in *C21*, a problem he remedied to some extent in *C&I*. This chapter shows that Post Keynesian economics is able to buttress many of these weaknesses. It provides a theoretical defense for r>g without running afoul of the Cambridge controversy, and it is able to explain the important negative macroeconomic consequences of inequality, especially when it comes to productivity growth.

Similarly, Post Keynesian economics has gotten a number of things right about inequality. Most important, inequality does affect both demand and productivity growth. Yet, Post Keynesians have gotten some things wrong, and the work of Piketty can buttress Post Keynesian economics here. Post Keynesians mainly focus on the functional distribution, when there is such good data on the personal distribution (as Piketty has shown), and when the distinction between wage and profit income is not a sharp distinction because some income has aspects of both wages and profit income – points made a long time ago by John Stuart Mill ([1848] (1994)). The positive reception of Piketty's work by both the economics profession and the general public shows the benefits of focusing on the share of income going to the very rich and analyzing the personal distribution of income rather than the functional distribution.

Finally, it should be noted that the work of Piketty and his colleagues and the work done by Post Keynesians has a great deal in common. Both groups are markedly to the left of center. Both groups take history and politics seriously. Both groups are concerned about inequality – its causes, consequences and policy implications. Piketty and Keynes share similar views regarding government debt. They both seem to want balanced government budgets over the business cycle. They look towards government investment spending to deal with the problems of insufficient demand and high unemployment. And last, but certainly not least, Piketty and Keynes looked towards fiscal policy to equalize the distribution of income in order to generate greater economic growth.

NOTE

1.   Post Keynesian John Kenneth Galbraith ([1958] 1976) was an important exception here.

REFERENCES

Advani, A., Chamberlain, E. & Summers, A. (2020) A Wealth Tax for the UK: Final Report (Wealth Tax Commission).

Baumol, W. (2012) *The Cost Disease* (New Haven, CT & London: Yale University Press).

Brown-Collier, E. & Collier, B. (1995) What Keynes Really Said about Deficit Spending, *Journal of Post Keynesian Economics* 17(3): 341–355.

Cohen, A. & Harcourt, G. (2003) Whatever Happened to the Cambridge Capital Theory Controversies? *Journal of Economic Perspectives* 17(1): 199–214.

Davidson, P. (2005) The Post Keynesian School. In B. Snowdon & H. Vane (Eds), *Modern Macroeconomics: Its Origins, Development and Current State* (Cheltenham, UK & Northampton, MA, USA: Edward Elgar Publishing), pp. 451–473.

Eichner, A. & Kregel, J. (1975) An Essay on Post-Keynesian Theory: A New Paradigm in Economics, *Journal of Economic Literature* 13(4): 1293–1314.

Galbraith, J.K. [1958] (1976) *The Affluent Society*, 3rd ed. (Boston: Houghton Mifflin).

Haavelmo, T. (1945) Multiplier Effects of a Balanced Budget, *Econometrica* 13(4): 311–318.

Hansen, A. (1939) Economic Progress and Declining Population Growth, *American Economic Review* 29(1): 1–15.

Harcourt, G. (1972) *Some Cambridge Controversies in the Theory of Capital* (Cambridge: Cambridge University Press).

Hein, E. & Vogel, L. (2008) Distribution and Growth Reconsidered: Empirical Results for Austria, France, Germany, the Netherlands, the UK and the US, *Cambridge Journal of Economics* 32(3): 479–511.

Hyman, L. (2012) *Borrow: The American Way of Debt* (New York: Vintage Books).

Judis, J. (2016) *The Populist Explosion* (New York: Columbia Global Reports).

Kaldor, N. (1955–56) Alternative Theories of Distribution, *Review of Economic Studies*, 23(2): 83–100.

Kaldor, N. (1967) Strategic Factors in Economic Development. (Ithaca, NY: Cornell University Press).

Kaldor, N. (1996) *Causes of Growth and Stagnation in the World Economy* (New York: Cambridge University Press).

Kalecki, M. (1954) *Theory of Economic Dynamics* (London: Allen & Unwin).

Kalecki, M. (1962) *Studies in the Theory of Business Cycles, 1933–1939* (Oxford: Basil Blackwell).

Kalecki, M. (1971) *Selected Essays on the Dynamics of the Capitalist Economy* (Cambridge: Cambridge University Press).

Kelton, S. (2020) *The Deficit Myth: Modern Monetary Theory and the Birth of the People's Economy* (cc: Public Affairs).

Keynes, J.M. (1930a) *Economic Possibilities for Our Grandchildren*, in *Essays in Persuasion* (New York: Norton, 1963), pp. 358–373.

Keynes, J.M. (1930b) The Question of High Wages, *The Political Quarterly* 1: 110–124.

Keynes, J.M. (1936) *The General Theory of Employment, Interest and Money* (London: Macmillan).

Keynes, J.M. (1940) *How to Pay for the War: A Radical Plan for the Chancellor of the Exchequer* (London: Macmillan).

Keynes, J.M. (1980) *The Collected Writings of John Maynard Keynes, Vol. XXVII: Activities 1940–1946: Shaping the Post-War World: Rethinking Employment and Unemployment Policy* (London: Macmillan).

King, J.E. (2002) *A History of Post Keynesian Economics Since 1936* (Cheltenham, UK and Northampton, MA, USA: Edward Elgar Publishing).

Kregel, J. (1983) Budget Deficits, Stabilisation Policy and Liquidity Preference: Keynes's Post-War Policy Proposals. In F. Vicarelli (Ed.), *Keynes's Relevance Today* (Philadelphia: University of Pennsylvania Press), pp. 28–50.

Lavoie, M. (2006) *Introduction to Post-Keynesian Economics* (Basingstoke, UK & New York: Palgrave Macmillan).

Messenger, J. (2018) *Working Time and the Future of Work* (Geneva: International Labour Organization).

Mill, J.S. [1848] (1994) *Principles of Political Economy* (New York: Oxford University Press).

Minsky, H. (1977) The Financial Instability Hypothesis: An Interpretation of Keynes and an Alternative to 'Standard' Theory, *Challenge* 20(1): 20–35.

Mitchell, W., Wray, L.R. & Watts, M. (2019) *Macroeconomics* (London: Macmillan & Red Globe Press).

Pasinetti, L. (1974) *Growth and Income Distribution: Essays in Economic Theory* (Cambridge: Cambridge University Press).

Piketty, T. (2014) *Capital in the Twenty-First Century* (Cambridge, MA: Harvard University Press).

Piketty, T. (2020) *Capital and Ideology* (Cambridge, MA: Harvard University Press).

Piketty, T. (2021) *Time for Socialism* (New Haven, CT & London: Yale University Press).

Pressman, S. (1994) *Quesnay's Tableau Économique: A Critique and Reconstruction.* Fairfield, NJ: Augustus Kelley.

Pressman, S. (2011) Microeconomics after Keynes: Post Keynesian Economics and Public Policy, *American Journal of Economics and Sociology* 70(2): 511–539.

Pressman, S. (2016) *Understanding Piketty's Capital in the Twenty-First Century* (London & New York: Routledge).

Pressman, S. (2021) Accumulating Capital: *Capital and Ideology* after *Capital in the Twenty-First Century*, *Analyse & Kritik* 43(1): 5–22.

Pressman, S. (2023) Review of *Time for Socialism* by Thomas Piketty, *Review of Political Economy* 35(3): 905–911.

Pressman, S. & Scott, R. (2009) Consumer Debt and the Measurement of Poverty and Inequality, *Review of Social Economy* 67(2): 127–148.

Samuelson, P. (1948) The Simple Mathematics of Income Determination, in *Income, Employment, and Public Policy: Essays in Honor of Alvin H. Hansen* (New York: Norton), pp. 133–155.

Scott, R. & Pressman, S. (2019) Financially Unstable Households, *Journal of Economic Issues* 53(3): 525–531.

Seccareccia, M. (1995) Keynesianism and Public Investment: A Left-Keynesian Perspective on the Role of Government Expenditures and Debt, *Studies in Political Economy* 46(1): 43–78.

Semieniuk, G. (2017) Piketty's Elasticity of Substitution: A Critique, *Review of Political Economy* 29(1): 64–79.

Setterfield, M. & Kim, Y.K. (2022) How Financially Fragile Can Households Become? Household Borrowing, the Welfare State, and Macroeconomic Resilience, New School for Social Research Working Paper.

Smith, A. [1776] (1937) *An Inquiry into the Nature and Causes of the Wealth of Nations* (New York: Modern Library).

Stockhammer, E. & Stehrer, R. (2011) Goodwin or Kalecki in Demand? Functional Income Distribution and Aggregate Demand in the Short Run, *Review of Radical Political Economics* 43(4): 506–522.

Sylos-Labini, P. (1983–84) Factors Affecting Changes in Productivity, *Journal of Post Keynesian Economics* 6(2): 161–179.

Thirlwall, A. (1983) A Plain Man's Guide to Kaldor's Growth Laws, *Journal of Post Keynesian Economics* 5(3): 345–358.

Thirlwall, A. (1987) *Nicholas Kaldor* (Washington Square, NY: New York University Press).

Widerquist, K. & McCall, G. (2021) *The Prehistory of Private Property* (Edinburgh: University of Edinburgh Press).

Wisman, J. (2022) *The Origins and Dynamics of Inequality: Sex, Politics, and Ideology* (New York: Oxford University Press).

Young, A. (1928) Increasing Returns and Economic Policy, *Economic Journal* 38(152): 527–542.

13. Concluding thoughts to *Post Keynesian Economics*

Therese Jefferson and John E. King

We hope to have shown in this book that Post Keynesians have contributed to some of the most interesting and important theoretical and policy questions of the present day, agreeing on many points but disagreeing on others, usually, if not always, in a friendly and courteous manner. Their broad agreement on most of the fundamentals is not surprising, as they are united in their endorsement of the principle of effective demand and the implication that aggregate employment and output are determined in the product market, not in the labour market. Thus, they agree that the achievement of full employment without inflation is very likely to require government intervention, and that fiscal policy is no less important (and probably more effective) than monetary policy. And they disagree with the neoclassical Keynesian belief that everything can be put right if only the appropriate interest rate structure is imposed by the monetary authorities, a conclusion reached via the IS-LM (investment-saving/liquidity preference-money supply) model and its more recent variant, the New Neoclassical Synthesis. With all this in common, Post Keynesians can afford to argue with each other over the very interesting but less fundamentally important issues that have been dealt with in previous chapters of this book.

The five broad issues that our authors were asked to address are not, of course, the only topics that Post Keynesians are debating in 2023. We considered soliciting contributions on several other questions, including issues of economic methodology, on the political implications of Post Keynesianism, on attitudes to pluralism in economic theory, on the Post Keynesian approach to microeconomics, and on questions of economic policy. The methodology chapters would have included questions of ontology, the thorny chestnut of providing micro-foundations for macroeconomics, and the role of formalism (mathematical modelling and econometrics) in Post Keynesian thinking. In the chapters on politics our contributors would have discussed whether their underlying economic ideas should be seen as 'liberal socialist', social democratic, or basically conservative. Those writing on Post Keynesian attitudes towards pluralism in economics might well have disagreed on the full implications of rejecting both a single monolithic theoretical apparatus and

225

its opposite, an 'anything goes' position. Finally, disagreements on economic policy would almost certainly have included a strong focus on fiscal policy and on policies for the labour market that might restore wage-led growth and do away with wage theft.

Such a book would have been at least twice as long as the present one. Perhaps a second volume, edited by younger colleagues in 2033, will cover some of these unresolved controversies.

Name index

Addo, F.R. 95, 105
Adorno, Theodor 154
Advani, A. 221, 222
Agenjó-Calderdon, Astrid 90, 92, 105
Agnew, Lord 179
Aguila, Nicholás 51, 61, 67, 68, 86
Aja, Alan 106
Albelda, Randy 94, 98, 105
Alchian, A.A. 24, 26
Aldana, Carolyn 98, 103, 106
Altringer, Levi 105, 106
Andresen, Todd 36
Arbuthnot, G. 166, 167, 168176, 187
Arena, Richard 35, 36, 37, 44
Arestis, Philip 36, 40, 44, 45, 46, 47, 74,
    108
Armstrong, Philip 48–70, 72, 73, 74, 75,
    76, 77, 78, 79, 80, 81, 84, 86
Asimakopoulos, Tom 36, 123, 124–5,
    127
Aspromourgos, Tony 36

Banks, N. 91, 105
Baran, Paul 159
Barnard, Anne 136, 143
Barrère, Alain 35, 43, 44, 45
Bartscher, A.K. 102, 105
Baumol, William J. 216, 222
Beach, W. 128
Beaud, Michael 161
Becares, L. 185, 188
Becker, Gary 92, 105
Bell-Kelton, Stephanie 78, 81, 86
    see also Kelton
Bell-Pasht, A. 94, 98, 105
Bellofiore, Riccardo 8–9, 10, 11, 33, 34,
    35, 37, 44, 145–65
Beneria, Lourdes 105
Bentham, Jeremy 203
Berkeley, A. 65, 67
Berlin, Isaiah 204

Berr, E. 31, 44
Berger, S. 23, 26, 69
Bhutta, N. 99, 105
Biden, Joe 127
Blecker, Robert A. 92, 106
Blinder, Alan 133, 143
Bloch, Harry 125, 127
Blume, E. 28
Blundell, R. 183, 187
Böhm, S. 122, 127
Bohren, J. Aislinn 105, 106
Bolsonaro, Jair 217
Bonefeld, W. 161, 164
Bonnizi, B.A. 84, 86, 106
Boschma, R.A. 23, 26
Bouhia, R. 93, 106
Bradford, Wylie 204
Bradley, R. 189
Braudel, Ferdinand 206
Braunstein, Elisa 92, 93, 102, 105, 106,
    109
Bright, S. 187
Brown-Collier, E. 219, 222
Buiter, W. 72, 86
Burbidge, J.B. 123, 127
Burke, Edmund 202

Cagatay, Nilufer 92, 103, 107
Calver, T. 175, 187
Calvert, J. 166, 167, 168, 176, 186, 187
Campbell, K. 128
Capps, Randy 103, 107
Carlock, Greg 135, 143
Carpenter, S.B. 102, 106
Carter, Michael 98, 106
Cassegärd, C. 164
Cattan, S. 182, 187
Chadlington, Lord 179
Chakraborty, Shouvik 144
Chamberlin, E. 222
Chang, A.C. 105

Subject index

Printed and bound by CPI Group (UK) Ltd, Croydon, CR0 4YY

23/04/2025

14660960-0005